P9-DTS-240

N

Consciousness: East and West

Published in Association with Robert Briggs

CONSCIOUSNESS: East and West

Kenneth R. Pelletier
and
Charles Garfield

HARPER & ROW, PUBLISHERS
New York, Hagerstown, San Francisco, London

Designed by Eve Callahan

LIBRARY OF CONGRESS CATALOG CARD NUMBER: 74–13791

STANDARD BOOK NUMBER: 06–090386–4 (PAPERBACK)

STANDARD BOOK NUMBER: 06–136178–X (HARDCOVER)

Grateful acknowledgment is made to the following for permission to reprint from:

John O. Beahrs, "The Hypnotic Psychotherapy of Milton Erickson," *The American Journal of Clinical Hypnosis*, vol. 14 (1971), pp. 73–90. Reprinted by permission of *The American Journal of Clinical Hypnosis* and the author.

Anton T. Boisen, "Onset in Acute Schizophrenia," *Psychiatry*, vol. 10 (1947), pp. 159–166. Copyright by the William Alanson White Psychiatric Foundation. Reprinted by special permission of the William Alanson White Psychiatric Foundation.

Daniel Goleman, "Meditation as Meta-Therapy: Hypotheses toward a Proposed Fifth State of Consciousness." Copyright 1971, Transpersonal Institute, 2637 Marshall Drive, Palo Alto, California 94303. Reprinted by permission from Volume 3, Number 1, of the *Journal of Transpersonal Psychology*.

Bernard E. Gorton, "Autogenic Training," *The American Journal of Clinical Hypnosis*, vol. 2 (1959), pp. 31–41. Reprinted by permission of *The American Journal of Clinical Hypnosis*.

R. D. Laing, Figures 1 and 2 from Chapter 5 of *The Divided Self*. Copyright © 1960 by Tavistock Publications Ltd. Copyright © 1969 by R. D. Laing. Reprinted by permission of Tavistock Publications Ltd and Pantheon Books, a Division of Random House, Inc.

Edward W. Maupin, "On Meditation," in *Altered States of Consciousness*, edited by Charles T. Tart. Copyright © 1969 by John Wiley & Sons, Inc. Reprinted by permission of John Wiley & Sons, Inc.

Julian Silverman, Tables I and III from "A Paradigm for the Study of Altered States of Consciousness," *The British Journal of Psychiatry*, vol. 114 (1968), pp. 1201–1218. Reprinted by permission of *The British Journal of Psychiatry*. Table I was adapted from Table I in Julian Silverman's "Shamans and Acute Schizophrenia," *American Anthropologist*, vol. 69 (1967), pp. 21–31.

To Linda and JLS

Contents

Preface

All of our conceptions of the nature of consciousness do not describe the phenomenology of the mind but are simply tenuous theories and constructions. These conceptions have endured because they explain and clarify at least some aspects of human behavior. It is the intention of this book to propose modifications in the accepted perspective from which we consider human consciousness.

Within the last decade, deep space probes, Eastern philosophies, incessant warfare, quantum physics, ecological crisis, and information overload have turned man's attention toward considering his place in the universe with urgency and humility. In this spirit, our book is offered as an explorer's sourcebook in the mapping of the mind of man. It is intended to articulate an emerging *Weltanschauung* for those of us who choose to work from, improve upon, and expand our conceptions of man and his universe. The contents are not intended to prove a point of view but to raise questions concerning the assumptions, orientations, and predispositions of researchers and laymen who are engaged in self-discovery. It is very likely that we will abandon, contradict, and even denounce these positions as our work progresses in future years, since viability and flexibility outweigh dogma and defense of an untenable position. All our observations are offered for scrutiny and evaluation in order that the insights be researched further and the misconceptions be discarded.

Our concern is not only with the theoretical considerations of altered states of consciousness but also with the innovative, pragmatic applications available when this new perspective is adopted. Throughout the book, we will consider the nature of psychotic, psychoactive, and meditative states of consciousness, as well as innovative systems of psychological and psychosomatic therapy, such as meditation and Biofeedback. In the Berkeley–San Francisco area, numerous forms of human potential, religious, and educational movements exist, and this book has grown out of the synthesis of our experiences with these systems and our professional training as clinical psychologists who have sought to understand the interaction of mind and body. For the last five years we have been engaged in theoretical research, clinical practice, and meditative disciplines that have expanded our awareness of the latent abilities within each of us. During this time, our friendship has grown and deepened on this mutual quest, and the order of authorship was elected by a fall of the I Ching yarrow stalks.

Much of the information contained here has been gleaned from ancient disciplines, such as Zen and Tibetan meditation, which are strikingly compatible with the most recent theories and technological innovations in neurophysiology. Our goal is to convey the sense of human consciousness as that aspect of being wherein the temporal and eternal, the complex and singular, the ancient and contemporary, the material and spiritual, the microcosm and macrocosm are resolved in a moment of comprehension and insight.

Acknowledgments

Throughout the preparation of this book, my colleagues and friends have been trusted guides with their encouragement and support. For their help, I acknowledge my gratitude to Philip Cowan, Elmer Green, Joe Kamiya, Christina Maslach, and Beverly Timmons. My special thanks are to Roger and Lucy Pelletier, Arthur M. Young, Ruth Young, and James Yandell for sharing their insight and wisdom.

Kenneth R. Pelletier
Berkeley, California
December 1974

All homage to the teachers! To Sheldon Korchin, Dale Larson, and Hilde Burton for their consistent support; to Jon, Sylvia, and Edward Garfield for their lifelong love and encouragement; and to Kahil Gibran, Gregory Bateson, and R. D. Laing, who have helped me "to cleave the domain of ignorance with the sword of discrimination."

Charles Garfield
Berkeley, California
December 1974

Our normal waking consciousness, rational consciousness as we call it, is but one special type of consciousness, whilst all about it, parted from it by the filmiest of screens, there lie potential forms of consciousness entirely different. We may go through life without suspecting their existence; but apply the requisite stimulus, and at a touch they are there in all their completeness, definite types of mentality which probably somewhere have their field of application and adaptation. No account of the universe in its totality can be final which leaves these other forms of consciousness quite disregarded. How to regard them is the question —for they are so discontinuous with ordinary consciousness. Yet they may determine attitudes though they cannot furnish formulas, and open a region though they fail to give a map. At any rate, they forbid a premature closing of our accounts with reality.

William James

1

Paradigms of Consciousness

How may we define the term *consciousness?* What relationship may we posit between the activation of the neural networks of the brain and the working of human cognitive systems? What are the specific determinants and concomitants of the various altered states of consciousness? Theorists and researchers in psychology, biochemistry, physics, mathematics, molecular biology, neurophysiology, anthropology, and philosophy are currently attempting to devise and evaluate comprehensive theories of consciousness. Yet, as Tart (1969) has indicated:

> There is a multitude of philosophical and semantic problems in defining just what "normal" consciousness and "altered" states of consciousness are, yet at this instant I have not the slightest doubt that I am in my normal state of consciousness. Yet there have been a number of occasions in my life when I have not had the slightest difficulty in realizing that I was in an altered state of consciousness (ASC).

Tart defines an altered state of consciousness for a given individual as "one in which he clearly feels a *qualitative* shift in his pattern of mental functioning, that is, he feels not just a quantitative shift (more or less alert, more or less visual imagery, sharper or duller, etc.), but also that some quality or qualities of his mental processes are *different*."

As White (1972) observes, efforts directed at altering consciousness inevitably confront obstacles that are both culturally and biologically determined. In discussing the former, White quotes anthropologist Edward T. Hall:

> Selective screening of sensory data admits some things while filtering others, so that experience as it is perceived through one set of culturally patterned sensory screens is quite different from the experience perceived through another. . . .

as well as Carlos Castaneda's *Teachings of Don Juan:*

> Anthropology has taught us that the world is differently defined in different places. . . . The very metaphysical presuppositions differ: space does not conform to Euclidean geometry, time does not form a continuous unidirectional flow, causation does not conform to Aristotelian logic, man is not differentiated from non-man or life from death, as in our world. . . . The central importance of entering into worlds other than our own . . . lies in the fact that the experience leads us to understand that our own world is also a cultural construct.

White states that biological factors pose further difficulties in the alteration of consciousness in that the processing of sensory data is the initial stage in the determination of reality. He offers the example of human vision as an active process which of necessity filters out, via the optic nerve and reticular activating system, all those signals and perceptions not attended to by the brain. Clearly, the directed deployment of attention necessary for species survival would be impossible if every datum of sensory input gained access to consciousness. McCollough's frog-eye experiment at Massachusetts Institute of Technology, in which it was found that frogs paid attention only to those moving objects approximating the size of an insect and that they repressed other visual perceptions, is offered by White as support for the contention that man is constructed on the basis of evolutionarily functional sensory repression.

In spite of the difficulties confronting any global conceptualization of consciousness and altered-state phenomena, several such ASC have figured prominently in both Eastern as well as primitive and civilized cultures. It is our aim to investigate two of the altered states of consciousness: the hypnotic and the meditative states, with the intention of focusing on their physiology, psychology, and applications to psychotherapy. As Wallace (1970) observes, although speculation about the nature of human consciousness and its alteration has gone on for millennia, only within the last half century has technology permitted researchers to describe the physiological and biochemical correlates of altered states of consciousness. The result has been a fuller comprehension of the fundamental processes and neural structures underlying these states.

Within the last decade, there has emerged an increasingly problematic area of inquiry in psychological theory and research termed *altered states of consciousness.* An altered state of consciousness (ASC) is defined as "a qualitative alteration in the overall pattern of mental functioning, such that the experiencer feels his consciousness is radically different from the 'normal' way it functions (Tart 1972)." Thus normal consciousness is defined as an individual's overall patterning of psychological functioning; an ASC differs from the normal conscious state in that ordinary stimuli are processed in a significantly different way, giving rise to experiences that are not normal in Western culture. Existence of an ASC can be established either by an individual's report of his own subjective experience or by the inference of another observer or observers. It is important to recognize that the criterion of statistically rare versus average levels of behavior neither validates nor invalidates an ASC experience. Value judgments concerning the validity or invalidity of various ASC experiences are largely dependent upon whether the state is acceptable or tabooed within a given culture or subculture. This inquiry should not be interpreted as an advocation or rationalization of altered-state experiences but an attempt to recognize, understand, and integrate such experiences for the benefit of those who seek to map the internal landscape of consciousness.

Given the breadth and complexity of the subject matter, our theoretical overview will follow this plan: (1) a brief inquiry into the Western paradigm of science as the pervasive philosophical basis from which researchers and laymen construct their concept of normal consciousness; (2) an examination of the process by which people internalize this paradigm subliminally, as it is manifested in certain cultural and social norms and sanctions, and a redefinition of the conflict of the individual and his culture as the necessary prerequisite to individual growth and transformation; and (3) a definition of the essential properties of all ASC experiences that provide people with the potential for individuation; (4) last, a hypothesized cartography of specific altered states of consciousness ranging from psychotic to transcendent, which clarifies various psychological functions that were formerly relegated to unconscious primary processes with few attempts to differentiate among the multiplicity of these states. In conclusion, this presentation will propose a systematic inquiry into the psychological processes underlying altered states of consciousness with an emphasis upon the phenomenology of such states. Also, the future directions and implications of such theory and research will be briefly explicated.

Primarily, the intent of this discussion is to formulate the basis of a cartography of consciousness. During a recent discussion, one researcher stated that the present research in mapping altered states of consciousness is analogous to maps of the known world before Columbus. Other researchers and theoreticians agree with this observation and recognize that this mapping constitutes one of the most stimulating areas of psychological inquiry. To date there are a few scattered research projects and reports suggesting some of the aspects of consciousness that must be included in any comprehensive cartography. There are indications of fundamental similarities between various states as well as evidence of significant differences that define each state as discrete. It is the purpose of this book to integrate these various aspects to illuminate the known features of the map as well as to define the parameters of the unknown terrain of consciousness.

INFLUENCE OF THE WESTERN SCIENTIFIC PARADIGM

One major reason underlying the reluctance of researchers and clinicians to approach ASC phenomena is the misconception that such inquiry is without support within the current methodology of scientific inquiry. However, a brief foray into the nature of scientific paradigms and formal logic will not only demonstrate the foundations for such research but will also explain the necessity for experimentation based on a newly evolving model of scientific inquiry. It is necessary to examine the philosophical and logical basis of any proposed inquiry into altered states of consciousness; all too frequently, researchers and theoreticians proceed into new areas of research without first examining their own sources, biases, assumptions, and influences from other disciplines. Such an examination is needed if the ensuing theory and research is to be well rooted and broadly based. Establishing the links between philosophy of science, formal logic, and research in altered states of consciousness is both a means of grounding such research and a means for transmitting the implications of this psychological research into other, related disciplines.

According to T. S. Kuhn in *The Structure of Scientific Revolutions,* a paradigm is a "supertheory" or a theoretical formulation of a wide diversity of existing data into an internally consistent and coherent body of knowledge. It is a philosophical predisposition that directs and interprets the scientific activity of the adherents to that paradigm. Unfortunately, a paradigm tends to become an increasingly rigidified "supertheory" in the sense that it becomes an implicit framework for the inclusion and exclusion of certain phenomena from scientific inquiry. Rather than a tentatively held theory of the structure of the universe, the paradigm becomes a dogma and defines the parameters within which the researchers conduct their inquiries. One clear deficiency of such a dogma is that it becomes self-perpetuating in that it is a self-fulfilling prophecy. This point is underscored by Alfred N. Whitehead in *Science and the Modern World,* where he observes that paradigms impose order upon a basically random order of phenomena. A paradigm serves as a "prism" through which certain phenomena are included for inquiry while others are excluded. This schema directs the attention of researchers to certain groupings and correlations of data that are themselves amenable to that kind of investigation, and the results of that predetermined investigation verify the paradigm. Whitehead points out that the narrow efficiency of the scheme is the very cause of its "supreme methodological success." For example, Einstein's equations helped initiate the current paradigm of physics, which in turn verifies Einstein's equations. Examples of earlier paradigms are Copernican astronomy, Newtonian physics, and Darwinian evolution. In each case, their acceptance necessitated the scientific community's rejection or radical modification of one scientific theory, such as Kepler's astronomy, in favor of another incompatible with it (McCain and Segal 1969). Each adoption of a new paradigm produced a shift in the problems recognized as available for scientific scrutiny and in what constituted a valid solution. Furthermore, this shift in perspective transformed the scientific imagination in a manner that can only be described as a profound alteration and transformation of the *Weltanschauung* of the researcher. Since culture and society are ultimately affected by the prevailing world views of their authorities, be it a Nobel Prize-winning scientist or shaman, such a paradigm alteration has the effect of radically restructuring the world view of all members of that society.

It is inevitable that pervasive alterations in world perspective be met with resistance despite the fact that certain demonstrable phenomena remain inexplicable in terms of the former paradigm. Such a process is explicated by Kuhn (1962, p. 64): "Novelty emerges only with difficulty, manifested by resistance against a background provided by expectation. Initially, only the anticipated and usual are experienced, even under circumstances where anomaly is later to be observed. The later awareness of anomaly opens a period in which conceptual categories are adjusted until the initially anomalous has become the anticipated." In effect, a paradigm is an agreed-upon set of expectancies that excludes other possibilities, and a revision of that paradigm introduces a new order of possibilities. The necessity of scientific disciplines to be based on a shared set of expectancies becomes manifest in the social order as the consensual validation of an order of reality. From this shared state of consensus derives the concept of normality of a certain mode of psychological functioning.

There are two concrete manifestations of Kuhn's observations that bear on the problem of researching altered states of consciousness. One affirmation of Kuhn's critique of dogmatic paradigms is Kurt Gödel's formal mathematical demonstration of a nonlogical, non-objective component of bias in all logical paradigms. This fundamental work of formal logic is known as Gödel's theorem. Words such as *nonlogical, nonobjective,* and *irrational* refer to the undiscovered order, or *psycho logic,* of the phenomenology of the mind, which cannot be researched under the present constraints and definitions of objectivity and the scientific method. Gödel demonstrates the incompleteness of logic by strictly formal methods, and proves that there must exist in logic a proposition that says that it is not a proposition. This proof has not been refuted and stands as a testimony that the hope of logicians to logicize mathematics and other sciences is ill-founded (Natanson 1963). In effect, the proposition that states it is not a proposition shows that not every proposition has an antecedent. Before Gödel, logical systems were based on the postulate (an a priori, unproven fundamental principle) that for every proposition p there must be an antecedent proposition q which implies it. In demonstrating the irrational aspect of the proposition that denies itself, Gödel presents a formal proof of the irrational component in all logical systems and undermines the internal coherence of logic as a closed system. The point of this rather circuitous digression is that research into the illogical phenomena of ASC is given formal sanction as a legitimate endeavor by the demonstration of the pre-rational aspect of all logical systems—that is, all paradigms.

Adherence to a particular paradigm is a function of belief or faith rather than a matter of necessity dictated by objective information (Pearce 1971; McCain and Segal 1969). Thus, Gödel's theorem remains a formal affirmation of a nonrational component adhering to an essentially rational, logical system. Since a universal quality of all ASC experiences is that they are of a transcendent nature, an inquiry into such phenomena is an attempt to comprehend those experiential phenomena that influence an individual's interpretation of and adherence to logical systems, ranging from scientific paradigms to explicit cultural and social codes of behavoir. In approaching ASC phenomena, the focus is necessarily upon the individual since an integral aspect of ASC phenomena is that they are often over-looked as falling outside normal conditions and dismissed as statistical variance.

There is a second foundation within existing natural-science para-digms on which research into the non-rational, individual, not read-ily observable aspects of ASC phenomena may be based. Verifica-tion that such an inquiry is necessary and yet untenable within existing scientific parameters comes from the unexpected quarter of quantum physics. This affirmation is the Heisenberg uncertainty prin-ciple, which demonstrates the limits of a deterministic interpretation of the physical universe (Koestler 1972). Rationality and objectivity are the underpinnings of the deterministic paradigm, but in order to affirm that rationality and objectivity it would be necessary that an observer be capable of determining the position of the most ele-mentary particles. Heisenberg demonstrated the impossibility of such an observation and, in a manner analogous to Gödel, affirmed the necessity of acknowledging the non-rational components of any logi-cal system. This observation of Heisenberg can be summarized as follows:

> In order for determinists to prove the assumption of predictability, then it is necessary to observe the position and momentum of this fundamental particle. In order to observe this fundamental particle or photon, the observer must cast light on the particle. However, the wavelength of light (10^{-5} cm) is a million times greater than the diameter of the observed particle. Thus it is impossible to make the requisite observation to affirm a deterministic paradigm (Young 1975).

This indeterminacy factor was formalized by Nobel laureate Max Planck as Planck's constant, which clearly defined the hypothesized limitations of objective observation. This dilemma reveals the impor-tance of research into ASC phenomena—there is a predetermined limit to the objectivity of observation even within physics, the most stringent of the natural sciences. A further and more important impli-cation of the Heisenberg uncertainty principle is that it imposes a limit on the accuracy of knowledge about individual entities (Koestler

1972; Townes 1970). Thus, in order to perform the task of science, which is to discover laws and derive predictions, physicists have declined to deal wth individual phenomena and, instead, have concentrated upon modal statistics. Clearly, the predominance of modal research in psychology demonstrates the pervasiveness of an analogous principle in the social sciences that circumvents the problem of individual, subjective phenomena since they are not readily observable under ordinary conditions.

This brief excursion into formal logic and quantum physics has been necessary in order to demonstrate the precedents for inquiries into phenomena such as ASC, which are considered to be outside the realm of objective inquiry. There is evidence pressing for a turning away from the notion of objectivity maintained by classical determinism (Townes 1970). Promising inquiries have already been made by Gödel's demonstration of the incompleteness of logic and by Heisenberg's uncertainty principle in quantum physics. Though grounded in the natural sciences, these contributions have had impact beyond their disciplines and range into epistemology (Koestler 1972; Young 1972). While these observations demonstrate the inadequacy of a deterministic science of behavior, they do not go far enough to provide a basis for supplanting the classical belief in objectivity.

These instances are not intended as a condemnation of objectivity but as a demonstration of the necessity of formulating a more comprehensive definition of objectivity so as to include the less readily observable psychological phenomena of individuals undergoing various ASC experiences. Without noting such sanctions within the natural sciences for the need of such an extended definition, researchers in ASC phenomena would remain in the untenable situation of trying to adhere to an anachronistic paradigm.

There is great degree of similarity between a paradigm and the concept of a normative state of consciousness. Each is "a complex, interdependent set of rules and theories for interacting with and interpreting experiences within a certain context" (Tart 1972). In both cases, the rules and theories have become implicit until they are no longer recognized as tentative but, instead, operate automatically. Misconceptions concerning the nature of objective inquiry have systematically excluded individual ASC phenomena as valid subjects for investigation. However, there are precedents for such inquiries, and ASC phenomena are clearly within the realm of the scientific method, as will be demonstrated in later sections.

2

Altered States of Consciousness: Cultural Relativity

Although paradigms do influence cultural and social values and interpretations of phenomena, the effect is difficult to assess except in terms of their influence on the scientific community. More evident is the effect of the socialization rules that determine and define how individuals will react to normative or non-normative behavior.

Socialization refers to the process of learning by which individuals are inducted into a specific culture. In its broadest sense, this learning encompasses all planned and inadvertent education, formal and informal learning throughout the life of the individual, "including not only explicitly cultural learning but also nominally non-cultural learning that affects cultural behavior, such as the learning of culturally relevant and desirable personality characteristics" (Berger and Luckmann 1966). As an analytic concept, socialization bridges the gap between the micro and macro aspects of interaction, that is, between individual behavior in one instance and the comprehensive performance of the social system in the other.

There is a tendency over time for the members of a society to develop similar individual paradigms or predispositions to comprehend their society in a manner analogous to other individuals within that social order. This process is termed *mazeway* construction by anthropologist Anthony F. C. Wallace (1956) and is defined as follows:

> It is functionally necessary for every person in society to maintain a mental image of the society and its culture, as well as of his own body and its behavioral regularities, in order to act in ways which reduce stress at all levels of the system. The person does, in fact, maintain such an image. This mental image I have called "mazeway," since as a model of the all-body-personality-nature-culture-society system or field, organized by the individual's own experience, it includes perceptions of both the maze of physical objects of the environment and also the ways in which this maze can be manipulated by the self and others in order to minimize stress. The "mazeway" is nature, society, culture, personality, and body image, as seen by one person.

Working from Wallace's concept of mazeway homeostasis, one would postulate that each individual constructs a mazeway that creates the least conflict between the social "collective mazeway" and his own "individual mazeway" and avoids dissonance (Festinger 1957). Another assumption of Wallace's theory is that individuals will modify their perception of social phenomena in order to remain socially acceptable and to avoid psychological conflict. Such cognitive manipulations as rationalization, projection, dissociation, and repression will serve to modify the individual's perceptions. However, in situations of severe stress, an individual's mazeway ceases to provide him with comprehensive, dissonance-free interpretations, even after the above defenses have been employed. An individual may then choose, either consciously or unconsciously, to modify his perceptions of the social reality in which he is immersed. Stress may induce a profound alteration in an individual's perception of himself and his social reality, and the experience of that dissonance may lead to the observation that "selective screening of sensory data admits some things while filtering others so that experience as it perceived through one set of socially patterned sensory screens is quite different from the experience perceived through another" (Hall 1966, p. 125). Such a perceptual shift involves a radical reorganization, which has been termed "conduct reorganization" (Sarbin and Adler 1967), "deindividuated behavior" (Zimbardo 1969), "individuation" (Jung 1969a), "reconstitution of the self" (Perry 1962), to cite a few of the major theorists who have recognized the profundity of such a reorganization of perception.

In order to provide a basis upon which to examine this process, it is necessary to cite the recent research of personality theorist Salvatore R. Maddi. Maddi postulates that an infant's sensory behavior mediates and conveys exteroceptive stimulation to the cortical areas of the brain. These stimuli are processed into an interoceptive, organismic "activation level" (Maddi 1968), which is maintained by the reticular formation. Activation level refers to an infant's customary level of autonomic activity, which is established in the course of early development and remains relatively constant through early adult maturation and then declines with the onset of advanced age. Although Maddi does not delineate specific developmental sequences, he does hypothesize that this cortical activation may constitute the physiological basis of "the underlying drive properties of cognitive processes" (1968). In effect, Maddi's theory maintains that an individual is psychophysiologically predisposed to maintain an activation level based on early sensory experiences even though socialization curtails direct sensory interaction between individuals (Maddi 1968; Miller and Dollard 1941; Dollard and Miller 1950). Theoretical and physiological evidence indicates that the primary sensory process by which each individual first relates to his animate and inanimate environment is through unmediated, high-intensity, impulsive behavior. In operant conditioning, this behavior, termed "affective proprioceptive feedback," is assumed to be pleasurable since it is uncontaminated by other stimuli. It is this volatile, intense, primary sensory behavior that forms the substratum on which all future rational social behavior is based.

Researchers must turn to the interaction between socially sanctioned behavior and the more fundamental impulsive drives in order to fully understand the range of ASC behavior initiated by an individual in the process of perceptual reorganization. Developmental and personality theories do account for moderate adaptive "regression in the service of the ego" (Kris 1952) or retreat under stress to more infantile behavior (White 1964), but they do not consider progressive reactions of perceptual reorganization that do not imply classical regression or retreat from stress. Just as higher-order cognitive functions retain vestiges of earlier stages, so will any "degeneration" of behavior retain certain higher-order functions (Werner 1948). It appears that the conventional definition of regressive-like behavior, which we will call "deindividuated behavior" (Zimbardo 1969), is a progressive reorganization of conceptual and social constructs of conventional reality. Thus, our definition challenges the assumption that underlies terming such regressive behavior "degenerate." Deindividuated behavior involves the reinstatement of primary drive states in an inexplicable interaction with higher-order cognitive functions and is distinct from the simplistic mode of infantile regressive behavior. Specific conditions under which this behavior can occur will be explicated in Chapter 3, and specific states that can be induced will be enumerated in Chapter 4.

Given that Maddi's hypothesis has been empirically verified (Fiske and Maddi 1961; Maddi and Propst 1963), *socialization* can be interpreted as the process by which an infant's sensory behavior is transformed into socially defined, mediated symbolic interaction (Birdwhistell 1960; Frank 1957; Hall 1966). What is often neglected in examining this transformation process is that the socially sanctioned modes of behavior may be too constrictive or too abstracted to permit adequate expression of mature forms of affective proprioceptive behavior. The coordination of sensory behavior and visual schemata signals the transition of the infant away from the purely tactile, sensory interchanges with his mother so that observable facial expressions and gestures become signs and symbols of interpersonal relations and provide the biological basis for language acquisition (Cassirer 1967). It is clear in the research of Salvatore Maddi and Lawrence K. Frank that the emergent language and personality of a child may be viewed as an elaboration, extension, refinement, and transformation of his basic sensory and biological functions. The signs and symbols of language and social systems function as surrogates for primary sensory signals (Birdwhistell 1960). Linguist Ernst Cassirer recognizes this process as essential to language acquisition.

If a child when learning to talk had simply to learn a certain vocabulary, if he only had to impress on his mind and memory a great mass of artificial and arbitrary sounds, this would be a purely mechanical process. It would be very laborious and tiresome, and would require too great conscious effort for the child to make without a certain reluctance since what he is expected to do would be entirely disconnected from actual biological needs (Cassirer 1967, p. 132).

These modes of symbolic discourse permit the individual to live in a symbolic world and seek symbolic fulfillment through the social patterns he has learned to use in his own idiosyncratic fashion. Frank considers the patterning of these infantile sensory responses to be "one of the earliest and most significant social conventions," and he notes that as the child grows older, "he learns to employ the group-sanctioned ceremonies, rituals, symbols for approaching persons, relying upon negotiating, barter, sale, contract, courtship, seduction, marriage, for setting aside the inviolability of the object, animal, or person with which he seeks to make direct tactual contacts or to establish 'tactual communication of immediacy" (1957, p. 239). In the transformation of egocentric, infantile behavior, society prescribes the parameters of acceptable, mediated behavior in order to maintain a social order. Penalties are enacted by the society to insure that an individual will not engage in unsanctioned behavior. Societal restraint is analogous to Frank's concept of the "inviolability" of certain rules, which he enumerates: "For each application of the inviolability principle there is a systematized declaration—legal, ethical, religious, moral—accompanied by a more or less well-organized scheme of explanations or rationalizations and a kind of sanction appropriate to its enforcement" (1955, p. 114). Not only must a society enact the appropriate sanctions, it must also allocate sufficient compensation to its members for their individual restraint in the service of social order. Current emphasis upon "encounters" and "involvement" may be symptomatic of the fact that this reciprocating contract has become estranged in the midst of an increasingly complex symbolic environment (Ruesch 1956) demanding patience and cognitive constraint. Non-productive activity is reluctantly condoned while control and restraint are certified normative behavior. An automated society demands a temporal ordering of individual activity for efficiency, and this ordering can lead to an overemphasis on the cognitive control of behavior. A study made by Edward Megargee in 1966 reveals most disturbing information, when viewed in the light of this pervasive emphasis on rational restraint and control. Megargee found that a basic personality trait of people who commit violent crimes was that they were *over*controlled in terms of affective physical expression. Irrational behavior resulted when these people felt that their rigidly constrained behavioral system was threatened by novel situations. Inordinate stress on rationality and control may very well invoke its opposite when there is insufficient redress for this restraint and a scarcity of sanctioned outlets for irrational behavior.

This conception of the individual versus society is hardly innovative, but the assessment of an individual's reactions to that conflict is essential and in need of significant revision. It is readily demonstrated that impulsive and irrational behavior will assume dominance in stressful situations where the symbolic interactions are inadequate. Such behavior is often termed *regression* in the classical sense of reverting to immature behavior, the most pathological version of this defense manifesting itself in the extreme passivity of some chronic schizophrenics on one extreme and the hyperresponsiveness of irrational rage or euphoria on the other. This latter pole of the irrational continuum cannot be simply dismissed as regressive, since it encompasses behavior ranging from Manson-like sadism to mystical revelation. It seems more likely that this mode of behavior is a "conscious" decision to violate the inadequate, repressive social dictates, with their inordinate stress on the cybernetic qualities of rationality, reason, control, premeditation, and individual responsibility. "Conscious" is the critical factor because one may observe that there are certain social situations an individual can consciously enter that minimize self-restraint and evaluation and virtually negate social sanctions. Under such conditions, voluntary deindividuated behavior may be manifest since the social contraints of guilt, fear, and commitment are purposefully debarred from consideration.

Returning to the concept of socialization, we can see that the interface between societal attitudes and an individual's ASC experience will determine how that experience is evaluated both by the society and by the individual. It is predicted that ASC experiences will be manifested differently in various cultures both in terms of the symptoms shown and in the interpretation of that behavior (Kiev 1964). In many non-Western cultures, a person undergoing an ASC experience is given the opportunity to integrate his ASC into a meaningful style of behavior sanctioned by cultural values (Murphy et al. 1963; Silverman 1967b). Psychiatrist David Kennedy suggests that the conveyance of cultural meaning through social reactions to an individual's ASC experience will determine whether he integrates that experience or degenerates into psychosis: "The first question to be answered . . . is whether the deviant individual is revered, ignored, or condemned by those who surround him. Many societies condone or even worship forms of exceptional behavior which we could classify as deviant or pathological" (1961). Perhaps the most interesting and convincing evidence of the importance of social acceptance of an ASC phenomenon comes from the study of reactions to a drug-induced rather than a stress-induced ASC. In 1956, James S. Slotkin compared the reactions of white-American and Indian-American subjects to peyote-induced ASC phenomena. Because of their cultural conditioning, the white Americans, with their emphasis on rational processes, found the experience "meaningless, frightening, and became uncontrolled in their behavior" (Watson and Guthrie 1972). By contrast, Indians were accustomed to induced altered states and accepted the intense religious experience of the hallucinatory state and were able to "maintain mood stability, react with reverence and respect, and receive deep inner satisfaction" (Watson and Guthrie 1972). There are a significant number of other investigations that indicate the unique variations in interpretation of ASC phenomena in non-Western cultures (Leighton et al. 1963; Lin 1953; Murphy et al. 1963; Carothers, 1953).

It is not necessary to pursue these investigations further since the main point is to demonstrate that the interaction of cultural meaning and setting with an individual's subjective reaction will determine his response to the unfolding and subsequent integration of the ASC phenomena. Second, it is significant to note the predominant attitude toward ASC experiences within Western culture. Most psychiatric treatment as practiced in Western culture is directed primarily at eliminating the ASC phenomena through pharmacological intervention analogous to administering an antidote for ingested toxins (Laing 1970; Weil 1972). Also, psychotherapy most frequently tries to identify sources of conflict and to lessen those that are believed to be factors that cause and maintain the ASC experience (Laing 1970; Perry, 1962). Western culture's aim of eliminating or suppressing ASC experiences is based more on political and social considerations than on psychological insight. Perhaps these experiences are opposed to social responsibility, individual initiative, and self-control, which are so revered in Western cultures. But these are social criteria and are distinct from the more psychological observation that these experiences are a source of profound personal inspiration and are invaluable sources of information in determining the transcultural functions of the human mind.

What is most important to note here is that the understanding and integration of altered-state experiences is culturally relative. This fact should not be misinterpreted as a naïve condonation of psychotic behavior, drug ingestion, or autistic mysticism. The fact that ASC experiences are relative culturally indicates that any one culture or subculture considers only one aspect of a highly complex experience which needs to be explored in its entirety beyond specific cultural limitations.

Within the next decade, there will arise an increasing need for a comprehensive classification or cartography of these various ASC experiences in order that they be neither unduly deified nor condemned categorically as psychotic. A comprehension of these states offers a much wider view of the range of human potentialities and the vast wealth of unexplored inner experiences.

HYPNOSIS AND PRIMITIVE CULTURE:
SOCIOCULTURAL FACTORS

There are indications that suggestion and hypnosis also occur in primitive society and are similar to Occidental phenomena of suggestion and hypnosis. An analysis of the cultural context and meaning of such data indicates that socio-cultural factors, usually related to supernaturalistic attitudes and practices, greatly enhance the hypnotizability of the primitive, by increasing the prestige ("power") of the hypnotist, who is usually a magician. This finding implies that, when he seeks to induce a state of hypnosis, the effectiveness of the primitive hypnotist's technical competence is appreciably enhanced by the fact that hypnotic powers are imputed to him by his society as a whole. In fact, it is possible to demonstrate that, in some instances, the group as a whole acts as the hypnotist, while in other instances social expectations facilitate the appearance of trance states in hermits or in people who temporarily withdraw from the group while questing for a vision (Benedict 1923).

Psychodynamics . . . suggest that an analysis of primitive cultural data may shed new light upon [this] psychological phenomenon in our own society (Devereux 1966).

Whatever the advantages of a Western, logical-positivist, psychological view of hypnosis, one must acknowledge the feasibility of alternative approaches. This section will attempt to deal with the role of social and cultural factors in hypnosis among primitive cultures. As the anthropologists assert, this approach is hindered neither by the biases and preconceptions of ethnocentrism nor those of the scientific *Weltanschauung*. In addition and relative to hypnosis at least, the analysis of primitive data may enable us to better understand this phenomenon in our own culture, "precisely because what is repressed, or at least only latently present, in one society, may be out in the open and formally institutionalized in another society" (Devereux 1955).

We may begin by differentiating between the ideas of suggestion and hypnotism. Suggestion differs from hypnosis, on a descriptive level, by the absence of a "trance state." From a psychoanalytic point of view, the difference is mainly that the content of a suggestion and the manifest behavior of the suggestee—that is, the expression of a repressed wish—are of prime importance in suggestion; paramount in hypnosis, however, is the liberation of ordinarily inhibited mechanisms or faculties and/or the inhibition of ordinarily freely functioning mechanisms or faculties. Anthropological investigators have repeatedly commented on the suggestibility of the primitive, particularly in stressful situations. What has been given scant attention but has been equally substantiated is the fact that normally the primitive is both rational and pragmatic. Primitive hypersuggestibility appears to be a function of the fact that he is less able than civilized man to comprehend reality, and, as Devereux (1939) has noted, he is more often subjected to states of stress related to disorientation. Devereux (1966) offers the following intriguing analysis:

> . . . if a Kansas businessman and a youthful Plains Indian questing for a power-giving vision saw the same vision, qualitatively both persons would be equally abnormal. Of the two, however, the Kansas businessman would be quantitatively more abnormal, since in his case the eruption of the primary process and of visual hallucinations would not be supported and facilitated on the ego level by cultural expectations and cultural conditioning. The same considerations are applicable also to suggestibility and hypnosis. When a Plains Indian medicine man told a mortally wounded man to rise and behave as though he were well, his suggestion fell on culturally sensitized ears. It had the full support of cultural conditioning and mobilized important ego mechanisms; hence, the man could and did rise and walk around for days, even though he inevitably died. A similar command given to an Occidental patient would probably not produce comparable results, because of the lack of a cultural reinforcement of the shaman's command.

> The effectiveness of a primitive shaman's suggestions and hypnotic interventions thus cannot be doubted. The shaman is, by definition, held capable of performing certain feats. This means that his commands are reinforced by cultural conditioning and are therefore highly effective. Also, the primitive is eager for miracles; his desire is overt and conscious, and above all, extremely ego-syntonic. The desire for miracles is, of course, present also in Occidental man; however, it is often only preconscious or unconscious, and in most cases, is certainly not ego-syntonic.

Clearly, the point to be emphasized is not that of primitive hyper-suggestibility but the presence of a culturally based assumption that primitive shamans are possessed of extraordinary "hypnotic" capabilities. The notion that primitive suggestibility is greatly affected by sociocultural factors is given further credence by two other observations noted by Devereux (1966). In certain forms of hypnotic alterations of consciousness, (1) the entire group functions as the hypnotist, or (2) a socially recognized signal serves to induce a particular and predictable pattern of hypnotic behavior without the necessity of additional induction procedures. The phenomenon of a mass-induced hypnotic state among primitives is seen as the result of techniques such as monotonous drumming and incessant dancing. It is noted that these techniques may induce "dissociational" or "possession" states, as evidenced in the Haitian voodoo rituals. From the current perspective, the most relevant aspect of this phenomenon is that "the social implementation of trance states, i.e., the expectation that they will occur in selected persons on certain occasions, tends to support and to mobilize the dissociative abilities inherent in every individual, by giving social support to unconscious impulses and to the primary process in their struggle against the restraining ego, and the competing secondary process" (Devereux 1966). The second phenomenon, that of the induction of predictable patterns of hypnotic behavior or dissociation through a socially recognized signal, is evidenced in numerous and diverse primitive societies. For example, Aberle (1952) and Yap (1952), respectively, observed that Siberian tribesmen and Malay women were triggered by a startle reaction into a hypnotic state in which they identified with the aggressor and exhibited echolalia (the habit of repeating what is said by other people as if echoing them) and echopraxia (the habit of repeating the actions of other people as if echoing them). Devereux (1966) includes Adelman's (1955) example of the Malayan who, in reacting to the unexpected presence of a tiger, so identified with the animal psychologically, and hence behaviorally, that he frightened the tiger out of its wits!

It now appears advantageous to consider the manner in which the primitive uses the sociocultural factors operant in the hypnotic context to implement behaviorally his unconscious impulses. The quasi-magical aura surrounding hypnosis in primitive cultures increases the likelihood that the phenomenon will be used as justification for the entire gamut of what so-called civilized culture terms "acting-out" behavior. This brings to light the notion of an individual's compliance while in an hypnotic state. The fact that it is most difficult to induce extremely uncharacteristic behavior under hypnosis is well known. In primitive cultures, however, an appropriate individual's —that is, the shaman's—hypnotic command supported by the entire magico-supernatural social context can easily elicit compliance. This is especially true when the command (1) gives social and ego support to a deeply repressed unconscious impulse and (2) provides a culturally sanctioned alibi for the socially tabooed behavior.

SCHIZOPHRENIA AND SHAMANISTIC ALTERATIONS OF CONSCIOUSNESS

Krippner (1972) defines a particular category of ASC called *state of rapture* as follows: "States of Rapture are characterized by intense feeling and overpowering emotion, subjectively evaluated as pleasurable and positive in nature. These states can be induced by sexual stimulation, frenzied dances (e.g., the 'whirling dervishes'), orgiastic rituals (e.g., witchcraft and voodoo), rites of passage (e.g., conversion, 'evangelistic' meetings, 'speaking-in-tongues'), and certain drugs." It is clear that those inspirational medicine men called shamans often attain a state of consciousness in their primitive rituals that falls within this descriptive category. Eliade (1964), whose work entitled *Shamanism: Archaic Techniques of Ecstasy* is a classic in the field, offers the following description of shamanism: "The shaman remains the dominating figure; for through this whole region in which ecstatic experience is considered the religious experience par excellence, the shaman, and he alone, is the great master of ecstasy. A first definition of this complex phenomenon, and perhaps the least hazardous, will be: shamanism = technique of ecstasy."

It appears that marked similarities exist between what Western civilization calls schizophrenic psychosis and the seemingly bizarre but socially sanctioned behavior of the primitive shaman. Ethno-psychiatric investigations support the belief of cross-cultural researchers that the schizophrenic process is a universal one. The experience of the shaman, whose esteemed position is often a direct result of intense schizophrenic-like ordeals of symbolic death and rebirth, may prove to be the closest parallel to the schizophrenic reaction. Such characteristics as hypersensitivity prior to the shamanistic experience, powerful emotional reactions to personal traumas and/or impasses, feelings of inadequacy, and difficulties in relating to others approximate, if not duplicate, the symptoms of the prepsychotic. In addition, Silverman (1967c) states that

> Significant differences between acute schizophrenics and shamans are not found in the sequence of underlying psychological events that define their abnormal experiences. One major difference is emphasized—a difference in the degree of cultural acceptance of a unique resolution of a basic life crisis. In primitive cultures in which such a unique life crisis resolution is tolerated, the abnormal experience (shamanism) is typically beneficial to the individual, cognitively and affectively; he is regarded as one with expanded consciousness. In a culture that does not provide referential guides for comprehending this kind of crisis experience, the individual (schizophrenic) typically undergoes an intensification of his suffering over and above his original anxieties.

He also observes that there are certain difficulties in defining both shamanism and schizophrenia, and restrictions on both terms are required. Ackerknecht (1934) acknowledges these difficulties in the former case:

> The mentality of medicine men all over the world, conditioned by their respective culture patterns can hardly be caught by one general label and least of all by the term shaman, the healed madman . . . nor can the different mentalities be arranged in an evolutionary scheme. It is more or less in the nature of things that the medicine men are autonormal [i.e., normal in the sense of functioning effectively in their own societies].

The effects of cultural relativism may be negated by directing our attention only to those "inspirational medicine men who communicate directly with the spirits and who exhibit the most blatant forms of psychotic-like behaviors. These include grossly nonreality-oriented ideation, abnormal perceptual experiences, profound emotional upheavals, and bizarre mannerisms" (Silverman 1967c). In the case of schizophrenic psychosis, we must impose two definite limitations on the use of this diagnostic classification. First, we will consider only those sets of behaviors and experiences that fall within the category of "reactive" psychosis, and not those categorized as "process" schizophrenia, that is, those individuals in whom "the prepsychotic personality is better integrated, the onset of the disorder rapid, and the clinical picture stormy." The second limitation is that within the "reactive" classification we will consider only nonparanoid schizophrenic types, that is, those individuals whose alteration in consciousness includes "the profoundest of emotional upheavals and often abounding religious and magical ideation [which] unfold under conditions of marked environmental detachment" (Silverman 1967c).

Silverman contends that both schizophrenic and shamanistic behavior and cognition are the result of a necessary and sufficient sequence or ordering of psychological events. He further asserts that this ordering is well defined and consists of the five stages listed and discussed below:

1. The precondition: fear, feelings of impotence and failure, guilt
2. Preoccupation, isolation, estrangement
3. Narrowing of attention, self-initiated sensory deprivation
4. The fusing of higher and lower referential processes
5. Cognitive reorganization

1. Schizophrenia and shamanism have both been described as all-encompassing psychological maneuvers to cope with a condition or conditions of impasse or extreme threat. The condition of the schizophrenic has been conceptualized by some in terms of double-bind theory. It occurs:

   a. When the individual is involved in an intense relationship; that is, a relationship in which he feels it is vitally important that he discriminate accurately what sort of message is being communicated so that he may respond appropriately.

b. And, the individual is caught in a situation in which the other person in the relationship is expressing two orders of message and one of these denies the other.

c. And, the individual is unable to comment on the message being expressed to correct his discrimination of what order of message to respond to, i.e., he cannot make a metacommunicative statement (Bateson et al. 1956).

The condition of threat or impasse for the shaman results from a psychological state in which he perceives himself as being inadequate to "(a) attain what are culturally acknowledged as the basic satisfactions or (b) solve the culturally defined basic problems of existence" (Silverman 1967c).

2. Heightened withdrawal and preoccupation with inner processes, that is, "inner space," mark both ASC. The shaman and the schizophrenic tend toward increased self-absorptive behaviors that promote feelings of isolation and estrangement and minimize social interaction. People in either state may progress to a point of perceptual fixation, that is, "autohypnotic induction," evidenced by the hyperintense staring of schizophrenics and the total deployment of attention by shamans to their frenzied, incessant drum beating.

3. Silverman states that the processional development of both states includes the (a) constriction of the range of stimuli to which these individuals are responsive and (b) their intense absorption with a narrow group of ideas. He further asserts that it is precisely these factors that account for the evolution of those perceptual and cognitive alterations characteristic of both the schizophrenic and the shaman. This deployment of attention to an increasingly more narrow ideational sphere brings about a profound alteration in "sensory and ideational figure-ground relationships," which effects a subsequent alteration in relationships of a cognitive structural nature. Additionally, this mode of attention deployment diminishes sensory input and effectively induces a self-initiated state of sensory deprivation. When considered as results of psychological processes such as the alteration of attention deployment, the diminution of substantive sensory input,

and the preoccupation with inner processes to the exclusion of external reality, the seemingly bizarre and idiosyncratic behavior of the
schizophrenic and the shaman are more readily understood.

4. The focal point of both the schizophrenic and shamanistic
experiences is an extremely vulnerable and negative sense of self.
In an effort to resist the total fragmentation and ultimate dissolution of the ego, individuals in both ASC exhibit behavior that has
been termed pathological. Sullivan (1953a) has noted that "the fragmentation of one's self-concept in the course of redefinition also
implies a fragmentation of reality as it has been culturally elaborated by and for the individual." Silverman offers a further comparison between the two chaotic states in quoting Eliade's (1964)
description of the shamanistic experience: "The total crisis of the
future shaman, sometimes leading to complete disintegration of the
personality and to madness, can be valuated not only as an initiatory
death, but also a symbolic return to the precosmogonic chaos, to the
amorphous and indescribable state that precedes any cosmogony"
and Sullivan's (1953b) description of the schizophrenic experience:
"The experience which the patient undergoes is of the most awe-
some, universal character; he seems to be living in the midst of a
struggle between personified cosmic forces of good and evil, surrounded by animistically enlivened natural objects which are engaged
in ominous performances that it is terribly necessary—and impossible—to understand."

5. The general course of events leading to the psychic and emotional reconstitution of the shaman is, for the most part, predetermined by the cultural context. That is, the shamanistic experience
is a function of the culture in which it occurs and, as such, is patterned by the expectations of that culture. Common to all cultures in
which such alterations in consciousness are evidenced is the esteemed
position held by the shaman.

> . . . He has succeeded in integrating into consciousness a considerable
> number of experiences that, for the profane world, are reserved for
> dreams, madness, and post-mortem states. The shamans and mystics
> of primitive societies are considered—and rightly—to be superior
> beings; their magico-religious powers also find expression in an ex-

tension of their mental capacities. The shaman is the man who *knows* and *remembers*, that is, who understands the mysteries of life and death (Eliade 1964).

Accompanying this esteem, however, are the expectations held by the culture for the shaman. While entranced in his state of ecstasy, he is expected to evidence ritualistic behavior requiring superhuman physical and psychological ability. It is precisely these abilities that offer ample support for the assertion that the shaman undergoes a profound alteration in consciousness. Silverman makes the excellent point that some schizophrenics, that is, catatonics, perform similar ritualistic behavior, but, since it is not part of a consensually validated reality (as the shaman's is), it is classified as invalid and accounts for nothing more than additional proof of insanity.

It appears that considerable similarities exist between the schizophrenic and shamanistic ASC. It may very well be that, given the original restrictive conditions imposed on our consideration of the two states, the only substantive difference is the following:

> The essential difference between the psychosocial environments of the schizophrenic and the shaman lies in the pervasiveness of the anxiety that complicates each of their lives. The emotional supports and the modes of collective solutions of the basic problems of existence available to the shaman greatly alleviate the strain of an otherwise excruciatingly painful existence. Such supports are all too often completely unavailable to the schizophrenic in our culture (Silverman 1967c).

3

Fundamental Properties of
Altered States of Consciousness

Since socialization is a pervasive process in all cultures, it is logical to examine next the fundamental psychodynamic processes whereby individuals become alienated from the dominant social structure and undergo an ASC experience. A minimum of three basic reactions to socialization are plausible: (1) adherence to the explicit and implicit rules of socialization that entail normalcy, social responsibility, and social stability, that is, being well adjusted to the norms propounded within a particular cultural-social enviroment; (2) refusal to accept the rules of socialization coupled with an inability to formulate an alternative model, which results in stress ranging from neurosis to extreme pathology; and (3) refusal to accept socialization norms allied with a subsequent constructive process whereby the individual or group breaks from the dominant mode of socialization to create an alternative model of appropriate behavior.

Adjustment of the individual, as cited in the first alternative, is more than amply demonstrated by the general adherence of most individuals to the codes of acceptable behavior within a given society. This discussion will propose a positive interpretation of the last two alternatives in order to demonstrate the applicability of ASC experiences to the process of *individuation*, a term first propounded by C. G. Jung and defined as

> the process of forming and specializing the individual nature; in particular, it is the development of the psychological individual as a

differentiated being from the general, collective psychology. Individuation, therefore, is a process of differentiation, having for its goal the development of the individual personality. The psychological process of individuation is clearly bound up with the transcendent function, since it alone can provide that individual line of development which would be quite unattainable upon the ways dictated by the collective norm (de Laszlo 1959, p. 259).

This concept is echoed in such major clinical and personality conceptions of an individual's functioning as Rogers's "fully functioning person" (Rogers 1961) and Maslow's "self-actualized person" (Maslow 1962*b*). This idealized state is most succinctly defined by Maslow (and paraphrased here by Maddi) as a state in which

> the person is characterized by realistic orientation; acceptance of self, others, and natural world; spontaneity; task orientation (rather than self-preoccupation); sense of privacy; independence; vivid appreciativeness; spirituality that is not necessarily religious in a formal sense; sense of identity with mankind; feelings of intimacy with a few loved ones; democratic values; recognition of the difference between means and ends; humor that is philosophical rather than hostile; creativeness; and non-conformism (Maddi 1968, p. 493).

In order to obtain such a state, Maslow stated that it was necessary for an individual to undergo a "peak experience" (Maslow 1962*b*) as a necessary prerequisite to establishing a more integrated and more fully functional identity. Furthermore, Maslow attempts to define the paradoxical quality of the peak experience by stating, "the greatest attainment of identity, autonomy or selfhood is itself simultaneously a transcending of itself, a going beyond and above selfhood" (DeRopp 1968, p. 65). An implicit assumption in the theories of Jung and Maslow is that the highest form of individual functioning is transcendent rather than adaptive or homeostatic. This hypothesis has received empirical verification in the creativity studies of MacKinnon (1962, 1965), Bruner (1962), and in the neurological-activation models based on the research of Maddi (1968), Simeons (1960), and Prince (1971). Furthermore, it is evident from the theories of Jung, Maslow, Fromm, and Rogers that the necessary prerequisite to this radical transformation of the individual identity is an ASC experience.

Despite the fact that such impelling ASC phenomena are considered to be statistically infrequent, Jung initiated a concept that is gaining increasing acceptance—that there is a fundamental tendency within all individuals to maximize the expression of their individual abilities. Jung termed the process *vocation* and defined it as

> an irrational factor that fatefully forces a man to emancipate himself from the herd and its trodden paths. This vocation acts like a law from which there is no escape. That many go to ruin upon their own way, means nothing to him who has vocation. He must obey his own law, as if it were a demon that whisperingly indicated to him new and strange ways. Who has vocation hears the voice of the inner man; he is called (Jung 1961, p. 283).

Again, an analogous concept is prominent in the theories of Bakan with "the attempt to maximize the expression of both agency and communion" (1966), Rogers's "tendency to actualize one's inherent potentialities" (1961), Maslow's "push toward actualization of inherent potentialities" (1962b), and Adler's "striving toward superiority or perfection" (1930), to cite major examples. The function inherent in an individual to strive toward a state of individuation is an absolutely critical concept to bear in mind in examining the occurrence of ASC phenomena. Instead of interpreting ASC experiences as necessarily indicative of pathology, it is possible to view them as the manifestation of the process of individuation, which may frequently be opposed to the predominant values of a given society. In Western culture, which values rationality and control, ASC phenomena are often termed psychotic, but Jung offers an alternative viewpoint when he states, "the primitive theory therefore does not seek the reason for insanity in a primary weakness of the consciousness, but rather in an inordinate strength of the unconscious" (de Laszlo 1959, p. 391). In essence, any interpretation of the positive attributes of ASC phenomena is dependent on this very alteration in values and perspective.

Most recently, Harvard psychiatrist Andrew Weil has asserted: "A desire to alter consciousness periodically is an innate, normal drive analogous to hunger or the sexual drive. . . . the omnipresence of the phenomenon argues that we are not dealing with something socially or culturally based but rather with a biological characteristic of the species" (1972, p. 66). It has, in fact, been demonstrated in a number of theoretical and research publications that ASC experiences in various cultures have much in common. Before proceeding to differentiate and elaborate upon the disparate aspects of ASC phenomena, it would be informative to enumerate the fundamental psychodynamic similarities underlying these states. Enumeration of the prerequisite social and psychological conditions for an individual to undergo an ASC experience is a formidable task. A search of the related literature reveals that only two experiments (Festinger, Pepitone, and Newcomb 1952; Singer, Brush, and Lublin 1965) and one conceptual article (Ziller 1964) approach this specific problem. There are, however, a number of factors that may be operative and have received some theoretical and experimental consideration. One such factor is anonymity, which has been demonstrated to lead to more overt "parental hostility" by Festinger and more frequent use of "obscene language" by Singer (1965). This phenomenon was further enhanced by allowing the individual subjects to become involved in a self-supportive group matrix where responsibility for the socially undesirable behavior was rendered collective. Another possible factor would be involvement in a relatively unstructured situation, such as in a demonstration or under the influence of alcohol or hallucinogens, since behavior would be less constrained by learned situation cues. Such a situation would permit, if not demand, more reliance on individual reactions and social interpretations, since the normative function of social constraints would be suspended. In this state, an individual may become absorbed in the immediacy of his actions rather than in their personal and social consequences. This irresponsibility is an essential characteristic of deindividuated behavior freed from social and personal constraints. A third related factor would be a generalized state of physiological arousal, since such arousal could override cognitive controls and lead to exaggerated, unconstrained behavior (Schacter 1962). This state may be induced by the above stimulants or by a "sensory input overload" (Zimbardo 1969), particularly when induced by the immediacy of physical contact, exemplified in fighting or sexual activity. Intense sensory input is conducive to a reactivation of the primary intensity of sensory behavior. The individual's behavior derives its impetus from a precognitive substrate of unmediated, physiological arousal or "activation level," as postulated by Maddi and Fiske. Thus, it is possible for social contraints to be suspended and for inidividuals to behave in a manner that places individual expression above the observation of social dictates. Behavior that is unconstrained, impulsive, and yet remains nondestructive to the individual or to others is likely to precipitate an ASC.

One of the most comprehensive paradigms of the social and psychological processes involved in inducing altered states of consciousness has been formulated by Philip G. Zimbardo. Using his conceptualization as a base, we will correlate and amplify his schema by reference to the only two other attempts to formulate such a paradigm. One is a theoretical article by Julian Silverman entitled "A Paradigm for the Study of Altered States of Consciousness" (1968a), and the second is a paper by Theodore R. Sarbin and Nathan Adler entitled "Commonalities in Systems of Conduct Reorganization" (1967). Zimbardo postulates a process termed *deindividuation,* which essentially prescribes the prerequisite conditions under which an individual would be likely to undergo an ASC experience. Deindividuation is defined as

a complex, hypothesized process in which a series of antecedent social conditions lead to changes in perception of self and others, and thereby to a lowered threshold of normally restrained behavior in violation of established norms of appropriateness. Such conditions permit overt expression of antisocial behavior, characterized as selfish, greedy, power seeking, hostile, lustful, and destructive. However, they also allow a range of "positive" behaviors which we normally do not express overtly, such as intense feelings of happiness or sorrow, and open love for others (1969, p. 13).

Included in the list of conditions prerequisite to deindividuated behavior is "altered states of consciousness." However, for purposes of this theoretical presentation, ASC will be eliminated from the list since the remaining factors are contributory to but not synonymous with ASC behavior. Factors listed are (1) anonymity, (2) responsibility, (3) group size, (4) altered temporal perspective, (5) arousal, (6) sensory-input overload, (7) reliance on noncognitive interactions and feedback, (8) physical involvement in the act, and (9) novel or unstructured situations. All of these factors are essential to the induction and prolongation of an ASC experience; individually or in interaction, they form the basis upon which the various ASC experiences are derived. Rather than discussing specific ASC states here, an attempt will be made to define the precedents for the ASC states, which will be enumerated in chapter 4.

Anonymity is a frequent precedent because if an individual cannot be identified he is less subject to social sanctions. This prerequisite can be fulfilled either by the immersion of the individual within a crowd or by means of physical isolation, as in sensory deprivation experiments (Lilly 1968). Physical isolation can often plunge an individual into an experience of symbolic death and rebirth, which Sarbin and Adler term "the surrender of the self." The individual usually becomes engulfed in subjective fantasies and hallucinations and perceives that he is losing grip on reality and self-control. It has been frequently reported that drug usage is essentially an asocial, isolating ritual that insures the anonymity necessary to experience an ASC (Osmond 1972; Metzner 1970). Establishing anonymity involves an experience of depersonalization, which allows an individual the capacity for disowning responsibility for his own actions.

Zimbardo uses the term in the responsible sense that one can avoid answering for his antisocial actions by sharing accountability with others. There are several narratives about rites among primitive peoples that insure collective responsibility for acts of sacrifice (Furst 1972); they bear a striking similarity to the idea of diffusion and lessening of individual responsibility in military organizations (Bettelheim 1967, p. 41).

Group size is a factor in the extension and enhancement of anonymity and diffused responsibility. In Sarbin and Adler's theory of conduct reorganization, the size of the group is a major factor in the sense that, if an individual has renounced his allegiance to his former rules of socialization, then the size of his reference group will determine the degree of assuredness with which he constructs his new identity. In effect, "the individual not only changes overt behavior to meet role expectations and demands but in the process his conception of self becomes modified" (Sarbin and Adler 1967).

Altered temporal perspective is one of the most important factors in initiating and sustaining an ASC experience. Present time expands and engulfs the individual in an extended present, free from past contraints and unheedful of future liabilities. This experience amounts to a prolongation of subjective time (Masters and Houston 1966), in which an individual experiences a multiplicity of temporal distortions, ranging from experiences of timelessness to an imploding of time into an accelerated present. According to Sarbin and Adler: "Such a bracketing and isolation of time may not only focus attention but also prepare the individual for the lack of earlier specific roles, and, given the failure of expectancies due to the absence of customary feedback, initiate the stripping of achieved roles" (1967). It is clear that a deviation in the normal temporal ordering of experience can induce subjective alterations in concentration, attention, memory, and judgment and thus provide the state of disequilibrium necessary before undergoing an ASC experience.

Arousal is another major factor closely allied with sensory-input overload. It is evident that profound alterations occur in a person's visual, auditory, tactile, olfactory, gustatory, and kinesthetic perceptions before the onset of an ASC experience. According to Silverman (1968b), either "sensory overload" or "sensory underload" can induce an ASC state since either marked increases or marked decreases in exteroceptive stimulation are precursors of general emotional arousal. Instances of such sensory alteration can be witnessed among primitive "rites of passage" (Eliade 1964) and also in the early stages of the onset of a schizophrenic reaction (Ludwig 1966). Arousal is also cited by Sarbin and Adler as achieved by the use of prolonged kneeling and swaying or fatigue to challenge and disrupt a person's dependence on external stimuli (Jung 1950; Sullivan 1968b). These rituals are intended to create an environment in which an individual is freed from societal constraints and encouraged to submit to the new group norm that sanctions the expression of formerly repressed behavior.

Recognition of this last statement leads directly to the most fundamental issue of all, which is Zimbardo's concept of reliance on noncognitive interaction and feedback. Most significantly, this last factor —the release of repressed behavior—is supported by the basic motivational assumption that much behavior that would be inherently pleasurable to manifest is denied expression because it conflicts with social norms. Consequently, the affect of this inhibited behavior increases in intensity until conditions permit deindividuated behavior and a release of the presumably gratifying behavior. By definition, expression of such pleasurable behavior is self-reinforcing and, once initiated, self-perpetuating and beyond the control of the usual external checks and constraints (Zimbardo 1969). The motivation to engage in such behavior results simply in the conscious reestablishment of denied pleasurable activity. Once this behavior is initiated, it becomes increasingly impulsive, erratic, and totally absorbing, since its dynamics are based on a noncognitive feedback system, which is aptly defined by Zimbardo: "Noncognitive feedback becomes an auxiliary input to a closed-loop system which results in spiraling intensity whose terminal state cannot be predicted from knowledge of the initial boundary conditions" (1969, p. 23). A self-amplification process is generated by the individual's purposive intent to reexperience the intensity of unconstrained behavior regardless of subsequent good-bad value judgment. Irrational behavior of this mode can be positively attributed to the vitalistic strength of early and underlying primary-process interaction rather than to a cognitive weakness or breakdown. Regressive behavior may be approached as a positive, developmentally progressive outstripping and reorganization of cognitive processes since its only link to infantile regressive behavior is in the individual's outward behavior. This closed-loop system may enable an individual to experience an intensely pleasurable experience. Closed-loop functioning is a basic psychodynamic process that, although it has not received sufficient attention, can explain all positive and negative ASC phenomena, including schizophrenic psychosis. Whereas a "noncognitive closed loop feedback system" (Zimbardo 1969) is a potential source of increasing pleasure, a cognitive closed-loop feedback system is viewed by R. D. Laing as one of the initiating factors in psychosis. Laing discusses a spiraling process of cognitive degeneration in which one becomes more and more caught up in his subjective thoughts about external reality and increasingly ignores the actual situation at hand. Autistic logic of this type is termed *synthesis* by Laing; he uses this concept to describe a triadic interaction of circuitous mental processes—a fundamental psychodynamic that, if left unchecked, would result in psychosis: "I interiorize your and his syntheses, you interiorize his and mine, he interiorizes mine and yours; I interiorize your interiorization of mine and his; you interiorize my interiorization of yours and his. Furthermore, he interiorizes my interiorization of his and yours—a logical ongoing spiral of reciprocal perspectives to infinity" (1967, p. 97). What is most significant in Laing's rather facetious observation is that an inward spiral of cognitive construction layered on cognitive construction leads to pathology as one becomes increasingly removed from direct sensory experience of external reality. However, if the closed-loop system allows the individual to experience external reality with heightened intensity, then there is the *potential* for that person to undergo a positive ASC experience. An internally spiraling process implies excessive rumination, fantasies, and withdrawal, whereas the externally spiraling noncognitive process implies increased reactivity, spontaneity, and involvement in the unabated sensory experience of external reality. Obviously, neither extreme leads to positive behavior since an internal spiral can proceed from productive introspection to autistic fantasy, and an external spiral can proceed from spontaneity and immediate reactivity to unconstrained violence. Our concern here is to examine the positive aspects of a person's intense, immediate involvement with the people and the world around him. Throughout the literature on all positive altered states of consciousness, one of the most notable qualities is found to be the rapid intensification of the experience of noncognitive external stimuli, such as colors, sounds, and smells. The concept of a "noncognitive, closed loop feedback system" is a truly outstanding contribution to the under-standing of all ASC phenomena, since semiautistic amplification is the fundamental psychodynamic process underlying all altered-state phenomena.

Physical involvement in the act is an example of a noncognitive feedback system because the sense of touch is the most primary one in an infant's initial orientation to the external environment (Wolff 1952). Such involvement is termed a *trigger* in the scheme of Sarbin and Adler; triggers are specific events, objects, or intense sensations likely to crystallize the process of conduct reorganization. "Positive triggers," such as religious artifacts, exercises, and movements, are differentiated from "negative triggers," such as illness, hunger, and cold.

Last, a novel or unstructured situation is conducive to spontane-ous, unpremeditated actions because, in it, an individual is less con-strained by "learned situation-bound cues" (Zimbardo 1969, p. 20). Certain environments are constructed to minimize distracting stimuli; through the use of a drone, incense, or uniform lighting, a person is induced to experience the environment in a novel manner. Silver-man (1971) describes such an alteration in environment as leading to "hyperattentiveness to a narrow range of sensory and ideational stimuli and hyposensitivity to ordinarily responded to attributes of the environment." In effect, this experience can be equated with an enhancement of perceptual attentiveness to ordinarily low-intensity stimuli, such as hearing the minute variations in the chords of a musical score. By attending to the low-intensity stimui of his environ-ment, a person experiences the environment in a novel manner since in the normal state of consciousness, the low-intensity stimuli are ignored or blocked by the more dominant stimuli. In the unstruc-tured or unfamiliar environment of novel stimuli, one would more readily undergo an ASC experience.

There are several other frequently cited precursors and charac-teristics of an ASC experience. It is difficult to establish causality in discussing ASC experiences since such phenomena are generated in a closed-loop system of spiraling intensity. However, the above nine observations are considered to be prerequisites to an ASC experience, while the following factors can be interpreted either as requisite to or characteristic of an altered state of consciousness. These other factors are: (1) emotional lability with increased intensity of emotion (Masters and Houston 1966; Leary, Metzner, and Alpert 1964); (2) changes in body chemistry and in neurophysiological-response systems (Silverman 1971); (3) body-image changes involving a dissolution of boundaries between self and others or self and inanimate objects (Silverman 1971); (4) perceptual distortions and psychotic changes, including thought disorder and delusional and referential thinking (Masters and Houston 1966); and (5) feelings of profound insight, illumination, and truth and a general increase in the sense of significance concerning common events (Silverman 1971). In summary, these factors comprise the fundamental psychodynamic substrates of all ASC experiences; all of them are present in varying degrees in any manifest ASC behavior. In chapter 4, the interaction and/or predominance of these factors will be considered as they define discrete ASC phenomena and their varying degrees of success in going beyond the transient disruption and achieving a state of individuation.

Despite cultural and social sanctions that inhibit mass expression of such irrational behavior, many individuals either willingly or unwillingly embark on a quest that begins in chaos but, it is hoped, terminates in a more profound integration. It is increasingly evident that psychotherapists need to be aware of the properties, dangers, and virtues of such states in order to most efficiently guide themselves and their patients through this terra incognita.

A CARTOGRAPHY OF CONSCIOUSNESS

According to Stanley Krippner (1972), there are twenty identifiable altered states of consciousness, including normal consciousness. Considerable overlap among these states is inevitable given the similarities of the processes by which these states are derived. This cartography will list Krippner's unelaborated states and will then explicate each state with reference to current theory and research.

We will examine those states on which research is available and in which we are interested and knowledgeable extensively, and we will deal with the others summarily.

Twenty semiautonomous states of consciousness can be categorized as follows: (1) dreaming state, (2) sleeping state, (3) hypnagogic state, (4) hypnopompic state, (5) hyperalert state, (6) lethargic state, (7) state of rapture, (8) state of hysteria, (9) state of fragmentation, (10) regressive state, (11) meditative state, (12) trance state, (13) reverie, (14) daydreaming state, (15) internal scanning, (16) stupor, (17) coma, (18) stored memory, (19) "expanded" conscious state, and (20) normal waking consciousness. These states are commonly agreed-upon differentiations of psychological functioning; however, there has been only one attempt (Fischer 1971) to place these states on a continuum and to define the similarities and differences of each discrete state. It is interesting to discover that the need for such an exploration of consciousness was evident at the roots of psychology in 1887:

> Narcotism, hypnotic catalepsy, hypnotic somnambulism, and the like . . . afford, as though by a painless and harmless physical vivisection, an unequalled insight into the mysteries of man. Then, again, after isolating and exaggerating one process after another for more convenient scrutiny, we may return to those normal states which lie open to our habitual introspection, having gained a new power of disentangling each particular thread in the complex of mentation, as when the microscopist stains his object with a dye that affects one tissue only among several which are indiscernibly intermixed (Myers 1887).

This presentation will focus primarily on three major altered states: (1) psychotic states or states of fragmentation, (2) psychedelic drug-induced states or expanded-conscious states, and (3) meditative or mystical states. These states are the ones that have been most extensively researched and written about in a wide variety of settings. Before concentrating upon these three altered states, we will consider relevant theory and research on the other seventeen altered states cited by Krippner. Most of them will be dealt with as briefly as possible because Krippner's taxonomy is quite comprehensive and is a basic reference for standardizing the number and contents of altered states. Further references will be noted when they are available, but we will not attempt to review existing literature.

Most research on the dream state has relied primarily on data obtained from the electroencephalogram (EEG) since this state can be readily identified on the EEG by noting the periods of rapid-eye movement (REM) and the absence of "slow" brain waves. NIMH research reporter Gay Gaer Luce has compiled a 125-page summation entitled "Current Research on Sleep and Dreams." Given the availability of this report, it would be redundant to recapitulate research on the dream state. However, despite the extensive review of current research, the report concludes with the observation that "voluntary control over sleep behavior and, indeed, some facets of waking consciousness, have come into systematic investigation only recently. Only a bare beginning has been made in the study of sleep behavior itself." As one aspect of ASC experience, the REM state most closely resembles the waking state in terms of EEG activity. During REM sleep, the EEG of the person is similar to the person's waking state yet the subjective experience is quite different from normal. In the REM state, there is a great degree of electrical and physiological stimulation, which induces a high degree of mental function. Such dream functions are free from the limitations imposed by the socially conditioned logical orientation of normal consciousness. In this state, a person is less responsive to external stimulation, and his high-activity mental processes are available for creative problem solving and inspiration. Stanley Krippner and William Hughes have documented major discoveries and insights that have been gained by individuals while in the REM state (Krippner and Hughes 1970). For example, Niels Bohr conceived of the existing model of the atom through a dream image; Otto Loewi, a Nobel Prize-winning pharmacologist in 1936, formulated his theory of the nervous system in a dream state; and Elias Howe solved a major mechanical shortcoming in the design of his sewing machine based on an insight he had during the REM state. In order to explicate this process, Gardner Murphy has described four phases of the creative process as "immersion, consolidation, illumination, and evaluation" (1958). In effect, Murphy is postulating an interaction effect between the cognitive acquisition of factual information and an irrational processing of that information as the basis of creativity. Like most research in ASC phenomena, this hypothesis is in need of further research and empirical verification.

Sleeping-state research is similarly based primarily on EEG interpretation, since the definition of this state is that it can be identified by the absence of REM and by a gradually emerging pattern of slow brain waves. A normal person will spend a considerable portion of the night in this stage, especially if he has been deprived of sleep (Agnew, Webb, and Williams 1964). In the sleeping state, the individual's muscles are very relaxed, respiration is slow and even, heart rate and temperature are at their lowest point, and it is most difficult to awaken a person from this stage of sleep, designated *stage four*. During this period of sleep, the EEG pattern is dominated by slow high-amplitude waves. Despite the fact that the individual appears to be physiologically unresponsive, the EEG indicates a sharp response to every external sound or the lightest touch. However, cortical systems, which would convert this stimulation into conscious sensation, appear to be not functioning in their normal manner, and this unusual altered state may account for the inexplicable ability of a somnambulist to perform quite adeptly while remaining in deep stage-four sleep (Hernandez-Peon 1963; Allison 1965). This stage of sleep is one of the least researched, and it used to be assumed that there was little or no mental activity in stage four. Recent research has indicated that dreams do in fact occur in stage-four sleep and that an individual awakened from this state is usually capable of reporting dreamlike imagery that is considerably less vivid than REM-state imagery.

Both the hypnagogic state entering into sleep and the hypnopompic before awakening from sleep are characterized by vivid visual imagery occasionally accompanied by auditory stimuli. Hypnagogic imagery occurs between waking and sleeping at the onset of the sleep cycle, while hypnopompic imagery occurs between sleeping and waking at the end of the sleep cycle (Krippner 1972). McKellar and Simpson (1954) reported the results of one of the few investigations of hypnagogic imagery by describing the four main characteristics of such imagery (as opposed to dream images) as "more vivid but usually static; independent of conscious control, more originality, and more rapid changefulness." There is no known research on hypnopompic imagery, and only one researcher, Elmer E. Green of the Menninger Foundation, has pursued an inquiry into hypnagogic imagery. It is Green's goal to develop a method by which individuals can sustain focused awareness of hypnagogic imagery and learn to manipulate it in a creative manner. Green has postulated, in accordance with L. E. Walkup (1965), that creative people have developed a high degree of ability to manipulate visual symbols for creative insight. All of Green's research has focused on the use of Biofeedback from the EEG, but this will be more fully discussed in chapter 9, which is concerned primarily with Biofeedback and its application to research and psychotherapy.

Krippner characterizes the hyperalert state as one of "prolonged and increased vigilance while one is awake. It can be induced by drugs which stimulate the brain by activities demanding intense concentration, or by measures necessary for survival" (1972). This state clearly involves an altered temporal perspective, which Zimbardo cites as a necessary prerequisite of an ASC experience. No research has been conducted on this state. Similarly, Krippner's recognition of a lethargic state can be most closely allied with theories concerning depression. This state is characterized by "dulled, sluggish mental activity which can be induced by fatigue, hypoglycemia, or by despondent moods and feelings" (Krippner 1972).

The state of rapture is determined by "intense feeling and overpowering emotion," subjectively evaluated as "pleasurable and positive in nature." For centuries, primitive cultures have made extensive use of this state in orgiastic rituals, rites of initiation, and rites of passage. According to Jungian analysts J. L. Henderson and M. Oakes in *The Wisdom of the Serpent,* "From the earliest sources of knowledge concerning the ritualistic behavior of prehistoric man, we find evidence of rites of passage performed to conduct the souls of human beings into death as well as to initiate the young into life" (1963, p. 46). Characteristically, these rituals involve the initiate in an anxiety-inducing situation in which his life may be threatened, in order for him to experience the rapture of living as fully as possible. Analogous to this state is Krippner's state of hysteria, which he defines as a state of overpowering emotions subjectively evaluated as "negative and destructive in nature," such as violent mob activity invoking rage, fear, or anger. Although the outward manifestations of these states are markedly different, they are both characterized by arousal, sensory-input overload, and physical involvement in the act, qualities conducive to ASC experiences. Primitive rituals are frequently intended to induce an ASC experience involving a death and rebirth cycle. This cycle plays a prominent part in certain stages of a psychotic episode and during mystical states of consciousness, as will be demonstrated later in this discussion. It is common among Eastern religions to invoke an ASC experience involving a symbolic death and rebirth, such as in the Hindu dance of Shiva, or death, where Shiva is recognized as "destruction—Shiva —is only the negative aspect of unending life" (Zimmer 1946). Death and rebirth are depicted in a dance or ritual as an unending cycle repeated throughout eternity. Rituals such as these are more graphic in Eastern and primitive cultures than in our own; yet Henderson and Oakes formulate this death and rebirth experience as a necessary step in achieving higher states of consciousness:

> This is the knowledge of death and rebirth forever withheld except at those times when some transcendent principle, emerging from the depths, makes it available to consciousness. For this reason, analytical psychology postulates the existence of a transcendent function of the psyche which has the power to relate contents of the unconscious to consciousness in a healing symbol (1963, p. 40).

Their emphasis on the healing potential of such an experience is extremely important to bear in mind because it becomes critical in the later discussions of the psychotic, drug, and meditation ASC states. Powerful ASC experiences bear both destruction and rejuvenation and only through a more thorough understanding of the content and processes of those experiences can a therapist weigh the outcome in favor of rejuvenation and renewal.

Listed in the taxonomy of Krippner's states are seven distinct categories of consciousness that will not be considered in detail, since the main states to be examined in this presentation are the psychotic, drug-induced, and meditative or mystical states. In order to present a comprehensive summation of Krippner's unique model, these seven states will be briefly defined before a more detailed examination of the three main categories of ASC states is given.

Although Krippner differentiates regressive states from stored-memory states, there is little or no qualitative difference between them. Essentially a regressive state is, in the classic sense of behavior, that which is clearly inappropriate for an individual's chronological age. Similarly, a stored-memory state involves the reenactment or remembrance of a past experience that is not immediately available to a person's conscious awareness.

Stupor is characterized by a suspended or greatly reduced ability to perceive incoming stimuli, while coma is defined as an inability to perceive incoming stimuli. In both cases, the individual is involved in an altered state of consciousness so far removed from normal consciousness as to render him virtually inaccessible to communication, as in extreme autism.

Trance states involve "hypersuggestibility, alertness, and the concentration of attention on a single stimulus" (Krippner 1972; Aaronson 1967). Closely allied to this state are reverie, which is usually induced under hypnosis, and the daydreaming state, which is considered to be a form of self-induced hypnosis. Voluminous research has been done on theory and application of hypnosis and autosuggestion (Van Nuys 1970; Barber 1970).

Last, three major ASC phenomena will be explicated and compared at length in order to determine the similarities and differences between states occurring (1) during a psychotic episode, (2) while under the influence of psychedelic drugs, and (3) following meditative practices. Information concerning these major states of consciousness is useful in understanding the contents and dynamics of all of the states cited in Krippner's taxonomy. In Western psychological literature, the dream state has received the most attention and consideration because it is believed to offer a clear representation of some of the major aspects of the landscape of consciousness. An examination of three related ASC states, which have not been as thoroughly researched, will serve to point out other prominent aspects in this cartography of consciousness.

4

Schizophrenic
States of Consciousness

While both qualitative and quantitative variations in consciousness
are regular intrapsychic occurrences, a number of major variations
have been categorized as definite alterations in the "normal," waking
state of consciousness, that is, they are altered states of consciousness. Ludwig (1966) offers the following definition of ASC:

> I shall regard altered states of consciousness . . . as any mental
> state(s) induced by various physiological, psychological or pharma-
> cological maneuvers or agents, which can be recognized subjectively
> by the individual himself (or by an objective observer of the in-
> dividual) as representing a sufficient deviation in subjective ex-
> perience or psychological functioning from certain general norms
> for that individual during alert, waking consciousness.

The generality of this definition of an ASC was recognized as and
intended to be an effort to encompass a formerly heterogeneous
grouping of clinical phenomena. Presumably, ASC can now be
regarded as related states with a greater possibility of reduction to a
common denominator. In *The Interpretations of Dreams,* Freud
attempted this reduction, and his work has been subsequently developed by Rapaport (1951). It is Rapaport's work that provides the
only systematic theory able to account for many of those clinical
phenomena falling under the rubric ASC. It should be noted, however, that this judgment is valid only for Western culture, since

many Eastern philosophical systems deal explicitly with the categorization of ASC.

Rapaport contends that consciousness is a superordinate sense organ that codes sensations at the sense receptors and also codes intrapsychic activity. Prototypically, all conscious experience is the hallucinatory gratification produced when (a) the image of previous drive discharge situations is activated following (b) the failure of a current drive cathexis to be discharged. More simply, all conscious experience corresponds to the cathexis of the memory trace of a previous gratification. The primitivistic formal aspects of such conscious experience may be "reexperienced" during such ASC as dreaming, drug, and psychotic states. In these ASC, the individual perceives intrapsychic activity as external reality that does not adhere to any formal logic but, rather, to "the prelogic of primary process based on the syncretic, diffuse, and undifferentiated character of primitive perception" (Van Nuys 1968).

Rapaport distinguishes the four following classes of altered states:

1. The continuum of normal states of consciousness ranging from wakefulness to the dream
2. The special states of normal consciousness, such as absorption, boredom, sensory deprivation, and hypnosis
3. Developmental states of consciousness, such as those of children and preliterates
4. Pathological states of consciousness, such as the definite qualitative changes in experiencing associated with the Korsakoff syndrome, fugue, amnesia, and so on

Krippner (1972), who has tentatively identified twenty states of consciousness, offers the following description of pathological states or states of fragmentation:

States of Fragmentation are characterized by lack of integration among important segments, aspects, or themes of the total personality. These states parallel conditions referred to as psychosis, severe psychoneurosis, dissociation, multiple personality, amnesia and fugue episodes (in which someone forgets his past and begins a new life pattern). These states, which may be either temporary or long lasting, can be induced by certain drugs, physical trauma to the brain, psychological stress, physiological predispositions (which interact with psychological stress in some types of schizophrenia), and experimental manipulation (e.g., sensory deprivation, hypnosis).

It is with the final class of ASC that this chapter is primarily concerned.

Inquiry into the nature of ASC is of high clinical relevance both as it examines diverse psychopathological conditions and as it relates to broader issues of psychodynamics and therapy. Indeed, it is possible that qualitative alterations in consciousness occur in any form of psychopathology and perhaps in so-called normal states as well. We intend, however, to examine specifically those alterations occurring in schizophrenic psychosis.

SCHIZOPHRENIA

The enigmatic aspects of schizophrenia theory and research are acknowledged by the majority of investigators of these psychotic states. The etiological obscurities of the varied non-mutually exclusive classes of schizophrenic syndromes and the unreliability of diagnostic criteria are evident. Bleuler (1965) examined a substantial number of contemporary perspectives ranging from genetic to environmental, from biochemical to psychological, from descriptive to dynamic and concluded that "no single specific cause for all schizophrenic psychoses has been found. I think that it does not exist." Yet diverse empirical findings have been reported indicating familial "disturbances," biochemical "abnormalities," and genetic factors. After acquainting ourselves with all the major theoretical perspectives, we became aware that fundamental difficulties existed on both the theoretical and metatheoretical levels. Perhaps the clearest statement on the current state of affairs in schizophrenia theory and research was made by Loren R. Mosher, Chief of the NIMH Center for Studies of Schizophrenia. In the conclusion of a *Special Report on Schizophrenia,* Mosher (1971) stated:

In the area of scientific fact, the schizophrenic disorder, as always, abounds in controversy. Some of the most pressing issues are detailed below:

1. Is schizophrenia a single disease or a heterogeneous syndrome? [Prevailing opinion favors "multiple entities within the disorder" as the most likely explanation.] Should this assumption prove correct, investigators will be released from the need to apply findings to all schizophrenics. But, even if freed of this obligation, investigators still must define and identify the subgroup to which findings *do* apply—a task that, thus far, has defied completion.

2. That heredity plays a role in the development of schizophrenia (in at least some individuals) is rarely disputed; yet the mode of the genetic transmission is unknown. Whether schizophrenia is transmitted by a single gene or reflects a polygenic mode of inheritance is still a mystery, although at present most investigators favor the latter possibility. Granted, "something" may be inherited, but precisely what that something is remains a matter of speculation. Is it an enzyme defect, a biochemical abnormality, a minor neurological deficit, or any one of a seemingly infinite number of factors? If a predisposition is inherited, what is it? How does it operate? What is the nature and course of the spiraling feedback mechanism set up in the individual, his family, and the social system?

3. Despite the recent proliferation of studies of family factors in schizophrenia, investigators have as yet been unable to determine whether the phenomena described are products or causes of the illness. Nor is it clear whether these factors are *specific* to schizophrenia or are more pathological conditions. The longitudinal prospective study of children thought to be at high risk for the development of schizophrenia should make it possible to deal more adequately with this question of cause and effect—a point of controversy which plagues almost all areas of schizophrenia research.

4. Infantile autism and childhood schizophrenia are still largely unresolved riddles (indeed, it is not even certain whether they constitute *one* riddle or *two*). Although evidence of central nervous system damage in afflicted children under 5 years of age (the group most commonly designated as autistic) continues to accumulate, infantile autism remains puzzling, and childhood schizophrenia, which is most often manifest in later childhood, is more mysterious

still. What, for example, is the family's role in the genesis of child-hood schizophrenia and/or autism? To what extent are either birth or family factors etiologically significant? The unanswered questions are myriad.*

Mogar (1968) recognizes this multiplicity of theories and overtly conflicting evidence and states that a reconciliation is possible if it is recognized that

(a) an ever-increasing range of experiences and behaviors are currently labeled schizophrenic, (b) there is nothing in schizophrenic phenomenology that would be quite strange to the healthy, i.e., there is nothing intrinsically pathological in the experience of ego loss, (c) a variety of avenues can lead to a schizoid state and (d) various levels of interpretation of the empirical evidence may have entirely different individual and social consequences and yet be simultaneously valid and consistent.

Mogar offers support for his contentions by comparing two opposing theoretical orientations, namely, the disease model and the social-existential perspective. The former is represented by the adrenochrome metabolite theory of Hoffer and Osmond (1960), which maintains that a genetic mechanism is responsible for the following chain of events:

genetic mechanism ⟶ physiological, biochemical and clinical peculiarities ⟶ perceptual and affective alterations ⟶ psychosocial consequences.

This hypothetical genetic factor is purported to increase the production of adrenochrome and adrenolutin, two psychotomimetic ("psychosis-mimicking") substances (Osmond and Hoffer 1966).

The contrasting theoretical perspective is the social-existential orientation of Laing, Szasz, and others, which emphasizes the familial-social origins of schizophrenia. Laing (1967) denies the existence of any such psychopathological condition as schizophrenia and maintains that

* L. R. Mosher, *Special Report on Schizophrenia* (Washington, D.C.: National Institute of Mental Health, 1971), p. 32.

schizophrenia is a diagnosis, a label applied by some people to others. This does not prove that the labeled person is subject to an essentially pathological process, of unknown nature and origin, going on *in* his or her body. It does not mean that the process is, primarily or secondarily a *psycho*pathological one, going on *in* the *psyche* of the person. But it does establish as a social fact that the person labeled is one of them. It is easy to forget that the process is a hypothesis, to assume that it is a fact, then to pass the judgment that it is biologically maladaptive and, as such, pathological. . . .

There is no such condition as schizophrenia, but the label is a social fact and the social fact a political event.

Laing describes the *schizophrenic as one whose experiences and behavior are atypical, from the vantage point of his relatives and psychiatrist.* He further asserts that, based on considerable research evidence, "no schizophrenic has been studied whose disturbed pattern of communication has not been shown to be a reflection of, and reaction to, the disturbed and disturbing pattern characterizing his family of origin and . . . without exception, the experience and behavior that gets labeled schizophrenic is a special strategy that a person invents in order to live in an unlivable situation." Mogar contends that no essential conflict exists between the genetic-disease and social-existential models of schizophrenia. Theorists of the social-existential persuasion do not ignore the possibility of a genetic factor but, rather, consider such a factor from an evolutionary perspective. For example, schizophrenics are referred to by Adolph Meyer as "experiments in nature," by Teilhard de Chardin as "children of a transitional period" and by the metaphorical Laing as follows: "If the human race survives, future men will, I suspect, look back on our enlightened epoch as a veritable Age of Darkness. . . . They will see that what we call schizophrenia was one of the forms in which, often through quite ordinary people, the light began to break through the cracks in our all-too-closed minds" (1967). Conversely, Hoffer (1966) appears to acknowledge the complexity of his genetic-disease position somewhat when he asserts that schizophrenia "is also psychological, sociological, and even theological. For like the psychedelic reaction, the molecular abnormality in schizophrenia merely sets off the train of events which is perceived and reacted to by a person in terms of his life's programming."

We are in accord with Mogar's crucial point that the only certain important variation among contemporary perspectives of schizophrenia involves the individual, familial, and social consequences of adhering to one theoretical orientation to the exclusion of alternative frames of reference. More precisely, the assumption of a disease entity lying outside the agency of the person—that is, as a disease "that the person is subject to or undergoes, whether genetic, constitutional, endogenous, exogenous, organic, or psychological, or some mixture of these" (Laing 1967)—has been responsible for the classification of certain extraordinary cognitive and perceptual experiences as pathological. Three antitherapeutic consequences of regarding schizophrenia as exclusively a pathological condition are (1) the rejection of the validity of multiple realities, (2) the definition of the schizophrenic as a nonresponsible object, and (3) the lack of attention directed at the positive aspects of altered states of awareness. It is the third consequence, that is, the conceptualization of schizophrenia as an altered state of awareness or ASC with both positive and negative potential for the individual, that is our major concern. More specifically, our focus will be the discovery and examination of relevant psychophysiological, perceptual, and subjective analogues of the schizophrenic experience and individual experiences of other ASC.

THE SCHIZOPHRENIC EXPERIENCE

The Metamorphosis from "Normal" to "Psychotic" Experience

Despite the wide variation in schizophrenic symptomology, one can depict a general pattern of common characteristics.

1. The conflict of having to deal with a consensually validated but unendurable life condition results in an extensive dependence on metaphor and fantasy.

2. Attention is inner directed and focused on a fragmented yet partially egoic symbolism.

3. Cognitive processes are prelogical, idiosyncratic, and, hence, out of synchronism with consensual reality.

4. The "hyperliterality" of the schizophrenic is evidenced by an inability or reluctance to deal with abstractions and, often, a preoccupation with the auditory or associational quality of words at the expense of their meaning.

5. The inability to differentiate between inner and outer space results in the cross-contamination of current perceptions and the contents of memory.

6. There are alterations in the schizophrenic's sense of time; he experiences temporal cessation rather than temporal progression and, more fundamentally, eonic time rather than mundane time.

7. On an interpersonal level, the schizophrenic's inability or reluctance to "re-cognize" social cues effects a diminished relatedness to others.

Above and beyond the etiology and characteristics of schizophrenic psychosis lies the fact that we are dealing with both an alteration in the content of consciousness and a metamorphosis of perception and experience from the "normal" to the "psychotic" modes.

Any analysis of an ASC must acknowledge, as did Bowers (1968), that

> The study of consciousness is frustrating. Though we utilize each day a basic faith that our experience is closely akin to that of our fellows, it is categorical that we can never demonstrate scientifically that we are in fact observing another's conscious experience. We can ask ("What are you thinking?" or "What were you feeling?"), but we can never be sure of the validity of the ensuing report. Yet we proceed operationally in all phases of human encounter, and we act on the notion that we can, for purposes of living, come close to understanding the experience of another. . . . At best this is an impure, approximate form of knowing; yet it can be important and fruitful if one is able to accept avenues of investigation which are not scientifically pure in order to get at experiences which are distinctively human.

Bowers notes four stages in the pathogenesis of acute schizophrenic psychosis: the setting, the destructuring of perception and affect, the destructuring of the sense of self, and the formation of delusions. At first, patients' accounts of their prepsychotic mental state often reveal the feeling that they were "struck by a bolt from the blue." Further discussions, however, often reveal a mental state suffused with conflict and impasse, where the emotional tone is "one of overwhelming guilt and dread as a crucial maturational step was confronted but retreated from" (Bowers 1968). One is reminded of the clinical accounts of the effects of the double-bind situation, in which the individual can neither approach, nor avoid, nor "leave the field" (see Bateson et al. 1956). The existential predicament of the prepsychotic will be discussed in detail elsewhere in this presentation.

As is the case in other ASC, that is, in various peak and nadir experiences, a change from a state of impasse and double-bindedness to one of heightened awareness often occurs in the prepsychotic's experience. He frantically searches for more visual and auditory cues, acting as if the impasse could be resolved by further environmental information. Information processing cannot keep pace with this overload condition; thus, the sensory attributes of significant stimuli (for example, intensity, magnitude, and color) are attended to more effectively than the perceptual and ideational attributes (for example, configuration, quality, and quantity). The psychotic may initially feel hyperfunctional, aware, and creative as he attempts to deal with the experience of sensory overload. The combined distortions of temporal experience and inner from outer reality confront the schizophrenic with an environment replete with elements of both the present and the intrapsychic past.

The incipient psychotic frequently experiences not only an elevated state of awareness but also a qualitative experiential alteration. Like a self-fulfilling prophecy, the schizophrenic's frantic search for environmental cues reveals "hidden meanings, neutral individuals are suddenly animated with strange ideas and designs, curious connections between feelings and perception are experienced" (Bowers 1968). A process of deautomatization occurs whereby habitually categorized sensory inputs are no longer scanned automatically. In a characteristically egocentric mode, the schizophrenic experiences all sensory input with regard to personal relevance. The development of this manner of perceptual field articulation is processional and, as is the case with "normal" crisis situations, basically an information-gathering mechanism. These ideas of relevance become "ideas of reference," and "the individual literally has the irrefutable cognitive experience that this or that object, person, event, or transaction has meaning for him" (Bowers 1968).

The intense processes of information gathering and field articulation, that is, "press for meaning," fail to resolve the schizophrenic impasse, and the psychotic literally takes this meaning personally; he is convinced that particular environmental elements are significant for him. Normal processes of logic and reason are suspended as the cognitive experience of the schizophrenic overwhelms him. In addition, the normally adaptive and interdependent systems of affect and perception "tend to cross-contaminate each other and lead to affectively-induced reality distortion or reality-induced alterations in affect and self-experience. This second process, tied as it is to individual experience, contributes further to the irrefutable quality of the idea of reference or influence" (Bowers 1968). Following this fundamentally egoic mode of heightened experience, the schizophrenic undergoes the opposite, that is, identity dissolution or ego loss. There is a deautomatization of normal self-representation and an experienced loss of an immediate and continuous sense of self.

The final stage is the onset of delusional ideation. Understanding the predelusional experience of the schizophrenic aids considerably to the comprehension of the experiential sequence involved in this restitutive process. Bowers offers the following sequence of events in the formation of delusional ideation: (1) impasse, dread, and overwhelming anxiety; (2) altered experience of self and world; (3) press for "making sense" of the experience; (4) overcoming of constraints imposed by normal reality guards; and (5) a certain relief and comfort (even elation) experienced with the delusional idea. Hence, delusions are seen as "understandable constructs derived from

experiences of heightened and altered sensory influx and self-experience, widened categories of relevance, and a push for closure or
meaning" (Bowers 1968).

It would appear that our examination of the experiential sequence
in the pathogenesis of acute schizophrenic psychosis strengthens
the psychoanalytic view of ego development and the formation of
object relations in infancy. Deindividuated regressive behavior and
experience are characteristic of the alterations in affect and perception evident in acute schizophrenic psychosis. In addition, prepsychotic individuals appear unable to act as effective agents in the
resolution of developmental impasse. Laing (1960) contends that this
inability to engage the elements of one's environment is accompanied by specific anxiety states experienced by the prepsychotic:
fear of engulfment, fear of the implosion of reality, and fear of
petrification or depersonalization. The cause of this ineffective resolution of crisis may be primary, that is, a defective development of
object relations, or secondary, that is, the result of the anxiety states
themselves. At present, the causal factor(s) are not clear; hence,
we will consider what may be relevant primary- and secondary-
process features in the evolution of the schizophrenic experience.
Our analysis of these features will compare the primary- and secondary-process views and rely heavily on the works of Freud
(1957), Hartmann (1939), Brody (1965), and Laing (1960).
Rather than support one perspective at the expense of the other, we
contend that primary- and/or secondary-process factors may be
causally related to schizophrenic psychosis.

Altered Ego Development and the Prepsychotic Schizoid

The construction of theoretical parallelisms between conceptualizations of the prepsychotic schizoid adult and of the infant has been
a relatively nonexistent area of inquiry. One might attribute this
fact to the significant observation that "this press toward reconstruction differs fundamentally—as a pathological process necessarily
must—from the normal genesis of personality. . . ." (Werner 1948).

We believe, however, that, although normal genesis of personality and the development of the prepsychotic state differ fundamentally, significant parallelisms exist between the product of a certain atypical mode of infant development and the prepsychotic schizoid personality. Since Arieti, Klein, and others have described the schizoid state from varied developmental perspectives, we do not intend to duplicate either previous descriptions of etiology or exhaustive psychoanalytic interpretation. Rather, our purpose is to investigate the basic conceptual similarities between the infant product of an altered ego development and the preschizophrenic individual. In developing similarities, we will use both the language and the framework of psychoanalytic theory and an extension of that framework through an examination of the adult schizoid from an existential and phenomenological perspective. It is evident that the interpretation of the earlier observable phenomena of infant development into psychological terms is immensely hazardous. Such translations of preverbal behavior are even more difficult to draw than hypotheses from the observable behavior of prepsychotics.

Psychoanalytic theory assumes an initially undifferentiated ego-id stage of psychic organization, in which the infant cannot distinguish between internal and external stimuli. It has been posited that the differentiation between *inner* and *outer* is learned as a function of ego development. In the initial phase, instinctual energy is guided by opposing states of general pleasure and displeasure, and environmental influences are undifferentially regarded in terms of tension and release of tension. The states of pleasure and pain involved in the feeding situation enable the child and mother to successfully pattern this central activity.

The second phase of the development of the ego is characterized by a differentiation of energy in terms of a general aim. The infant develops a rudimentary conception of distantiation without separation; the nipple, now a more differentiated tension releaser, is conceived as distanced from the mother but not separate. No true object relations yet exist, since identity is intimately associated with function rather than with external performing agent. Expressions of distress are signals for relief—not a call for mother—and are indicative of a wish requiring fulfillment rather than an intended communication to another being.

It is in the subsequent stage of ego development, that of the differentiated object, that the infant first experiences a separation between self and other. This differentiation between self and notself is accomplished via the experience of distancing an "as-if" separate self.* It precedes a stage of true object relatedness, since the child is capable only of relating to images. Before the child can experience an interpersonal relatedness, it is necessary that he conceive of the image of the nipple as being discontinuous. He must be capable of realizing separation before he can experience being nourished by mother. In this stage of ego development, the psychophysiological communication loop between mother and child serves a most vital function. Within the framework of the feeding situation, a critical timing is established by the mother that enables her at once to satisfy the needs of the child and to compel him to become aware of her separateness without fearing abandonment. Consequently, the child learns to communicate his being objectively, that is, as an object, and, in psychoanalytic terms, this learning develops through the use of libidinal energies subservient to the ego. Hopefully, but, as we will show, not universally, this energy is expended in the course of normal development.

Developmental psychology has rightfully shown great concern for the growth of the child's capacity for object relationship. However, it is the mother's capacity for such relationship that determines the extent of the resolution of the child's abandonment-separateness conflict. Optimally, her intent should fall between responding exclusively to the child's wish and introducing and responding to environmental fluctuations necessary for the alteration of his schemata. Similarly, the child's responses alter the mother's image of him. The gratification received by the mother is externally generated and their mutual experiences enrich both their personal spheres (von Uexkull 1934). Through the use of what may be termed *auditory hyper-*

* This term, to be discussed more fully later, was introduced by Helene Deutsch and has no connection with Vaihinger's "as-if" philosophical concept.

cathexis, the mother responds to the child's vague and nebulous signals of distress. Gradually, she requires the child to offer more intentional and *re-cognizable* signs. Originally, the child regards the nipple, that is, mother, merely as an extension of his wish. As he experiences the state of separation, the physiological communication loop with mother enables him to consider the nipple as time controlled by his wish. Ultimately, the presence of the nipple is divorced from his wish, and he learns to experience occurrences uninitiated by his inner wish—that is, the child learns separateness. Unlike the first stage of ego development, when mother is a diffuse, undifferentiated rage gratifier, or the second stage, when she is the "feeding mother," the child now attributes an existence to the mother unrelated to survival. She has attained the status of a significant other.

Serious difficulties arise when the mother is incapable of coordinating her inner image of the child with the continuum of existential evidence he manifests. Burlingham (1935) attributes her inability to establish a true object relationship to her failure in resolving her own fear of abandonment. We might theoretically envision such a mother as fixated in the second stage of ego development and, hence, able only to cathect the child, not as a separate other, but as a continuation of self. The very existence of the child is determined by this maternal imagery rather than by the libidinization of an existent, that is, a real, other. Only when he validates his mother's projection is the child re-cognized, since he is merely his mother's image devoid of any originality or spontaneity. This as-if child undergoes a slow, existential "death."

The developmental process is now radically divergent. The child's learning process is founded on the validation of delusion rather than on true object relatedness. The timing inherent in the normal psychophysiological communication loop between child and mother is gone because timing is now exclusively a function of the mother's inner world. If the child's desire to eat coincides with his mother's attempt to feed him, he receives approval. If he attempts to signal distress out of phase with his mother's internal timing, he is ignored. Despite her appearance of attentiveness, she is not cognizant of any independent action on the part of the child nor of any environmental incongruities. Not atypical are such distorted deductions as "Since I have not seen him vomit, he could not have vomited. Therefore, his stomach must be terribly upset." That the child in question is contented is not recognized as evidence to the contrary and can offer nothing inconsistent with expectation. In actuality, the as-if child is an ambiguous locus of causality. The more the child is confined to such a system, the more he must adhere to expectation to avoid acute psychological impoverishment. The characteristic intensity of such as-if relationships is directly related to the child's consistency in validating his mother's projection. When he fails to validate her projection, "he" worries her. Having herself not achieved the level of objective relationship, she seems to experience separation anxiety and draws further away from such relationship. The cycle is vicious and mutually impoverishing. The mother's manifested concern is not the product of the true object relationship but of the infantile relationship where function is independent of the existent other. *He* may worry her, but the existent *he* is punished by actual or intimated abandonment. His terror of abandonment is continually reinforced whenever his spontaneous behavior is incongruent with his mother's expectations. Eventually, he feels that he is no longer within her *Umwelt*.

The symbiosis inherent in the psychophysiological communication loop is now nonexistent. Temporality is exclusively a function of the mother's level of tension, and the child is related to as if his aims were consistent with his mother's. His learning mode remains characteristically preobjective, while the conflict between separation and abandonment remains unresolved. The child is fixated in the functional stage and undergoes a significant variation in ego development. The existent child continues to regard mother as a feeder-nonfeeder while he increasingly identifies with her projected image. The more he complies with this process, the more he exists as an image—a pseudo ego, a false self. Psychologically the real child is literally split off from himself, while existentially he is dying or dead.

As mentioned previously, the child's mode of learning remains preobjective, and the consequences of this fixation are substantial. His mode of perception and attempts at communication are taught to coincide with his mother's cathected as-if child, and he is compelled to accept the *Umwelt* of her image child as his own. Behavior of the real child incongruent with that of the as-if image is not reinforced, and attempts to interact with the unknown are forbidden. Maternal action is based solely on the perpetuation of this false relationship, and the child is forced to interact through a false self consonant with his mother's projection. One can envision the evolution of the false self in terms of Bateson's (1956) double-bind theory. If the existent child responds according to his own wishes, he is ignored and/or threatened with abandonment; if he does not respond, his real needs are unmet. In addition, there is the added condition of his dependency preventing him from "leaving the field," that is, evading the choice. He is doubly bound, and his solution is to be not real—to be a false self.

The false self is a stagnated, immobile identity. Environmental information is either refined to fit this nonequilibrating system or ignored. Ultimately, this identity becomes a *concrete abstraction* and the child devotes his existence to the verification of the false self. If the child is constricted beyond control in the double bind, reality may be abruptly and completely lost. It is at this point that similarities with the schizoid adult become most apparent.

The Schizoid False-Self System

> . . . if a man is not two-dimensional, having a two-dimensional identity established by a conjunction of identity-for-others and identity-for-oneself, if he does not exist objectively as well as subjectively, but has only a subjective identity, an identity-for-himself, he cannot be real (Laing 1960).

The term *schizoid* refers to the personality state that has been frequently found to be the prepsychotic state of the schizophrenic. Kretschmer has characterized the schizoid personality as indifferent, apathetic, antisocial, eccentric, timid, hypersensitive, and nervous. These diverse labels are sometimes helpful but more frequently antithetical and confusing. What is consequential is that the schizoid may use such overtly divergent postures to cope with a feeling of failure in communication and an increasing sense of inadequacy and estrangement. Theorists in both psychology and psychiatry have posited the emergence of a false-self system as characteristic of the schizoid's experienced mode of *being-in-the-world*. The developmental origins of this system are intimately bound to an underlying existential insecurity.*

> People who lack a fundamental security . . . do not seem to have a sense of that basic unity which can abide through the most intense conflicts with oneself, but seem rather to have come to experience themselves as primarily split into a mind and a body. Usually they feel most closely identified with the "mind." . . . Here we have a basic difference in the self's position in life. We would almost have, if the embodiment or unembodiment were ever complete in either direction two different ways of being human. . . . The embodied person has a sense of being flesh and blood and bones, of being biologically alive and real: he knows himself to be substantial. To the extent that he is thoroughly "in" his body, he is likely to have a sense of personal continuity in time. He will experience himself as subject to the dangers of attack, mutilation, disease, decay, and death. He is implicated in bodily desire, and the gratification and frustration of the body. The individual thus has as his starting-point an experience of his body as a base from which he can be a person with other human beings. . . . He has a starting point integral in this respect at least. Such a starting-point will be a precondition for a different hierarchy of possibilities from those open to the person who experiences himself in terms of a self-body dualism (Laing 1960).

Thus, the unembodied schizoid, like the as-if child, lacks a self-referential framework on which to accumulate experience. We speak alternatively of his "ego split," "weak body image," or "inadequate body schema"—all of which are descriptive of his [inability to feel that his body is a base of operations for his real self.]

When examining the phenomenon of ego splitting of the schizoid, existential psychology is inclined to utilize the aforementioned notion of a mind-body split. Interaction with the environment is delegated to a false-self system, while the real self is experienced as disem-

* The intention here is not to establish continuity between the state of the as-if child and that of the schizoid adult but to construct existential parallelisms.

bodied. Impassivity and detachment in times of extreme stress are also observable in the normal adult and may be accompanied by the appearance of a temporary schizoid state. One is attempting to transcend a threatening situation as he observes the fate befalling his physical being. It appears, however, that the schizoid, whose mind-body split is his mode of being-in-the-world, experiences that world as a permanent threat. Impassivity and detachment are the schizoid's prerequisites for survival—he experiences persecutory anxiety, of which the source is reality itself.

As was the case with the as-if child, a result of this mind-body split is that the real self is never communicated through spontaneous expression. All perception and overt behavior are products of the false-self system and are themselves false. Comments by schizoid individuals to the effect that their experiential world is unreal are existentially correct. Schematically, the difference between the normal system of perception and action and that of the schizoid adult is shown in the following diagram from Laing (1960).

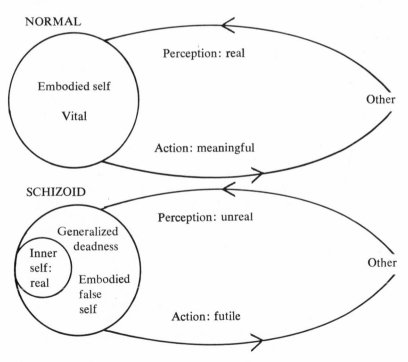

The real self is denied the opportunity to establish a relatedness with others. Experientially, a *pseudo identity* is established as the basis of the schizoid's existence in the world. Not only does he lose his chance at objective relatedness with the world, but he actually disowns part of his own being in the process. This is represented by Laing (1960) as follows:

Instead of (Self/body) $\rightleftarrows$ Other
The situation is Self $\rightleftarrows$ (body-other)

Laing further notes that the mode of relatedness with others is not that of two real selves interacting or, in Buber's terms, an "I-Thou" relationship. It is rather the dead, sterile relationship of a *quasi-it–it* interaction. The consequence of this substitution is that the individual incessantly feels Kierkegaard's experience of *dread*. The schizoid is convinced, as was the as-if child, that any real, spontaneous interaction will be lethal.

Laing (1960) offers the following example of the inner-outer schizoid split:

> The patient, who conducted his life along relatively "normal" lines outwardly but operated this inner split, presented as his original complaint the fact that he could never have intercourse with his wife but only with his own image of her. That is, his body had physical relations with her body, but his mental self, while this was going on, could only look on at what his body was doing and/or "imagine" himself having intercourse with his wife as an object of his imagination. The wife of the above patient was quite unaware that he felt that "he" had never had intercourse directly with her; he had had intercourse only with his image of her which happened to coincide sufficiently well with her in reality for no one but himself to know the difference. . . . Thus the above patient said that, although Kinsey might have put down that he had intercourse two to four times per week for ten years, "he" knew that he had never had intercourse "really." Generally, the self can relate itself with immediacy to an object which is an object of its own imagination or memory but not to a real person.

The false-self system is clearly distinguished from the primarily mechanical role behavior adopted by the "normal" individual. Mechanistic, nonspontaneous behavior is not characteristic of every overt action or expression of the "normal" person. The schizoid individual, however, regards expressive spontaneity as an "alien reality within himself" (Laing 1960), and he attempts to attribute to that reality an existentially independent character. So fearful is the schizoid person of this estranged segment of his being that he feels compelled to "objectively" interact through a false-self system. The unfortunate consequence of this development is that the false self is experienced as both alien and unreal. The futility and aim-lessness which permeate the cognitive and affective realms of the schizoid individual are not manifested defense mechanisms, as is often contended; rather, they are the immediate consequences of the dynamic structure of the schizoid mode of being.

Another brief illustration of the emergence of the schizoid false self may prove fruitful. We note that, from an existential point of view, this illustration bears marked similarities to the case of the as-if child.

> James said that he was not a person in his own right. In his behavior he had allowed himself to become a "thing" for other people. His mother, he felt, had never recognized his existence. One can say, I suppose, that one can recognize the existence of another person perfectly well in Woolworth's, but this was quite clearly not what he had in mind. He felt that she never recognized his freedom and right to have a subjective life of his own from out of which his actions would emerge as an expression of his own autonomous and integral self-being. On the contrary, he was merely her puppet, "I was simply a symbol of her reality." What had happened was that he had developed his subjectivity inwardly without daring to allow it any objective expression. In his case, this was not total, since he could express his "true" self very clearly and forcibly in *words*. He knew this: "I can only make sounds." There was, however, hardly anything else "he" did, for all his other actions were ruled not by his will but by an alien will, which had formed itself within his own being (Laing 1960).

The schizoid adult, like the as-if child, presents a quality of apparent compliance. The affirmation of will counter to that of the significant other is nonexistent, as the mask of the ideal husband or conscientious student is entirely compliant with the intent and expectation

of the other. This overt acquiescence is not a product of social conformity or active superego functioning. It is a negative submission
to the expectation of an other perpetuated by an intense fear of self-
realization. Again, the cycle is vicious and the process self-perpetuating. As the schizoid individual fails to get adequate feedback from
his acts, he withdraws further from external object relatedness. The
real self remains impoverished since it fails to secure its aliment,
that is, authentic interpersonal contact. Thus, the schizoid, as Sullivan observed, "never knows what the next person will be like, and
never suspects that he can be pleasant." His *Umwelt* is suffused with
fear and anxiety, and he relies more heavily on the false-self
system. Action and reality approach a syntonic relationship only if
the former encompasses not only outer reality but inner reality as
well. A diminished capacity for object relatedness prevents both the
as-if child and the schizoid adult from integrating outer- and inner-
related expectancies of inner consequences.

Interaction through a false-self system implies a renunciation of
accountability for one's acts. It denies the process of individuation
and, on any level of development, seems tantamount to abdication
from life itself. Indeed, as Kafka observed: "You can hold yourself
back from the sufferings of the world, this is something you are
to do and is in accord with your nature, but precisely this holding
back is the only suffering that you might be able to avoid."

SCHIZOPHRENIA AND PSYCHEDELIC
ALTERATIONS OF CONSCIOUSNESS

The issue of whether hallucinogens such as LSD-25 are truly
psychotomimetic (psychosis-mimicking) has been instrumental in
understanding of the schizophrenic state of consciousness (SSC).
In focusing on the individual's experience as well as on the control
and inhibition of sensory stimulation, Silverman (1969a) has identified the following core characteristics common to the two ASC:

1. Heightened sensory experience
2. Distractibility and figure-ground disorders

3. Thought disorder
4. Blocking
5. Withdrawal
6. Loss of spontaneity in movement and speech
7. Changes in space perspective
8. Stimulus intensity reduction

HEIGHTENED SENSORY EXPERIENCE. "Heightened sensitivity to stimulation is a primary characteristic of incipient schizophrenia and LSD reactions" (Silverman, 1969a). McGhie and Chapman (1961) and Bowers and Freedman (1966) have noted that elevated sensitivity to sensory quality and color are the initial perceptual alterations. Personal accounts of these altered sensitivities stress the fact that "sights and sounds possessed a keenness that I had never experienced before. . . . My senses were sharpened, sounds were more intense and I could see with greater clarity, everything seemed clear to me. Even my sense of taste seemed more acute" (Bowers and Freedman 1966). Patients often express feelings of marked elation at this time and frequently attach a profound significance to this portion of their psychotic episode.

Subjective accounts of the LSD experience are extremely similar. Following the ingestion of the drug, the individual is often acutely aware of a heightened sensitivity to sensory stimulation. In an effort to avoid drowning in the onslaught, the individual struggles merely to attend to increases in sensory impression. This is the "implosion of reality and refers to the full terror of the experience of the world as liable at any moment to crash in and obliterate all identity as a gas will rush in and obliterate a vacuum" (Laing 1960). In both incipient schizophrenic psychosis and LSD reactions, the individual attempts to defend against this state of disequilibrium and enhance the restoration of sensory control. Silverman (1968a) points out that such clinically noted defensive maneuvers as distractibility, blocking, withdrawal, and loss of spontaneity in movement and speech are designed to "reduce the overwhelming intensity of ordinarily regarded, minimal-to-moderate intensity stimulation."

DISTRACTIBILITY AND FIGURE-GROUND DISORDERS. Silverman and

others have employed the term *stimulus bound* to denote the inordinately powerful attraction of the sensory qualities of varied stimuli to highly sensitive or sensitized individuals. As a response to heightened sensory stimulation, both the schizophrenic and the LSD user experience themselves as bound to incidental stimuli. Often distressing is the fact that these stimuli may be incidental while the compulsion to attend is experienced as intense and unpredictable. The results of this lack-of-attention inhibition may vary from irritability and confusion to the experience of dissolution of perceptual gestalts. We agree with Silverman's (1969a) observation that hyperresponsiveness to minutiae and hyporesponsiveness to logically higher-order aspects of the perceptual field are, at minimum, antecedents to thought disorder.

THOUGHT DISORDER.   As this decrease of attention to logically higher-order aspects of the perceptual field continues, there is a corresponding decrease in the schizophrenic's ability to willingness to deal with the symbolic features of his world. As the individual becomes less of an *agent,* attention is less governed by an active mode of functioning and more directly bound by the stimulus configurations themselves. As thinking in both the schizophrenic and LSD user becomes increasingly stimulus bound, both higher- and lower-order logical processes (problem solving) are rendered ineffectual. As noted by Silverman (1969a), a logical extreme of this stimulus boundedness is the dissolution of the experience of the temporal continuity and linearity prerequisite to goal-directed thought.

BLOCKING.   Another coping mechanism related to the experience of hyperresponsiveness to sensory input is the trancelike state called *blocking.* Silverman (1969a) notes that "blocking phenomena are regarded as transient disturbances in consciousness which are associated with failure to exclude irrelevant stimulation." Chapman (1966) quotes the following report of a schizophrenic patient: "I don't like dividing my attention at anytime because it leads to confusion and I don't know where I am or who I am. When this starts I just go into a trance and I just turn off all my senses and I don't see anything and I don't hear anything." When confronted with information inputs that are conceptually too difficult, individuals in both ASC will be perceptibly more distracted and anxious. As the distraction and anxiety mount, the schizophrenic or LSD user effectively tunes out the other individual and freezes himself, both physically and cognitively.

As Silverman has observed and most LSD users will attest, the ingestion of the drug leads to a state in which words and thoughts fail to convey the "intense kaleidoscope of feelings and visions. . . . When you ask a psychedelic subject what is happening, he can't tell you. He looks at you blankly or he gasps: WOW!" (Leary 1966).

WITHDRAWAL. Perhaps the most impressive accounts of schizophrenic withdrawal are found in Laing (1960). From the current vantage point, however, the hypersensitive person's attempt to avoid other individuals is an adjunct of his effort to reduce sensory stimulation. Behavioral manifestations such as those evidenced in blocking may culminate in a total withdrawal from interpersonal contact. In order to avoid the implosion of sensory input and maintain some control over excessive levels of stimulation, catatoniclike withdrawal may appear to both the schizophrenic and the LSD user as the sole recourse.

LOSS OF SPONTANEITY IN MOVEMENT AND SPEECH. The reduction of kinesthetic and proprioceptive responses occurs in both ASC. As there is little qualitative differentiation between internal and external stimuli in either state, both are experienced as excessive stimulation. McGhie and Chapman (1961) quote the following accounts:

> When I move quickly it's a strain on me. Things go too quick for my mind. They get blurred and it's like being blind. It's as if you were seeing a picture one moment and another picture the next. I just stop and watch my feet. Everything is alright if I stop, but if I start moving again I lose control.

> My brain is not working right. . . . I can't speak properly. . . . The words won't come.

Fischer (1972) notes that there is a characteristically high sensory-to-motor ratio in such ASC as schizophrenic psychosis, LSD reactions, daydreaming, and sensory deprivation. Silverman (1969a) notes that the prototype of this "predominance of the sensory over the motor component of behavior" is in the catatonic hallucinatory state, where there is no motoric component and levels of sensory experiencing are elevated.

CHANGES IN SPACE PERSPECTIVE. In the articulation of the perceptual field in both schizophrenia and LSD reactions, the deployment of attention is bound by the most compelling objects in the field. Silverman (1968a) has found that this effects an alteration in the perception of space, causing an exaggeration in the size of nearby objects and an underestimation in the size of distant objects. McGhie and Chapman (1961) are aware of this distortion of depth perspective and believe it is causally related to the loss of spontaneity in the normal coordination of body movement. "The things I look at seem to be flatter as if you were looking just at a surface. Maybe its because I notice so much more about things and find myself looking at them for a longer time."

STIMULUS INTENSITY REDUCTION. "There is a paradoxical quality to sensory experience which is exemplified in some of the experiential reports of schizophrenics and LSD-drugged individuals. On the one hand, hypersensitivity is reported in response to ordinary range stimulation. On the other hand, hyposensitivity is reported to extremely strong stimulation." Cohen (1963) and Chapman (1966) have found that, when exposed to reduced levels of sensory stimulation, both schizophrenics and LSD users exhibit less evidence of undergoing an alteration of consciousness. This is, of course, common knowledge to "indoctrinated" members of the psychedelic-drug culture who, in an attempt to maximize alterations of consciousness, will seek exposure to heightened sensory environments. Silverman and others have reasoned that reduced responsivity to stimulation, that is, greater alterations in consciousness, serves as a compensatory mechanism for the experience of overstimulation. In Table 1, Cohen (1970) offers the comparison of an LSD reaction and a particular class of schizophrenic reaction—acute catatonic.

Our comparison between the schizophrenic and psychedelic experiences has identified several core features characteristic of both

Table 1. Characteristics of Psychotic and Psychotomimetic Reactions

Type of Change	Model Psychosis Produced by LSD	Acute Catatonic Excitement (Schizophrenic Reaction)
Perception	Illusions, frequent intensified visual perception; pseudohallucinations; hallucinations, mainly visual; other sensory hallucinations are rare	Illusions, rarely intensified perceptions; hallucinations, mainly auditory but also visual; other sensory hallucinations are rare
Cognition	Impairment of judgment and abstract reasoning for practical problem-solving purposes; blocking; ideas of reference; delusions; disorganized ideation	Marked impairment of judgment and abstract reasoning; blocking; use of metaphor; ideas of reference; bizarre delusions; disorganized ideation
Affect	Anxiety, depression or elation, ecstasy; uncontrollable laughter or tears	Anxiety, terror; rarely euphoria or ecstasy; mutism, inappropriate moods, stupor
Behavior	Passive, rarely restless, and overactive	Gesturing, grimacing, destructive, withdrawn, automatism, negativism, hostility
Posture	Slight tremor; slight unsteadiness	Complete immobility; pacing, "caged animal"; posturing
Consciousness	Relatively clear	Relatively clear but preoccupied
Reality testing	Slightly or moderately impaired	Greatly impaired
Speech	Blocking, halting, sometimes unimpaired	Condensations, alliterations, blocking, echolalia, slang associations
Ego boundaries	Depersonalization; derealization	Depersonalization; derealization

states. Of course, we do not intend a blanket equation of the two altered states but, rather, wish to suggest a continuum unifying varied alterations in consciousness. We will now focus specifically on the psychedelic state in an effort to better locate this experiential mode relative to other altered states of consciousness.

5

Psychedelic
States of Consciousness

Given the controversy surrounding both schizophrenic and drug-induced altered states and the overriding importance of the cultural context in which they occur, it is not surprising that psychotomimetic research and theory have yielded equivocal results. In several extensive reviews of psychedelic-drug studies, Robert Mogar has concluded that the research and theory fit two mutually exclusive research paradigms; one regards psychedelic drugs as an agent of liberation and insight, while the other approach views the drug as an escape mechanism that can induce chronic psychosis. All states referred to as drug states in this presentation are those states induced by the psychedelic compounds (Osmond 1972) such as marijuana, LSD, pscylocibin, and mescaline (Marin and Cohen 1971), As in the case of schizophrenia (disease or panacea?) neither position is tenable, and judgments must remain largely dependent on the harmful or beneficial outcome for the individual who has undergone the ASC experience. After emphasizing the similarities between acute psychotic episodes and drug-induced experiences, Prince concludes that the major differences between them lie in their positive or negative consequences for the individual (Prince 1971). What is most important here is not to decide that debate but to glean information from opposing positions in order to insure that individuals who are in drug-induced ASC states can be treated or helped in the most constructive manner possible.

There is general agreement that psychedelic drugs can enhance schizoid deviation from conventional thinking and perception. However, recent research and theory emphasize that the psychotic state differs from the drug-induced ASC in a number of significant criteria. These differentiations are based on the observation that psychotic episodes are uniformly disruptive, while drug-induced states are frequently anxiety free and essentially pleasurable under supportive circumstances. This analysis acknowledges that drug-induced states occasionally result in extreme anxiety that closely approximates psychosis and that drug use can elicit or precipitate a psychotic episode. However, the question of causality in these cases is debatable, and in this presentation, the primary focus will be on the similarities and differences between the psychotic and drug ASC experiences.

One difference between the two experiences lies in how the individual experiences his personal identity. In both psychotic and drug states, the person experiences himself as depersonalized and derealized (Marin and Cohen 1971). Since there is a general sense of identity instability and fragmentation, psychotics experience feelings of invasion by other people or alien forces. Extreme conflict is experienced between the individual and his social environment, leading to chronic anxiety. Accompanying this conflict are sensations of being insignificant and an experience of the "indifference of the universe" (Siegler, Osmond, and Mann 1971). There is an ensuing state of nightmarish fantasies and a feeling of becoming increasingly isolated (Alvarez 1961; Wapnick 1969). In contrast to this, people in the midst of a drug-induced ASC report markedly different perceptions of their identity. Frequently, they tell of a pleasurable sensation of unity with other people and material objects and a general feeling of being at one with the world; rather than being intimidated by their environment, they indicate feelings of humility and awe at the grandeur of the universe. Generally, there are sensations of ego integrity and the capacity for creative controlled fantasies (Caldwell 1968; Osmond 1972).

One key dimension in contrasting the two states is the individual's experience of time. Psychotics experience a sense of stasis, where time contracts into an experience in which nothing ever changes. Both internal and external time may slow down, leading to an inhibition of action and the creation of despair. Future time offers no consolation since it induces further feelings of dread, anxiety, and danger (Cohen and Marin 1971). These experiences are quite distinct from those of drug-induced ASC states, where individuals often report a liberation from time that expands or contracts at will; the future becomes an eagerly anticipated realm of new sensations and insights (Masters and Houston 1966).

Affect is also considerably different in the two states; psychotics seldomly exhibit euphoria or ecstasy whereas people in drug-induced states frequently laugh spontaneously. There is a general flattening of affect in psychosis, exemplified by mutism, stupor, chronic depression, and feelings of disgust. An overriding sensation of isolation, fear, hatred, and suspicion is often manifest during psychotic episodes. This general pattern insures that the individual will remain withdrawn since his basic desire is to reduce his intake of sensory stimulation. Behavior such as maintaining a fixed gaze, closing the eyes, and hiding in corners is an attempt to avoid interaction. Most patients report a blocking phenomena that is most aptly defined by the following subjective report: "I don't like dividing my attention at anytime because it leads to confusion and I don't know where I am or who I am. When this starts I just go into a trance and I just turn off all my senses and I don't see anything and I don't hear anything" (Chapman 1966). This phenomenon was recognized and defined by Bleuler in 1911 when he observed: "The most extraordinary formal element of schizophrenic thought processes is that term 'blocking.' The associative activity often seems to come to an abrupt and complete standstill" (Bleuler 1950, p. 32). This mechanism determines that effect will frequently be blocked or nonexistent for prolonged periods of time. Directly opposed to this is the occurrence reported in drug-induced states of an elevated mood and experience of everything as meaningful and exhilarating. Frequently, individuals report transient feelings of anxiety and depression that are offset by elation and ecstasy, often manifested by uncontrollable tears or laughter (Caldwell 1968). They are delighted with the world and express empathy, consideration, and positive affection. There is a marked increase in their appreciation of sensory stimuli as sources of affective delight. This experience is common to the onset of psychosis as well as to the onset of a drug state, but the psychotic individual is then plunged into anxiety and despair while the individual in the drug-induced state may remain delighted for prolonged periods of time. This theoretical observation is attested to by one hospitalized schizophrenic: "I feel my tactile senses are enhanced as well as my visual ones, to a point of great power. Patterns and designs begin to distinguish themselves and take on significance. It's the same now as with the drug [LSD], only then I knew I was coming back" (Bowers and Freedman 1966). People in drug-induced states seek out rather than avoid sensory stimulation in order to promote the onset of a system of noncognitive interaction and feedback. Distinction between a psychotic and a drug-induced ASC depends on whether an effect is flattened or heightened and on the duration and lability of that effect.

Cognition is another major area of distinction. In schizophrenia, there is a marked impairment of judgment and abstract reasoning; there are frequent ideas of reference, bizarre delusions, disorganized ideation, and the awareness of so many possibilities that action becomes impossible (Siegler 1971). In contrast, individuals in drug states exhibit more selective impairment of abstract reasoning—for example, a resistance or reluctance to address themselves to practical problem-solving tasks. In addition, they frequently manifest ideas of reference and disorganized ideation; yet they seek these changes in thought patterns and place a high value on innovative cognitions. They experience multitudes of possibilities but they do so with the attitude of welcoming these new possibilities as opportunities for innovation and novel experience (Siegler, Osmond, and Mann 1971; Caldwell 1968). Closely affiliated with alterations in cognitive processes are the accompanying alterations in perceptual processes. Psychotics can become stimulus bound (Silverman 1967*b*) or be compelled to attend to irrelevant and otherwise innocuous events in unpredictable ways. According to Coate, "In psychotic states, where the fate of the whole universe may be at stake, awareness of material objects and trivial events can be heightened to an extent that is outside the range of normal experience" (1965). This behavior is evident in both psychosis and drug-induced states, but it ranges from disruptive hallucinations and personality fragmentation in psychosis to simple annoyance and perplexity in drug-induced states. In schizophrenia, such distortions are mainly auditory; they are predominantly visual in psychedelic states. Last, perceptual changes are frequently felt as exhilarating and pleasurable in drug-induced states, but they are experienced as frightening and threatening in psychosis.

All of the above distinctions between psychotic and psychedelic-drug-induced states obviously are blurred or indistinguishable in certain individual cases. These subtle differentiations are noted so that they may be more fully explored in order that both states can be more completely understood. It is of the utmost importance that clinicians and researchers be aware of their personal assumptions about these states—that is, are they analogous or distinct? Perhaps these few preliminary differentiations will influence those researchers who are of the former disposition. Instead of belaboring the distinctions between two states of "pathology," we will cite the preliminary evidence that psychotic and drug-induced states share a commonality in terms of transcendent rather than pathological experience.

According to psychiatrist Stanislav Grof's clinical observation and research, drug-induced states have definite implications for a deeper understanding of religion, artistic creativity, philosophical insights, and for psychology's understanding of the mind. At the Maryland State Psychiatric Research Center, Grof has conducted the most extensive clinical and research investigation into drug-induced ASC phenomena and has reported distinct stages, or motifs, that are recurrent in an individual's experience. These stages closely approximate the mythic themes of individuals undergoing psychotic episodes noted by John Perry. Grof's attention has been focused primarily on the parallels between drug-induced ASC phenomena and similar phenomena reported in the annals of the major religions of the world, ranging from Buddhism to Christianity. Such religious inspirations are clearly rooted in episodes that were termed either psychotic or transcendent, depending on the cultural context in which they occurred. In his clinical observation, Grof notes that it is "virtually impossible to distinguish phenomenologically between the spontaneous (i.e., genuine or psychotic) and drug-induced religious experience" (1970). This observation is more fully documented by numerous case histories cited by W. V. Caldwell in his recent book *LSD Psychotherapy,* where he cites approximately ten "universal images" that are pervasive in the reports of patients undergoing psychedelic psychotherapy. What is clear from these observations is that individuals exhibit a finite set of transcultural behavior patterns while undergoing either a psychotic, drug-induced, or meditation-induced altered state experience. This evidence lends support to Jung's concept of a "collective unconscious" dimension of the human mind and, furthermore, provides the theoretical basis from which these various states might be more adequately comprehended. These transpersonal behavior patterns and themes offer the possibility of adducing a coherent and vitally important message from the formerly unintelligible utterings of an individual in the midst of such an ASC experience. Actually, these themes are frequently focused on the Jungian interpretation of dreams—the clearest example of a recognized altered state experience in Western culture. The use of these themes in comprehending psychotic, drug-induced, and mystical ASC experiences is less well developed, since these states have remained largely unrecognized or unacceptable. If they were to be interpreted in terms of themes and processes, as in dream interpretation, they would become sources of insight rather than symptoms of pathology. It seems that distinctions among psychotic, drug-induced, and meditative ASC are qualitative and are based on how adequately the experience is integrated into the life of the individual undergoing it. It is not at all surprising that the desire to experience an ASC state should become manifest in drug ingestion when one considers the American cultural context, with its emphasis on pharmacological bliss ranging from regular bowel movements to a restful night's sleep. This last statement is not intended to provide a rationalization for the extremely dangerous and potentially destructive act of ingesting a psychedelic drug. What is noted here is an essential agreement with Andrew Weil's observation that "when I say that persons take drugs in response to an innate drive to alter consciousness, I do not make any judgment about the taking of drugs. The drive itself must not be equated with the forms of its expression" (Weil 1972, p. 83). It has been amply demonstrated that the prolonged use of psychedelic drugs in order to produce an ASC experience is debilitating and self-destructive. For this reason, people in Western culture have increasingly sought more disciplined techniques for achieving various perspectives on social reality. This phenomenon is an attempt to retain the profundity of an ASC experience and a recognition that drug dependency is an individual and social anathema. Weil's observations are based on his hypothesis that drug-induced ASC experiences are viewed as positive or negative depending on the cultural or subcultural context in which that ASC occurs. By citing a number of primitive and modern Indian tribes who use psychedelic drugs in their religious rituals, Weil raises the question of why the Indians have been capable of avoiding the negative manifestations of drug abuse. There are several major factors that distinguish their use of psychedelic substances in a supportive cultural context from the use of psychedelic drugs under illegal circumstances. For example: "1) Indians use drugs in their natural forms . . . do not attempt to refine the substances into pure potent forms; 2) Use drugs ritually; 3) Seek advice from elders who know the experience; and 4) Use drugs for positive, religious ends rather than escape from boredom" (Weil 1972, p. 94). All Weil's evidence is intended to support his concept of an "innate drive" in people to alter their states of consciousness. Meditation disciplines have proved to be intelligent ways of fulfilling this postulated innate drive that are distinct from its negative manifestation of drug ingestion. Implications of this widespread interest in meditation will be more fully explored in chapter 7.

It is significant that a research project by Turner et al. (1959) determined that, when schizophrenics were given LSD, they denied that the experience was anything at all like their psychotic episodes. There is a marked degree of similarity between the *initial* experiences of psychotic and drug-induced altered states, but these similarities are slight, considering the difference between a chronic psychosis and a transient drug-induced state. Whereas psychosis is initiated by withdrawal and fear of the external environment, psychedelic states are often initiated in order to transcend the limits of the external environment and are characterized by perceptual expansion and a commitment to personal growth. Even an essentially negative drug-induced state is usually of a finite duration and seldom approximates the total disability experienced by schizophrenic patients. Additionally, there is no reason to suspect that either a negative psychotic or a negative drug-induced state is inherently pathological (in the sense of chronically disabling), since such adverse experiences can lead to profoundly positive ends. Most significant is the recognition that psychotic and drug-induced states are not totally synonymous and, furthermore, that each offers the individual the possibility to achieve a higher order of self-awareness and individuation; each of these states also bears the potential for self-destruction or self-realization. The outcome depends solely on the ability of future theories and research to more adequately comprehend these states and to formulate more decisive and effective interventions. Although there are meaningful, subtle differences between the schizophrenic and psychedelic altered states, the recognition of those differences is most helpful as a diagnostic aid in determining whether the outcome of such an experience will be detrimental or beneficial to the individual.

PSYCHOTOMIMETIC RESEARCH

The term *psychotomimetic* (psychosis-mimicking) has been applied to those psychedelics whose effects approximate psychotic-like phenomena. Mogar (1965, 1967) has indicated that virtually all the psychotomimetic research conducted fits one of two divergent research paradigms that are entirely mutually exclusive, that is, the clinical investigation and the laboratory investigation.

The clinical investigation views the drug as a liberator that facilitates accurate perception and insight (psychedelic orientation), pays particular attention to intrapersonal and interpersonal factors, optimizes the conditions under which the drug is taken, and obtains results indicating various kinds and degrees of performance enhancement. . . . The laboratory investigation, on the other hand, views LSD as a stresser capable of stimulating psychotic behavior (psychoto-mimetic orientation), ignores non-drug factors, employs impersonal, "objective" procedures, and obtains results indicating various kinds and degrees of performance impairment (Mogar 1968).

There is relative consensus on the point that LSD can mimic schizo-phrenic deviations from "normal" perception and thought processes. However, it has been emphasized that the drug experience cannot duplicate a chronic psychotic state (Cole and Katz 1964; Hoffer 1965). This appears explicable in view of the fact that clinical processes are not as rigorously bound temporally nor as circum-scribed by built-in socialized restrictions as is the laboratory situa-tion. The differences in the two ASC may serve to highlight those aspects of schizophrenic psychosis that must be explained in terms of "developmental factors and restitutive and compensatory sequences" (Bowers and Freedman 1966).

We are certainly in accord with the theorists and researchers who posit an essential similarity between the two ASC and agree that

The basic similarity is variously termed a dissolution of the ego, an expansion of consciousness, a regression to infantile modes of functioning, a grossly impaired cognitive/perceptual filter mechanism, a breakdown of self/world boundaries, or less judgmentally, a heightened state of emotional arousal, an increased sensitivity to stimuli in all modalities, a marked lowering of the threshold between conscious and unconscious activity, or a lessened capacity to think and perceive abstractly in conventional terms. These views of the communality among altered states of consciousness all imply a wider, more inclusive experiential mode—whether enlightening or chaotic (Mogar 1968).

In common, however, is the fact that the research evidence on both ASC indicates that many so-called "adverse" reactions are due to non-drug factors. Mogar notes that, in the case of the LSD reaction, negative expectancies, character deficits or disorders, inadequate preparation, and ill-managed sessions contribute to the "adverse" experience; in the psychotic state, an uncongenial milieu and/or character deficiencies may result in a similar effect. Echoing the age-old contention of Eastern religion as well as the view of more "enlightened" Western philosophers and scientists (for example, Mogar), we contend that whether its determinants are genetic, biochemical, familial or social, there is nothing intrinsically pathological about ego dissolution. Psychotomimetic researchers have chosen to view all unpleasant effects of LSD as schizoid in nature and all pleasant effects as transcendental or psychedelic. This overwhelming concern with the psychotomimetic aspects of LSD states and the exclusion from consideration of possible psychedelic features of the psychotic state is consistent with the prevailing "focus on disease entities as opposed to transactional processes." Mogar makes the point that different reactions to similar ASC are not effective indicators of different experiences, whether the latter are pharmacologically induced or spontaneous; that is, reactional differences "do not clearly differentiate schizophrenic from psychotomimetic or psychedelic experiences." It would appear that most reactional features to varied ASC are dynamic combinations of "awe and dread, terror and ecstasy, delusion and revelation." In addition, Mogar offers two major hypotheses: (1) the subject undergoing a pharmacologically induced alteration of consciousness, for example, LSD experience, is clearly distinguishable from the chronic schizophrenic; and (2) unpleasant and pathological reaction features in both ASC are not identical nor necessarily covariable.

Striking similarities exist between the initial experiences of *some* schizophrenic individuals and reports of the LSD experience. Bowers and Freedman (1966) identified a common core experience characterized by a dialectical quality, that is, a discomforting feeling of dread combined with an intense happiness—a fear of egoic disintegration together with an awareness of profound breakthrough. They concluded that

> *psychedelic and psychotomimetic phenomena are closely related.* Our hypothesis is that these states demonstrate to varying degrees the subjective phenomena of intrapsychic alteration, that they are fluid states whose outcome is determined by both intrapsychic and environmental factors. There are clearly quantitative, inter-individual differences in the way such experiences can be tolerated, interpreted,

terminated, and assimilated into the ongoing context of experience. To account for such differences in terms of discrete ego liabilities *and* assets would be to explicate many crucial psychological phenomena, including certain forms of psychosis, therapeutic personality change, and creative insight.

This determination that the consequences of a heightened state of awareness—as in certain psychotic and drug states—may be either harmful or beneficial appears significant. Bowers and Freedman emphasize that one must determine the degree to which these experiences are delusional or adaptive prior to any judgments of their validity. Prince and Savage (1972) note several key similarities between acute schizophrenia and the LSD experience and conclude that the primary differences lie in their consequences for the individual. Common features such as regression to preverbal, magical modes of thought, renunciation of worldly interests, ineffability, the noetic quality, ecstatic feelings, and a sense of cosmic union or suspension of self-nonself boundaries are pointed out. What both Mogar and Prince and Savage feel is highly significant is that such experiences may alternately construct and expand consciousness. In comparing the psychotic and psychedelic states, Prince and Savage contend that "a psychosis is a pressured withdrawal with—in many cases —an incomplete return. A psychedelic state is a controlled withdrawal and return; a death and rebirth, often a rebirth into a world with a radical shift in its iconography—a death and transfiguration."

PHYSIOLOGICAL DIMENSIONS IN THE SCHIZOPHRENIC AND PSYCHEDELIC STATES

When considering acute and/or chronic schizophrenia, the physiological evidence is conflicting or, at minimum, ambiguous. Lindsley (1944), Venables (1964), and Kennard (1965) have reported that chronic schizophrenics appear to have EEGs indicating cortical activation and elevated anxiety levels. Whatmore (1967), in an investigation of hospitalized schizophrenics undergoing acute decompensation, found increases and considerable variability of muscle tension.

Salamon and Post (1965), however, found that increments in alpha-wave production in schizophrenics compared to controls seemed to be indicative of decreased levels of anxiety and muscle tension. The contradictory nature of this experimental evidence may be understood in terms of psychiatrist Arthur J. Deikman's (1971) model of bimodal consciousness. Deikman maintains that "the human organism has two basic modes of function: (1) the receptive mode oriented toward the intake of the environment, and (2) the action mode oriented toward manipulation of the environment. Both physiological and psychological dimensions are integrated in these modes." On the basis of his model, he predicts that schizophrenic patients undergoing acute decompensation are functioning in the receptive mode and, hence, should exhibit decreased muscle tension rather than the increases reported by Whatmore. He would, however, be in accord with the findings of Salamon and Post, as increased alpha-wave production is consistent with receptive-mode functioning. He further notes that investigations of autonomic functioning show similar variability and lack of clarity, with diagnosis, drug effects, and chronicity as the major confounding variables.

Although there exists a distinct lack of data in the area of the physiological effects of the LSD state, the clinical variability of the states and the high incidence of anxiety suggest a situation resembling the schizophrenic psychoses. Deikman, while maintaining that more detailed and systematic research is needed, feels that functioning in the LSD state is in "an unintegrated mixture of modes." This concept may be understood by considering the schizophrenic state, in which the shift to the receptive mode may be accompanied by heightened anxiety and a "compensatory attempt to control the receptive mode experience, an attempt that is an action mode response." The fact that an analogous response is existent in the LSD state as well is indicated by the folklore of the psychedelic subculture, which advises drug users not to resist the experience—"go with it," and allow yourself to experience a dissolution of the ego.

—— 6 ——

Toward a Theory of Regeneration: Psychotic and Psychedelic States

Stanley Krippner refers to "states of fragmentation" as characterized by "lack of integration among important segments, aspects, or themes of the total personality" (1972). Within this realm fall conditions referred to as severe psychoneurosis, psychosis, or fugue episodes, in which an individual may delete all memory of his past and assume a radically new life pattern. In this chapter, the terms *psychosis* and *psychotic* will refer only to those disorders diagnosed as schizophrenia, since we are not considering here other forms of psychopathology, such as chronic depression and manic-depressive states. During schizophrenic episodes, individuals graphically reveal both the contents and processes of the unconscious in an extremely confused manner. However, this psychotic process also offers an invaluable source of information concerning the structure and dynamics of the psyche if the confused and obscure information can be constructively sorted out and understood by both the patient and the therapist.

For over sixty years, such psychotic conditions have been classi-fied as progressively degenerative mental diseases, based on the observations of Eugene Bleuler (Sarbin 1972). However, there is a new direction emerging in the comprehension and treatment of psy-chosis, which is now regarded as a potentially constructive rather than an inherently degenerative process. Any adherent to this new formulation should proceed with this concept of *potentially* regenerative versus *necessarily* degenerative clearly in mind in order to avoid being considered either an advocate of psychiatric chemotherapy or a proselytizer of the psychosis panacea. A primary tenet of the regenerative-psychosis position is that psychosis can be viewed as part of an ongoing, constructive process, wherein the individual attempts to correct the inadequacy of his functioning. The position has been summarized by Kaplan, who states: "so called 'symptoms,' rather than being ego alien manifestations of a disease process that has somehow gotten a grip on the person, are instead purposeful acts of the individual, which have intentionality and are motivated. The 'illness' is something the individual 'wills' to happen" (1964). In a similar manner, this position is echoed by Gregory Bateson, who attests to the purposeful quality of schizophrenia: "the mind contains, in some form, such wisdom that it can create an *attack* upon itself that will lead to a later resolution of the pathology" (1972). Undoubtedly, the most prominent authority for this position is R. D. Laing, who considers that "schizophrenia could be construed as the mind's natural way of healing that appalling state of alienation called normality . . . [and] that it is an inner voyage of self discovery, of ego death and rebirth, which ought to have society's sanction and be guided by cicerones including ex-patients, who have been on that trip themselves" (1965). Unfortunately, the profundity of Laing's observations is frequently lost in his tendency to translate his theoretical formulation of schizophrenia as a regenerative process into a categorical condemnation of society as essentially pathological. What is important to recognize here is Laing's metaphor of an inner journey, for the purpose here is to more clearly define the map in order to more adequately comprehend that journey. In essence, we wish to propose that the psychotic experience is a potential source of individual rejuvenation and regeneration of sufficient magnitude to rival that of mystical revelation.

Despite recent attention, the conceptual link of schizophrenia and mystical experience was recognized in 1902 by William James, who noted:

The same sense of ineffable importance in the smallest events, the same texts and words coming with new meanings, the same voices and visions and leadings and missions, the same controlling by extraneous powers . . . It is evident that from the point of view of their psychological mechanism, the classic mysticism and these lower mysticisms spring from the same mental level, from that great subliminal or transmarginal region of which science is beginning to admit the existence, but of which so little is really known. That region contains every kind of matter: "seraph and snake" abide there side by side (1961, p. 326).

In James's terms, schizophrenia is viewed as lower or diabolical mysticism as opposed to classic mystic experiences. Though the similarity of many aspects of these two experiences is striking, it should not obscure the significant differences between them, which will be described after an analysis of their similar components. There are three fundamental continuums along which researchers have differentiated psychotic, drug-induced, and meditative or mystical states. The first is that psychosis is a pressured withdrawal from external reality with an incomplete return, that drug-induced states are more voluntary and elected with potentially less permanent disability, and that mystical states are consciously chosen, experienced, and then usually followed by a higher order of cognitive integration and sense of well-being (Cohen 1967). Second, psychotic episodes are spontaneous in the sense of not being consciously planned and leave the individual unprepared or unable to cope with the experience, a drug state requires minimal preparation within a supportive subcultural environment, and mystical states require years of preparation within a disciplined system of prescribed techniques, interpretive instructions, and guidance (Wapnick 1969). Third, and most important, all three ASC phenomena can be comprehended in terms of various categories of depersonalized or transpersonalized themes that Jung terms *mythic* or *collective*. As he states in *Psychological Reflections:* "The deeper 'layers' of the psyche lose their individual uniqueness as they retreat farther and farther into darkness. 'Lower down'—that is to say, as they approach the autonomous functional systems—they become increasingly collective until they are universalized" (1961, p. 39). In psychotic episodes, these themes engulf the individual in a confusing manner; in the drug-induced state, they are subject to more conscious control and can be experienced as sources of inspiration rather than disorientation; in the mediative states, one lives out and consciously experiences them over a long period of time in order to alter and expand his subjective conception of time and space. In effect, Jung postulates a collective unconscious which is "the ancestral heritage of possibilities of representation" (Campbell 1963, p. 38) and consists of mythological motifs or primordial images. This collective dimension is composed of the fundamental a priori determinants of all psychological processes, which Jung terms *archetypes*. According to Jung, these archetypes are the predispositions for men of all ages, cultures, and circumstances to behave in certain basis patterns. The concept of the archetype is defined as follows:

> An instinct is a pattern of behavior which is inborn and characteristic for a certain species. . . . Instincts determine an animal's behavior on the biological level. . . . Just as instincts common to a species are postulated by observing the uniformities in biological behavior, so archetypes are inferred by observing the uniformities in psychological phenomena. Archetypes are the psychic instincts of the human species (Edinger 1968).

It is an invaluable concept in comprehending the contents of altered state experiences. These mythic patterns are strikingly evident—in the observed behavior, subjective reports, and theoretical literature on psychosis, drug states, and mystical states. An understanding of such ritualistic behavior and content is an invaluable asset when it is therapeutically employed in conjunction with psychodynamic inferences and an individual's past history. In this manner, the "psychotic" utterances and behavior of individuals in these altered states can be interpreted as "part of potentially orderly, natural sequence of experiences . . . the behavioral expressions of an experiential drama" (Laing 1967, p. 85). In essence, this is a basic assumption of the theory of regenerative psychosis that underlies such psychotomimetic experiences as drug-induced and mystical altered-state phenomena.

While many theorists and therapists have formulated theories of regenerative psychosis (Laing 1965b; Jung 1969a; Maslow 1962b; Van Dusen 1972; Bowers 1965; Alvarez 1961), the most comprehensive delineation of the stages of this process has been formulated by Jungian psychiatrist John Perry. In an attempt to understand the psychotic process, Perry has enumerated a ten-stage interpretation of its dominant transpersonal themes. Initially, the individual experiences negative self-perceptions accompanied by frustration, insecurity, guilt, anxiety, and other symptoms of severe neurosis or incipient psychosis. Frequently, he feels that he is participating in some form of drama or ritual. According to Perry's schema, the ritual unfolds according to the following transpersonal experiences:

1. World center. A location is established at the center of the world or cosmic axis
2. Death and afterlife. A predominant theme is of having died and being in an afterlife state. Themes of dismemberment are frequent (Bowers 1965; Boisen 1962; Henderson 1963)
3. Return to beginnings. A regression is expressed that takes the individual back to the beginnings of time and the creation of the cosmos. Infantile behavior is also manifest
4. Cosmic conflict. There arises a cosmic conflict between forces of good and evil or light and darkness (Bowers 1965; Boisen 1962)
5. Threat of other sex. There is a fear that one is being overcome by the opposite sex or being turned into it
6. Apotheosis. Patient experiences an apotheosis as royalty or divinity (Bowers 1965)
7. Sacred marriage. The individual enters into a sacred or royal marriage
8. New birth. A new birth takes place or is expected of a superhuman child or of oneself as an infant savior (Bowers 1965)
9. New society. A new order of society of an ideal or sacred quality is envisioned (Bowers 1965)
10. Quadrated world. A fourfold structure of the world or cosmos is established, usually in the form of a quadrated circle.

The steps do not all occur in order, and they may be fused for a long period of time, but these identifiable themes are prominent in the experiences and behavior of psychotic patients. These transpersonal and transcultural themes, either singly or in combination, are repeated in the great myths of the world. Individuals and societies as a whole do participate in these rituals either individually or collectively. In fact, the enactment of these rituals is the basis of shamanism, or primitive psychiatry. According to Cornell psychiatrist Ari Kiev, "the shaman's role may thus involve aspects of the roles of physician, magician, priest, moral arbiter, representative of the group's world view, and agent of social control" (Kiev 1964, p. 9). Even a cursory discussion of the prominence of Perry's themes in world religions, cultures, and the healing process of folk psychiatry is beyond the scope of this discussion. Two books, Kiev's *Magic, Faith, and Healing* and Mirceau Eliade's *Shamanism: Archaic Techniques of Ectasy*, point out the transpersonal and transcultural use of these themes in primitive and modern healing rituals. The point here is that these experiences have been demonstrated to be of profound influence on all people of all times and geographic locations. Perry's observation that these powerful themes occur during an individual's psychotic episode is strong evidence that more is taking place in certain forms of psychosis than a simple degeneration of coping mechanisms or regression under duress. Both the themes and psychodynamic processes occurring during psychosis can be most fruitfully examined as altered-state experiences of great importance.

Based on their theories of psychosis as an inner journey, both Perry and R. D. Laing have established institutions where patients are encouraged to enter into the psychotic process under supervision designed to promote a regenerative experience. These developments are consistent with Laing's plea for replacing "the degradation ceremonial of psychiatric examination with an initiation ceremonial, through which the person will be guided with full social encouragement and sanction into inner space and time by people who have been there and back again" (Mogar 1968). Much of what Laing has to say can be understood simply as an overreaction to the stance of orthodox psychiatry that views schizophrenia as a disease with no redeeming social value—that is, obscene. There are many practitioners who attempt to ignore the insights of Perry and Laing by making a parody of their arguments and deriding them as advocates of psychosis. Hopefully, what will emerge from this argumentation and debate will be a more enlightened view of schizophrenia, which will recognize that it is potentially a degenerative process but that it can sometimes be a source of regeneration and renewal. Exactly what the criteria will be to sort disease from renewal or death from rebirth is the challenge involved in considering these two opposing views of schizophrenia. Perry's theory represents a major attempt to comprehend the potential of psychosis as a regenerative process and provides an outline of processes that are also prominent in the experience of drug-induced and mystical altered states.

In *Minds That Came Back,* psychiatrist Walter C. Alvarez documents sixty-five biographical and autobiographical accounts of individuals who underwent the ASC experience of a regenerative psychosis. These cases were selected from over 850 accounts of such experiences and include accounts from Clifford Beers, William James, Anton T. Boisen, Nietzsche, Dostoevski, and van Gogh. Another document of a similar nature is Bert Kaplan's *The Inner World of Mental Illness,* which explicitly links themes of psychopathology to recurrent themes in the experiences of creative artists such as Tolstoi and mystics such as Saint Augustine. In reading the autobiographical and biographical passages from these works, one finds that, when excerpts are taken out of context, it is virtually impossible to distinguish among the psychotic, drug-induced, and mystical insights. Such presentations are not intended to imply that the schizophrenic individual is a more enlightened human being for his psychosis, since it is decidedly clear that such a patient is suffering from disabling chronic anxiety and is autistically bound by unbridled fantasies. However, because of the patient's journey out of the consensual construction of external social reality, he has had the opportunity to question the previously implicit assumptions concerning the nature of "normality." Whether such an experience degenerates into chronic psychosis or is integrated following a regenerative psychosis is dependent on the recognition of the transpersonal themes that lend a degree of coherence to the chaotic behavior of a diagnosed psychotic. States that have variously been called psychotic episodes, drug-induced delusions, and mystical states may at times lead to misery and helplessness and at others to personal growth and individuation. A primary result of our comparison of the schizophrenic state of consciousness (SSC) examined herein is the realization that "under pathological as well as normal conditions, we operate on, or relate ourselves to, many different levels of 'reality' and are able to shift, or are forced to shift, from one level to another" (Kluver 1965). Individual experience and response in all ASC appear to be functionally related to a finite number of internal (intrapsychic) and external (environmental) factors. Such characteristics as temporal continuity or discontinuity and the pleasure-pain dimension are intimately related to interactions between these sets of factors. Experientially, any ASC may be symbolic of rejection or expansion of self, or death with or without reconstitution. However, as noted by Laing, Mogar, and others, any attempts at assessing the validity or desirability of particular altered-state experiences reveal the fact that no universal criteria exist for such evaluaations. It appears inappropriate to judge their validity only as a function of culture-specific definitions of pathology and normality. Altered-state experiences such as the mystical state, the psychedelic-drug reaction, the shamanistic-trance state, and the schizophrenic episode are equally valid whether labeled pathological or normal and may best be judged as personal expressions of these diverse levels of reality. As a number of theorists have so aptly observed, all these states may result in either despair and self-renunciation or expansion and self-actualization.

When they occur within the sociopsychological context of modern post-industrial civilization, an increasing number of experiences are seen to be categorized as pathological, unreal, and, in effect, tabooed. The logical concomitant of this phenomenon has been the gradual constriction of consensual definitions of *normal, sane,* and *real.* To extend Mogar's point, this position seems tantamount to the assertion that all ASC, which are by definition *loss of reality* experiences (that is, relative to waking-state reality), are *unreal* and, hence, pathological. It is this equation of *unreal* with pathological that is the foundation of the social-existential, psychedelic, and, most recently, psychophysiological challenges to prior approaches to ASC. These alternative conceptualizations of altered-state phenomena emphasize recognition of "multiple, equally valid realities, the sterility of conventional experience, and the continuum of normal, psychotomimetic, and psychedelic states" (Mogar 1968). The notion of a continuum incorporating normal, ecstatic and schizophrenic states establishes a further relatedness among the varied ASC. This has attracted the attention of the physical sciences.

> Normal, creative, schizophrenic and ecstatic states, are conceived as symbolic interpretations (i.e., perception-behavior) on the perception-hallucination continuum of increasingly higher states of arousal. These states are experienced in terms of increasing data content and increasing rate of data processing, and may result in a creative (artistic or religious) state. Eventually, however, the rate of processing cannot keep step with the ever-increasing data content—"the torrential flood of inner sensation"—and results in the schizophrenic "jammed computer" state. At the peak of ecstatic states, interpretive activity ceases or, in biocybernetic terminology, there is no data content from without, and, therefore no rate of data processing from within, the only content of the experience at the height of rapture being the reflection of the mystic in his own "program" (Fischer 1972).

Much detailed experimental analysis of state-specific psychological, physiological, and neurological correlates of the SSC has yet to be done. In addition, an all-inclusive set of necessary and sufficient conditions for shifts along any ASC continuum, whether state-specific or not, has yet to be determined. The relevance and validity of such inquiries appear well founded and perhaps best expressed by Santayana in *Dialogues in Limbo:* "The physician knows madness in one way; he collects the symptoms of it, the causes and the cure; but the madman in his way knows it far better. The terror and the glory of the illusion, which, after all, are the madness itself, are open only to the madman and to some sympathetic spirit as prone to madness as he is."

THE SCHIZOPHRENIC STATE OF CONSCIOUSNESS

It is now our intention to examine the SSC directly in terms of Silverman's paradigm for the study of ASC (1968a). The rationale behind the elaboration of a systematic paradigm centers around the inability of previous theoretical constructs to remain free of contamination by traditional notions of reality while endeavoring to explain non-reality-oriented psychological states. "A research paradigm for the study of abnormal psychological states is needed which is less encumbered by conventional conceptions of 'reality,' 'reality adaptation' and 'psychopathology' " (Sarbin 1967).

Silverman, after defining an ASC as "an inference from behaviors and verbal reports which are indicative of nonconsensually validated, supernatural, and mystical experiences," offers the following list of characteristics of altered-state behavior:

1. Subjective disturbances in concentration, attention, memory, and judgment
2. Disturbed time sense
3. Difficulty in control
4. Changes in emotional tone
5. Body image change
6. Perceptual distortions
7. Changes in meaning or significance

In addition, he delineates three major factors, one or more of which usually precede the onset of an ASC. These are:

1. Sensory overload or sensory underload. "Either marked increases or marked decreases in exteroceptive stimulation typically associated with profound emotional arousal and 'mental fatigue,' induce ASC" (1968a).
2. "(1) Hyperattentiveness to a narrow range of sensory and ideational stimuli and (2) hypoattentiveness to ordinarily responded to attributes of the environment" (1968a).
3. Changes in body chemistry and in neurophysiological response patterns

Silverman's paradigm for the study of ASC is founded on recent research advances in the areas of neurophysiology and computer technology. Our examination of the SSC will be related to the process of attention deployment "in terms of three attention response factors which regulate reception and utilization of environmental and internal stimuli" (1968a). The three attentional factors under consideration are intensiveness, extensiveness (scanning), and selectiveness (field articulation).

INTENSIVENESS AND ATTENTION. Silverman (1967b) seemingly points out a paradox in the sensory functioning of individuals in ASC—that is, persons in the SSC, for instance, are shown to be hypersensitive to minimal-intensity stimulation. This is characterized by diminished sensory thresholds and overreactivity to subliminal or marginal stimuli. Paradoxically, people in the SSC also evidence a hyposensitivity to maximal-intensity stimulation, that is, elevated sensory-pain thresholds. The explanation of this apparent paradox requires an understanding of the output variations of the schizophrenic physiological-response system. In brief, individuals in the SSC do manifest a hypersensitivity to low-to-moderate range intensity stimulation. Since they are focusing on and responding to marginal stimuli more intensely, they need protection from maximal-intensity stimulation. The compensatory adaptation of hyporesponsiveness to the latter range of stimuli serves as the necessary protective adjustment.

EXTENSIVENESS (OR SCANNING) AND ATTENTION. Information gathering for individuals in the SSC is frequently restricted to an extremely narrow environmental field. "An individual in an ASC is preoccupied with a very narrow circle of ideas; the range of environmental stimuli to which he responds in a systematic way is constricted markedly" (Silverman 1968a). Research evidence indicates that individuals in an ASC who scan their environment minimally tend to overestimate on size judgments of standard stimuli and on size constancy of nearer stimuli. Reverse estimation errors are evident in maximal scanners (Silverman 1964b, 1967b). These results may be incorporated into our analysis of the SSC. A hypoattentiveness to ordinarily responded to environmental stimuli (minimal scanning) is characteristic of nonparanoid schizophrenics. On the other hand, a hyperattentiveness to a restricted range of sensory and ideational stimuli (maximal scanning) is characteristic of paranoid schizophrenics. These basic forms of the SSC show extreme experiential variations.

> In the acute nonparanoid or "essential" schizophrenic state, the individual may undergo the profoundest of emotional upheavals, often with abounding religious and magical ideation, in a markedly detached (minimal scanning) manner. He is beyond commonplace acts, he may not talk, he may not even recognize the personal meaning of other people's actions. . . . In the paranoid schizophrenic resolution of an altered state experience, the individual ". . . caught up in the spread of meaning, magic and transcendental forces, suddenly 'understands' it all as the work of some other concrete person or persons." (Sullivan, 1953) His direction of attention is thereafter primarily upon environmental events and people (Silverman 1968a).

SELECTIVENESS (OR FIELD ARTICULATION) AND ATTENTION. Silverman (1968a) notes that hypersensitive individuals such as those in an SSC articulate their perceptual fields in a manner that tends to be "(a) global and diffuse rather than analytic, and (b) strongly affected by minimal changes in internal and external stimulus conditions." This fluidity of perceptual orientation is related to Laing's notion of the "implosion of reality," or the overwhelming of consciousness by monumental (cosmic) imagery and ideation. Silverman notes Deikman's use of the term *deautomatization,* referring to a suspension and/or alteration of those psychological mechanisms that "organize, limit, select and interpret perceptual stimuli or the undoing of automatic perceptual and cognitive structures [which] permit a gain in sensory intensity and richness at the expense of abstract categorization and differentiation" (Deikman 1966). The results of this deautomatization are that "Thinking is grossly subjective and egocentric; concepts are experienced as percepts. Causal relationships may be perceived between the most distantly related of events; everything is capable of being connected with everything else in an irrational manner" (Silverman 1968a). Table 3 indicates the

Table 2. Two Types of ASC Associated with the Diagnostic Term Schizophrenia

Stage of Disorder	Essential Schizophrenia (Nonparanoid)	Paranoid Schizophrenia
Preconditions: fear; feelings of impotence and failure; guilt; high physiological arousal		Same in both
Preoccupation; isolation; estrangement		Same in both
Narrowing of attention; self-initiated sensory restriction		Same in both
Perceptual-cognitive reorganization: regression; religious and/or magical ideation	Themes of death and rebirth quite common	Themes of death and rebirth less common
	Concentration upon internal "other-world" events	Sudden understanding. Objectification of the "spread of meaning"
Perceptual-cognitive reorganization: change in problem-solving orientation in paranoid type	Impersonal, detached orientation toward the world. Relatively minimal scanning of the environment	Objectified orientation to the world. Extensive scanning of the environment

SOURCE: Silverman 1968a.

Table 3. Attentional Response in the Waking State and Altered States of Consciousness

Response	Ordinary Waking State	Altered States of Consciousness	References
Stimulus intensity control	Midrange sensitivity	Hypersensitivity	Silverman 1967b Fischer et al. 1965 Keeler 1965
	Either augmentation or reduction of the experienced intensity of stimulation	Pronounced reduction of the experienced intensity of stimulation (e.g., high pain tolerance)	Buchsbaum and Silverman 1968 Kast and Collins 1964 Chapman and Walter 1964
Scanning control	Balanced scanning of the environment	Minimal scanning of the environment	Carlson 1962 Silverman 1964b
	High saccadic rate associated with balanced scanning	High saccadic rate associated with minimal scanning	Hebbard and Fischer 1966 Silverman and Gaarder 1967
Field articulation control	Active analytical-segmentalizing perceptual responsiveness	Passive global-relational perceptual responsiveness	DeLuca 1967 Levine et al. 1955 Witkin 1965
	Capacity for shifting and sustaining a focus of attention on varying external stimulus patterns	Inability to shift and to sustain a focus of attention on varying external stimulus patterns	Shakow 1962 Wapner 1964 Wikler et al. 1965

SOURCE: Silverman 1968a.

attentional response characteristics associated with the "normal" waking state of consciousness and with ASC in general.

This paradigmatic emphasis on defining the SSC in terms of physiological-, sensory-, and perceptual-response patterns has two noted advantages over previous attempts. Namely, "(1) it provides an empirically derived, multi-dimensional framework for the study of behavior in ordinary waking states and in ASC, and (2) it avoids the pitfalls of inferences based on inadequate comparisons between abnormal behavior and behavior which occurs in the normal waking state. . . . Such an approach greatly facilitates investigation of the process underlying abnormal behavior and experiences" (Silverman 1968a).

Altered states of consciousness constitute a substantial portion of an individual's psychological processes and functioning. Ordinary perceptual processes, which normally dominate conscious mentation, are modified or suspended, permitting altered experiences of ordinary stimuli. Certain phases of acute psychosis, drug-induced states, or meditation states represent conditions of special receptivity to external and internal stimuli that are ordinarily excluded from awareness. Access to these states is either imposed or consciously sought out, and it is incumbent upon psychology to synthesize Eastern and Western concepts of altered states into a comprehensive system in order to derive maximum possible insight into these altered perceptions of reality.

At the beginning of the book, it was demonstrated that both Gödel and Heisenberg had formally proved the limitations of classical objective inquiry into certain nonrational phenomena. In psychology, analogous phenomena that have come to be recognized as requiring investigation are those categorized as altered states of consciousness. One proposal for extending the concept of classical objectivity to include such phenomena is offered by Charles Tart of the University of California at Davis. He proposes that there are four basic rules that constitute the scientific method; they are:

1. Good observation. A scientist is committed to observe the phenomena as well as possible.

2. Public observation. A scientist is obligated to report what he observes—to report the techniques and conditions of observation in enough detail so that any *trained* observer can replicate the observations.
3. Theoretical consistency. The theory a scientist develops must consistently account for all that he has observed up to this point and should have a logical structure that other scientists can comprehend.
4. Observable consequences of theories. Any theory must have observable consequences and must make predictions that can be verified by observation. If such verification does not occur, the theory must be considered invalid, regardless of how elegant, logical, or otherwise appealing it is (1972).

After a lengthy discussion of these factors, Tart proposes that it is possible to initiate a science of altered states of consciousness that does adhere to all the requirements of a scientific method despite the fact that the experimental variables are not manifest in the external environment. In effect, Tart proposes a true science of consciousness, which he terms a *state-specific science;* he defines it as follows:

> A group of highly skilled, dedicated, and trained practitioners are able to achieve a certain state of consciousness and agree with one another that they have attained a common state. Given that state of consciousness, they may then investigate further problem areas of interest, whether they be totally "internal" phenomena of that given state, or the interaction of that state with "external," physical reality or people in other states of consciousness (1972).

According to Tart's hypothetical construct, Western science has failed to develop state-specific sciences for states other than the normal waking one. As we have demonstrated, there are significant states of consciousness that are clearly in need of research yet remain inaccessible under the current misconceptions of the scientific method. Such a vast body of information cannot remain inexplicable if a true science of psychology is to develop.

What is not recognized in Tart's article is that Western scientists have tended to study the behavioral correlates of consciousness rather than consciousness itself. An example of this trend is the current emphasis on the psychophysiological monitoring of brain waves with little or no attention given to the accompanying subjective experience and imagery. In contrast to this, the Eastern psychological science of meditation considers subjective states to be more directly available for investigation than the objective phenomena of behavior. Accordingly, Eastern systems of meditation have developed a magnificent state-specific science, but no attempt has been made to verify, correlate, and expand these systems by reference to Western knowledge of the human nervous system. In the exploration of ASC phenomena, this synthesis is absolutely necessary for the inquiry to proceed on a scientific basis. One manifestation of the synthesis between science and transpersonal psychology would be the integration of clinical interview techniques with psychophysiological monitoring. This procedure would enable one to obtain the most information possible concerning the nature of a specific altered state. Further research and observation along the lines of John Perry, Julian Silverman, and the Polish psychiatrist Kazimierz Dabrowski would greatly enhance a therapist's ability to comprehend the context of ASC phenomena and deal with it accordingly. State-specific sciences of altered states will have profound impact on individuals and the culture as a whole when theory dictates application.

It is increasingly evident in the United States that large numbers of people are investing considerable time and money in meditation instruction. This phenomenon could be dismissed as a passing fad, or it could be viewed as reflecting a basic change in our culture—that is, an increasing emphasis is being placed on the individual and the spiritual in the midst of an increasingly collective and materialistic society. Any such radical shift demands that the therapists operating within that culture be aware of its dynamics in order to decide consciously on the issues that affect his relationship to his patients. Also of interest to psychology is the fact that meditation constitutes a systematic presentation of practices that leads individuals to con-

duct reorganization and profound insights. In this respect, an understanding of the process of such systems represents an invaluable
adjunct to psychotherapy.

Of particular interest is the potential of ASC phenomena to
illuminate many of the mysteries of the phenomenology of the self,
which is the core consideration of any psychological science. Comparisons between various modes of consciousness can provide information about how an individual constructs his reality, how he
experiences himself and others, and it can also provide a tool for the
discovery of hidden capacities of the mind that are manifest only in
creative genius. Furthermore, the striking similarity of perceptions
during ASC phenomena suggests that people are actually perceiving
their own internal psychological structures and modes of experiencing reality that existed before the effects of socialization. Evidence
that the conditions prior to the onset of the ASC experience and
the content of the phenomena are similar cross-culturally lends support to Jung's concept of the collective unconscious. Since American
psychology comprises ninety-two percent of the world's personnel
and publications in that field, this concept of a collective dimension
of consciousness would infuse respect for other cultures into psychology as it spreads its influence throughout the world. Beneath cultural
divergency lies a capacity in all peoples to reexperience their commonalities with all other peoples of the world.

Preliminary mappings of unknown territories are always more suggestive than definitive of the terrain, and such is the state of this
cartography of consciousness. Primary-process functions can be differentiated and classified according to the criteria suggested in this
discussion. Thus, researchers and theoreticians will be able to recognize the links between these states and the differences that mark
them as distinct and discrete. Once the properties of certain states
have been determined, it may become possible to predict the properties of other states of mind that have remained unrecognized because
researchers have had no adequate means of classifying their characteristics. By enumerating the attributes of several altered states, a
cartography of altered states of consciousness can serve as a tool to

refine and differentiate future observations concerning the nature and interrelationship of a variety of states of consciousness.

Finally, altered states pose a most enigmatic problem—to determine how the reinstatement of primary-process functions interacts with higher-order cognitive functions in a manner significantly different from infantile regressive behavior. It is inexplicable how stimulus-bound, autistic, inflexible behavior may preclude highly innovative and creative insights. The enigma exists and cannot be dismissed; deindividuated behavior is a frequent prelude to marked personal transformation. It would be of enormous benefit to more adequately comprehend this process, which need not be castigated for serving individual needs rather than institutionalized social goals —the two are not necessarily incompatible. Whereas a child knows no sense of individual identity and social responsibility, the individuated adult is often unduly constrained by those very factors. Altered-state experiences offer the individual adult the opportunity to reestablish contact with his innermost energies—a necessary prerequisite to individual growth and transformation innovation.

7

Meditative
States of Consciousness

The similarities between the mystic and schizophrenic experiences were noted as far back as 1902 by William James. James delineated two forms of mysticism: classic, or higher, and diabolical, or lower, and concluded: "It is evident that from the point of view of their psychological mechanism, the classic mysticism and these lower mysticisms spring from the same mental level, from that great subliminal or transmarginal region of which science is beginning to admit the existence, but of which so little is really known" (James 1958). Attempts to equate the two ASC or to indicate that the mystic state is a subclass of schizophrenic psychosis have been noted in the literature (Freud 1961). More recent investigations, such as Laing (1965, 1967) and Bateson (1961), have been criticized for excessively metaphorical portrayals of the schizophrenic experience. These criticisms are usually directed against proselytizing for schizophrenia, that is, against viewing it as a "desirable" experience similar to the psychedelic experience. However, as Wapnick (1969) has noted, the use of the actual metaphoric language associated with particular experiences, although subjective and experiential, is more expressive than objective terminology that inadvertently transforms the experience.

THE MYSTIC STATE

The tendency of Western psychology has been to regard mystical experience as hallucinatory and neurotic, or psychotic. An in-depth explanation of this tendency is a problem for investigation in the areas of sociology of knowledge and philosophy of science. In brief, this phenomenon may be attributed to the fact that most accounts and interpretations of mystical experience are highly individual and presented in nonscientific and metaphorical language. More recently, many "third force" (humanistic) psychologists are considering the mystic state to be an integral part of the process of self-realization and, hence, an area for legitimate consideration. Such investigators have become increasingly more open to the enormous amount of data that has been accumulated by Indian scholars in past centuries. Their realization has been that, even by current scientific standards, much of this material is well documented and deserving of objective evaluation.

Stace (1960) has described the mystic state as the experience of unity or "the apprehension of an ultimate nonsensuous unity in all things, a oneness or a One to which neither the sense nor the reason can penetrate." The most comprehensive description of the mystic state found in the literature is that of Underhill (1961). Mysticism is

the name of that organic process . . . which is the act of man's establishing his conscious relation with the Absolute. The movement of the mystic consciousness towards this consummation, is not merely the sudden admission to an overwhelming vision of Truth: though such dazzling glimpses may from time to time be vouchsafed to the soul. It is rather an ordered movement towards ever higher levels of reality, even closer identification with the Infinite.

It is this characteristic of an "ordered movement" that constitutes the major commonality unifying mystics across spiritual disciplines. This movement has been conceptualized as a succession of stages of experience through which the mystic progresses. These stages, as outlined by Wapnick (1969) as an extension of Underhill (1961), are as follows:

1. As experienced and reported by the mystics, there is the sudden conversion that follows a long period of great unrest and disquiet. Known as "The Awakening of the Self," it is the sudden realization of a strikingly new and different emotional experience that seems to exist beyond sensation, and that carries with it the awareness of a "higher," more desirable level of experience. James referred to this conversion as the breakthrough of the transmarginal consciousness, the sudden "possession of an active subliminal self."

2. After the mystic experiences this deeper level of consciousness he finds that his former patterns of living are no longer satisfying. He feels that they must be purged or mortified, what Underhill refers to as "The Purification of the Self." In the language of James' dichotomy of levels of consciousness, the new subliminal consciousness with which the person has just come into contact is markedly different from the everyday consciousness of his ordinary experience. Thus, the behaviors that involved his everyday functioning in the social world are not applicable to this more personal experience and so must be discarded. . . . The goal of mortification for the mystic is life, but this life can only come through the "death" of the "old self."

3. After the person has purged himself of his former interest and involvement with the social world, he enters the third stage or what Underhill terms "The Illumination of the Self." Here, he experiences more fully what lies beyond the boundaries of his immediate senses. The main reported characteristic of this stage is the joyous apprehension of what the mystic experiences to be the Absolute, including effulgent outpourings of ecstasy and rapture in which the individual glories in his relationship to the Absolute. What distinguishes this stage from latter stages, however, is that the person still experiences himself as a separate entity, not yet unified with what he considers to be the Ultimate. There is yet a sense of I-hood, of ego, of self.

4. This is perhaps the most striking stage of the mystical process. Although it may be found in all mystic experiences, its emotional expression appears only in the Western tradition, where it has taken its name from the evocative phrase of St. John of the Cross: "The Dark Night of the Soul." Here, there is total negation and rejection of the joy of the preceding stage. The person feels totally removed and alienated from his previous experiences and feels very much alone and depressed. . . . During the first purgative period, the individual had to purge himself of his former attachments to the social world. Now, he must purge himself of his experience of self.

5. Though not the final stage, this is the culmination of the

mystic's quest: the complete and total absorption in the asocial, personal world, what has been called "The Unitive Life." It consists of the obliteration of the senses, and even the sense of self, resulting in the experience of unity with the universe. This state has been described as a state of pure consciousness, in which the individual experiences nothing—no thing. The individual has seemingly made contact with the deepest regions of his consciousness and experiences the process as having been completed. Emotionally, the person feels totally tranquil and at peace.

6. Though not mentioned as an independent stage by commentators, the return of the mystic from the experience of oneness with the universe to the requirements of social living constitutes the most important part of his path. In most mystics, it may be observed that they renew their practical involvement in social situations with a new vitality and strength. . . . The mystic now no longer finds his involvement with the world to be abhorrent, but, in fact, seems to welcome the opportunity to move in the social world he had abandoned. This seeming paradox becomes understandable when one considers that it was not the world that the mystic was renouncing, but merely his attachments and needs relating to it, which precluded the development of his personal, asocial experience. Once he was able to abandon these dependent, social needs, and felt freed of the pull of the social world, he experienced the freedom to live within society in conjunction with his inner strivings, rather than experiencing society's customs and institutions as obstacles to his self-fulfillment.

SCHIZOPHRENIC PSYCHOSIS AS A RECONSTITUTIVE PROCESS: POSITIVE DISINTEGRATION

The highly idiosyncratic nature of the schizophrenic experience and its lack of consensual validation appear to be generally accepted facts. What are usually termed "distortions" of time and space—including undifferentiated experiences of "inner and outer space"—as well as "inappropriateness" of behavior from a social vantage point have been recognized as characteristic of the schizophrenic. Perhaps equally lacking in consensual validation is a single etiological equation for schizophrenic psychosis.

minority position, albeit one that is gaining favor, is the contention that "some of the most profound schizophrenic disorganizations
are preludes to impressive reorganization and personality growth—
not so much breakdown as breakthrough" (Silverman 1970). Basic
to this position is the belief that schizophrenic psychosis is a natural
reaction and/or coping mechanism to intensely stressful situations—
a spontaneous reconstitutive process undergone by individuals whose
"normal" attempts to correct inadequate functioning, that is, problem
solving, fail to be operative. This model of schizophrenia is described
by some of its leading proponents as follows:

> The so-called symptoms, rather than being ego-alien manifestations
> of a disease process that has somehow gotten a grip on the person,
> are instead purposeful acts of the individual, which have intention-
> ality and are motivated. The "illness" is something the individual
> "wills" to happen (Kaplan 1964).

> The mind contains, in some form, such wisdom that it can create
> that attack upon itself that will lead to a later resolution of the
> pathology (Bateson 1961).

> Schizophrenia is itself a natural way of healing our own appalling
> state of alienation called normality. . . . Madness need not be all
> breakdown. . . . It may also be breakthrough. It is potentially libera-
> tion and renewal as well as enslavement and existential death. It is
> not an illness to be treated, but a "voyage." Socially, madness may
> be a form in which . . . often through quite ordinary people, the light
> begins to break through the cracks in our all-too-closed minds
> (Laing 1967).

> Our basic hypothesis is that the organism's wisdom is greater than
> our limited intellectual appreciation of it. The daemonic symptoms
> may, like fever, be benign responses to the deeper trials of life that
> the patient may never solve if the therapist encourages escape or
> drugs him into a permanent state of psychic helplessness (Silverman
> 1970).

> Some patients have a mental illness and then get well and then they
> get weller! I mean they get better than they ever were. . . . This is
> an extraordinary and little-realized truth (Menninger 1959).

Laing (1966) suggests the label *metanoia,* meaning "beyond the
mind," for what is called schizophrenic psychosis. The purpose is to

redefine schizophrenia as a process or individual experience that transcends the general conceptualization of mind or ego—one that goes "beyond the horizons of our communal sense" (Laing 1967). If the schizophrenic experience is considered as an expression of the individual's asocial "inner world" as opposed to the manifestations of mental derangement, it may "appear to be part of a potentially orderly, natural sequence" taking the form of a series of stages not unlike the stages previously associated with the mystic experience.

Boisen (1947) noted the following sequence of stages in the onset of acute schizophrenia:

1. Initially, there is a period of preparation or frustration in which we find evidence of some unsolved problem relating to the patient's role in life—a problem which arouses intense emotions. Nearly always this problem involves some sense of fear and guilt. It has usually been on the patient's mind for many years as a source of distress and uneasiness until finally . . . there comes a desperate attempt at solution.

2. Next is a period of narrowed attention and preoccupation lasting from a few days to a few weeks. There is mention of praying and reading the Bible. In discussing a particular patient, we note a narrowing of attention that is so characteristic as to justify a question as to whether his suggestion regarding autohypnosis may not be worthy of consideration. Certainly we know that Hindu holy men and others of the shaman type employ techniques for the narrowing of attention in order to induce the trance condition.

3. Following this period is a stage in which the individual is confronted with an upsetting idea most frequently associated with contact with the superhuman and/or cosmic identification. Although the term "voice" is the one most frequently used, most of the patients will explain it is not something they heard with their ears. . . . The point to notice is that the mechanism involved in these voices is not different from the "insights" or "inspirations" of normal persons. The important consideration is what the voices say and the fact that they are attributed to a superhuman source.

4. The stage following is a period of elaboration and largely depends upon what the voices say. The most frequent of all the ideas found in the schizophrenic reaction is that of death. . . . After the initial idea of death which is accepted with a spirit of sacrificial renunciation . . . other strange ideas come surging in. Ideas of cosmic catastrophe, cosmic identification, previous incarnation and

prophetic mission are frequent. What claims our attention here is the fact that this period is not only characterized by elation, exaltation, and a great profusion of new ideas but is also marked by bewilderment and perplexity, with the central problem pertaining usually to the patient's own role. . . . As in mystical experience generally, the mind is stirred to its profoundest levels. There is great enlargement of the field within which intuition is valid, as the critical faculties are in abeyance. They are however by no means absent. One sees it in the overwhelming perplexity which is so often present. In many instances, the patient is sure of only one thing—that things are not what they seem to be. He seeks communication from above not merely in ideas which come into his head but also in all sorts of trivial happenings. . . . Subsequently, the patient may build up a new concept of his role in life . . . or conclude he was going right the way he was. In such cases the perplexity gives place to some degree of self-assurance.

He added the following commentary:

That there is much similarity between the process of creative thinking and that of the schizophrenic reaction is apparent. They have in common the period of preparation or frustration, the unpredicted insight which comes as "inspired" or "given" carrying authority because of the way in which it comes and producing a mood of exaltation and criticism represented in the flood of new ideas and a consequent strain upon the critical faculties. What is not so clear is the period of "renunciation" or "recession." We do find in a large proportion of our cases the renunciation of some longed-for hope and the sacrificial acceptance of the idea of death. It is generally following this that the idea of cosmic identification makes its appearance. But there is no recession in the sense of turning the attention to irrelevant matters. In most schizophrenic reactions, the new idea or insight follows a period of intense preoccupation and concentration. . . . It follows then that the schizophrenic condition results when, in some desperate problem-solving effort, the creative intuitive forces take possession at the expense of the organized self.

SCHIZOPHRENIC PSYCHOSIS AND THE MYSTICAL EXPERIENCE

In comparing the developments preceding the onset of the mystic and schizophrenic states of consciousness, Wapnick (1969) notes certain similarities as well as differences. Among the similarities are the experienced dichotomy between outer, or social, reality and inner, or personal, reality, the dissolution of all social attachments, the total entrance into the inner world with attendant feelings of pain and terror, the sense of pervading tranquility following the preceding terror, and, in some instances, the reentrance into the social world with improved functioning.

The differences noted are: while the mystical process is most often of long duration, the schizophrenic experience may be compressed into a much shorter time span; while the mystic state culminates in the experience of unity with one's environment, the schizophrenic has no such experience; while the mystical process is often accompanied by some contact with the social world and conscious control on the part of the individual, the schizophrenic often undergoes a total breakdown in social functioning and loss of conscious control. Perhaps the most marked contrast between the two ASC is in the ability of the individual to deal with the dissolution of the ego and with his break with outer reality. While the psychotic condition is characterized by an ineffective internal locus of control —that is, the schizophrenic is overwhelmed by his inner experience —the mystic retains a tolerance for this immersion in inner reality. This is comprehensible in view of the fact that, for the mystic, the entire process is directed at developing a tolerance for confrontation with one's inner world. As he increases his ability to "own" his inner world, the mystic gradually incorporates these experiences into his social existence. Wapnick (1969) notes that Jung (1961) stresses the functionality of external contact in shielding him from the "implosion" by the inner world of the unconscious.

> Particularly at this time, when I was working on the fantasies, I needed a point of support in "this world," and I may say that my family and my professional work were that to me. It was most essential for me to have a normal life in the real world as a counterpoise to that strange inner world. My family and my profession remained the base to which I could always return, assuring me that I was an actually existing, ordinary person. The unconscious contents could have drawn me out of my wits . . . [as they did Nietzsche] who was

a blank page whirling about in the winds of the spirit . . . [who] had lost the ground under his feet because he possessed nothing more than the inner world of his thoughts—which incidentally possessed him more than he it. He was uprooted and hovered above the earth, and therefore he succumbed to exaggeration and irreality. For me, such irreality was the quintessence of horror, for I aimed, after all, at this world and this life. No matter how deeply absorbed or how blown about I was, I always knew that everything I was experiencing was ultimately directed at this real life of mine.

The schizophrenic, on the other hand, is exposed to no such training regimen and, when immersed in inner experience, is both unable to cope with the sudden onslaught of asocial, personal feelings and unsure of survival.

In terms of Deikman's aforementioned model of bimodal consciousness, both the schizophrenic and mystic experiences are characterized by sudden and extreme shifts to the receptive mode of functioning: "decreased self-object differentiation, heightened sensory intake, and nonverbal, nonlogical thought process" (Deikman 1971). However, the results of this radical shift in functioning are quite dissimilar. In Deikman's terms, the mystic emerges from the "cloud of unknowing" or the "dark night of the soul" with the ecstatic experience of Unity—union with God, or the Infinite, and a harmonious integration of self and world. For the schizophrenic, the implosion of reality remains unintegrated, and there is no experience of "the harmony of mystico unio or satori." Instead, the psychotic copes with this implosion by structuring a delusional system directed at establishing a minimal ordering and control of the experience.

Mednick and Schulsinger (1970) note that maternal deprivation in the case of children and rejection by a loved one in adulthood are frequent precursors or precipitants of psychosis. We concur with Deikman's observation that these factors, coupled with the intense but unacknowledged hatred and destructive fantasies directed at a loved one, suggest the possibility that the schizophrenic ASC is defensive in nature and directed at the organization of a cognitive and perceptual mode of functioning (the receptive mode) that will effectively eliminate destructive action against the significant other(s). "If someone is ecstatic, Christlike, overcome with the significance of a thousand details, buffeted by alternate winds of fear, exultation, grief and rapture, he is in a state that maximizes what comes in and minimizes the possibility of aggressive action on someone else. Not incidentally, maximum sensory intake can be viewed as dealing with the painful emptiness following deprivation of love" (Deikman 1971). As the action mode of functioning is discarded and normal filtering mechanisms fail to impede sensory overload (implosion of reality), the schizophrenic endeavors to structure his experiences via delusional ideation. In addition to imposing partial structure and order, the delusional system provides the schizophrenic with an effective alternative "object" to the significant other(s). In Table 4, Cohen (1970) presents a comparison between the acute schizophrenic (catatonic) state, the mystic (visionary) state, and the sequential nature of "normal" insight.

The essence of mystical experience admittedly is difficult to grasp when one is limited solely to the workings of the intellect. The fact that we have made a comparison between the revered study of mysticism and schizophrenia is somewhat unusual in itself. Can a tradition so long held in high esteem by both Eastern and Western cultures possibly be translated as a form of mental derangement merely by a shift in perspective? Is it feasible that each of us might experience, albeit with diminished intensity, what mystics have described through the ages? We now turn our attention to the meditative state of consciousness in an effort to deal with these and related issues long neglected in the West.

MEDITATION-INDUCED ALTERED STATES

Before the last decade, members of Western culture were exposed to altered states of consciousness primarily in psychotic or drug-induced states. However, concurrent with this Western view there has existed a tradition in Eastern cultures of deliberately seeking and cultivating altered-state experiences through various systems of meditation. All of the major Eastern religions have the essential characteris-

Table 4. A Comparison between Acute Catatonic Schizophrenia, Visionary Experience, and "Normal" Insight

	Acute Schizophrenia (Acute Catatonic Excitement)	The Visionary State (Spontaneous Type)	The Inspiration (The Unifying Idea)
Predisposing factors	Frustration, insecurity, guilt, and anxiety in a predisposed individual	Frustration, insecurity, and intense emotion in a predisposed individual	Acquisition of background information and experience necessary for eventual problem solving. In instances of artistic inspiration, the technical ability must be available (preparation)
Latent period	Gradual mobilization of available defenses to maintain acceptable interpersonal relationships. These are inadequate and crumble	Intellectual and psychological efforts at personal problem solving culminating in periods of physical and mental exhaustion	Conscious striving to solve the scientific or artistic problem has been fruitless. It is set aside and attention is turned to other matters (incubation)
The idea	The sudden delusional projection of the conflict ("I am God"). Emotional discharge as ecstasy, furor, depression, stupor	The revelation, the Light. Emotional discharge as exaltation	The inspiration, a subliminal problem-solving process with only the final solution springing to consciousness. Emotional discharge as elation (illumination)
Developmental period	Further paranoid elaboration of the central delusion	Reshuffling of ego defenses (sudden personality change). Restructuring old patterns of behavior	Elaboration of the central idea, critical inspection with modifications (elaboration)
Final result	1. Reestablishment of the prepsychotic level of ego function. 2. Chronicity, flattening, increased mental disorganization (chronic schizophrenia)	1. Return to old patterns of living. 2. Continuing personal and group change in a direction of greater effectiveness (cults, religions, movements)	1. Discarding the idea. 2. Final polishing, new applications, testing of validity or value by others (verification)

tic of propounding a disciplined methodology by which an adherent may experience a transcendent or profound religious experience; the experience would affirm that religion's doctrine of a higher order of reality. For many centuries, meditation has been prescribed as a technique to bring about an altered perception of the world and the self. This altered mode of perception is usually characterized by a sense of unity, heightened sensory perception, strong affect, a sense of timelessness, and a sense of expanded awareness (Deikman 1971). The fundamental principle underlying all the disparate systems of meditation is the honing of introspection to such a refined quality of self-observation that one is fully able to observe himself with complete detachment (DeRopp 1968). This process involves a progressive detachment from social definitions of identity and a recognition that the individual is not defined or identified by his emotions, opinions, intellect, or by any metathoughts about any of these aspects of personality (Sen 1952). Meditation is, in essence, a profound state of passivity accompanied by an apparently paradoxical state of complete awareness.

Mastery of this state of focused awareness is an extraordinarily difficult task; in the process of achieving this state of self-awareness, the initiate will frequently undergo ASC experiences strikingly similar to those experienced by psychotics or drug-intoxicated individuals (Wapnick 1972). However, it is the explicit purpose of Eastern religion to provide the individual with an interpretive system through which he can comprehend these states and minimize the disruption to his former sense of ego identity. Meditatively induced ASC are similar to drug-induced states in the sense that they are voluntarily and consciously pursued, but the major difference is that the initiate engages in a rigorous discipline designed to prepare him to undergo and meaningfully integrate the ASC experience. In fact, every major religion and system of meditation stresses the avoidance of drug-induced altered states. Their reasoning in this matter is clear: "Drug experience strongly reinforces the illusion that highs come from external, material things rather than from one's own nervous system, and it is precisely this illusion that one strives to overcome by means of meditation" (Weil 1972, p. 90). It is significant that the meditative disciplines have evolved predominantly from the Indian, Chinese, and Japanese cultures, where there are significant amounts of psychoactive drugs, such as hashish and opiates, available to the general population. Systems of meditation have evolved both as religious systems and as systems of social drug control by presenting an alternative means of achieving the end of ASC experience. These aforementioned cultures have come to recognize that drugs are an ineffective means of attaining altered states and yet have not inextricably confused the means with the experiences themselves.

Before explaining meditation-induced ASC phenomena, we must note that we are not advocating either the Eastern or the Western means of achieving individuation; either culture has achieved an integrated view of the individual that would satisfy the contemporary psychologist or psychiatrist. Yet, there is a great deal to be learned by comparing them because it is from that comparison that a more comprehensive understanding of ASC phenomena will arise. Harvard psychiatrist Andrew Weil states this position most eloquently:

> I have complained about the materialism of the West, its attachment to the intellect, and its blindness to the reality of nonordinary reality. . . . Easterners tend to fall into the complementary trap of equating reality with nonmaterial reality, of dismissing the physical world as illusion. Consequently, they are no better able than we are to change the physical world for the better (Weil 1972, p. 65).

What both the Eastern and Western systems of psychological insight need is a more comprehensive synthesis in order to more adequately understand the various modes of experience and functioning of which an individual is capable.

In psychological terminology, the aim of meditation is to allow a person to gain awareness of these feelings, motives, and values that had been previously held out of awareness. Accomplishment of this end is achieved by engaging in prescribed techniques for freeing attention from immediate and distracting sensory stimuli in order to pay closer attention to the more subtle stimuli that unconsciously shape perceptions and behavior (Naranjo and Ornstein 1971). The intent is analogous to the goals of all psychotherapeutic systems. However, there is one added dimension in meditation—the process leads to a transcendent experience. Deikman has attempted to translate this concept of a transcendent ASC experience into psychological terminology. After a review of the literature on meditation-induced ASC phenomena, Deikman noted three general characteristics linking meditation to these altered states:

> 1) that the procedure of contemplative meditation is a principal agent in producing the mystic experience; 2) that training in contemplative meditation leads to the building up of intrapsychic barriers against distracting stimuli; and 3) that many of the phenomena described in mystic accounts can be regarded as the consequence of a partial deautomatization of the psychic structures that organize and interpret perceptual stimuli (Deikman 1971).

A basic assumption of this theory is that repeated acts of perception result in the construction of set categories of perception that eventually become unconscious and, therefore, are no longer subject to ready alteration (Naranjo and Ornstein 1971). "Deautomatization" is the undoing of this process "by the reinvestment of actions and perceptions with attention (Deikman 1971). This reinvestment of attention in otherwise unconscious processes of behavior and perception is precisely that state of awareness advocated by all systems of meditation.

Various techniques are used to achieve this state of awareness, but they are too numerous and complex to be discussed at this point; also, the focus here is on the states achieved rather than on the method of induction. Meditation techniques foster a cognitive attitude of empty receptiveness with an emphasis on immediate perception of present stimuli (Allison 1967). One psychophysiological study, made in 1961 by Anand, China, and Singh, is of paramount importance in demonstrating the validity of this state. They reported that there was no alteration in the quiescent alpha pattern of the EEG when meditating yogis were exposed to loud, distracting external stimuli. This demonstrates that the yogis were in fact capable of focusing on subtle internal cues in a deeply relaxed state despite external distractions. This same project provides evidence that supports both the claim of the yogis to experience each moment and Deikman's hypothesis that mediators can achieve a state of deautomatized attention. When the yogis were out of their state of meditation, the same stimulus produced an EEG response which did not lessen upon repetition. Under normal conditions, when a stimulus is introduced to a person, there is a tendency for the EEG to show a spike or large amplitude wave in response. The amplitude of this spike tends to decrease with each subsequent repetition until no overt response is noted. This gradual decrease in response is termed habituation and was previously thought to be an invariable norm of the autonomic nervous system. In the Zen meditators, the spiking continued with equal amplitude each time the stimulus was presented over a prolonged period of time, indicating a significant variation in nervous system reactivity. Subjects responded to each presentation of the stimuli as though it were a new event and demonstrated a continuing fresh receptiveness to the external world. This state is assumed to be a dominant characteristic of the individuated or fully functioning person and has been recognized by Jung, Maslow, and Fromm (who has most clearly attempted to incorporate Eastern concepts into Western psychology). Fromm expresses this present-time orientation in his concept of *well-being*, which he defines as follows: "Well-being means to drop one's ego, to give up greed, to cease chasing after the preservation and the aggrandizement of the ego, to be and to experience one's self in the act of being" (Fromm 1960, p. 91). Meditation does not seek to destroy the ego but rather to demonstrate the finiteness of ego consciousness, which is considered to be a social contruct. To psychoanalysts, the meditator's stress on loss of self and the unitive state of being is likely to suggest that there ensues a psychotic confusion of the inner and the outer—a loss of the self-object distinction, as in hallucinations and paranoid delusions—but such is not the case (Fingarette 1958). Freud suggested that the "oceanic feeling" of oneness was a concomitant of infantile regression to a maternal primal unity. However, meditation is a process that differs from infantile regression in that it is not a retreat from stress but is, in fact, a consciously willed, arduous task of controlled regression accompanied by a heightened state of self-observation (Allison 1967; Prince and Savage 1972). In support of this conception is a project by Edward W. Maupin (1965) in which he reported that if one has the "capacity for regression in the service of the ego" and "tolerance for unrealistic experiences," a positive response to meditation exercises can be predicted. Egocentrism is transcended in meditation; the result is that the ego is strengthened through the more conscious awareness of formerly subliminal processes. It is this deeper awareness of an individual's psychological functioning that permits him to live increasingly in the moment, free of past distortions and future anticipations.

Characteristics of meditation states fulfill several of Zimbardo's requisites for the induction of an altered-state experience. Initiates are (1) subjected to increasingly long periods of isolation analogous to sensory deprivation; (2) encouraged to expand their present awareness, which results in an altered temporal perspective; (3) taught to engage in physical involvement, in acts ranging from sitting to complex yoga postures; (4) placed in novel situations, such as extremely quiet rooms or darkened cubicles; and (5) trained to rely heavily on noncognitive interactions and feedback, especially from their own physiological processes (for example, breathing or heartbeat). All of these factors frequently contribute to inducing an ASC experience analogous to psychotic or drug-induced episodes but under maximally controlled conditions. Emphasis here is on the fact that meditative systems acknowledge the existence of and need for experiencing ASC phenomena and proceed on that basis to construct a system to insure the beneficial comprehension and integration of that experience for the individual. There is very little theoretical or research literature that has attempted to interpret the implications of these systems for Western psychology. One major obstacle to such a dialogue between Eastern and Western systems of psychological insight has been the obscure, esoteric metaphors of the East on one extreme and the rationalistic, mechanistic, and reductionistic jargon of the West on the other. Quite frequently, an initiate may undergo a psychotic episode during the initial stages of intensive meditation; it would be of enormous benefit for meditation instructors to become informed of specific therapeutic interventions.

From an extensive survey of the literature concerning meditation-induced and spontaneously occurring transcendent states, it is evident that all such accounts are attempts to describe what constitutes the core of a universal psychological experience. Excerpts from phenomenological accounts indicate that transpersonal, transcultural, and transcendent experiences have fundamental similarities. According to psychiatrists Walter N. Pahnke and William A. Richards, the fundamental aspects of all of them are (1) an experience of undifferentiated unity; (2) states of insight into depths of truth unplumbed by the intellect; (3) transcendence of space and time; (4) sense of sacredness characterized by awe; (5) deeply felt positive emotion; (6) paradoxical experiences, such as being reborn through death; (7) alleged ineffability, resulting in difficulty in communicating about the experience; (8) transiency, since all such states are relatively brief; and (9) positive changes in attitude and/or behavior (1966). Experiences of transcendence are not the exclusive province of meditators, mystics, or psychotics; one of the most insightful statements about the nature of these experiences is that of Albert Einstein:

> The most beautiful and most profound emotion we can experience is the sensation of the mystical. It is the source of all true science. He to whom this emotion is a stranger, who can no longer stand rapt in awe, is as good as dead. That deeply emotional conviction of a superior reasoning power, which is revealed in the incomprehensible universe, forms my idea of God.

Whether such experiences are validated or esteemed is largely dependent on the cultural context, but their effect on individual behavior is undisputed. Their ability to inspire is surpassed only by their ability to disrupt, for such an experience must be translated into terms that are comprehensible to the ego. Transmuting these transcendent insights into some socially or artistically acceptable symbolic form constitutes the essence of creativity, according to psychiatrist Lawrence S. Kubie in *The Neurotic Distortion of the Creative Process*. Drawing on Kubie's work, psychologist Lawrence Le Shan attempted to compare the theoretical positions of modern physicists and mystics. Le Shan reasoned that the goal of both groups was to understand the nature of reality more completely and to describe their conclusions on its nature. Obviously, the mathematics of the physicist is different from the poetry or prose of the mystics. Therefore, Le Shan decided to use autobiographical accounts of physicists who attempted to describe their thoughts and affect concerning an insight before translating that insight into mathematical symbolism. What resulted is a remarkable article (1969), containing sixty-two quotations from physicists and mystics arranged according to certain categories. It is immediately evident that it is difficult—if not impossible—to separate the quotations according to profession, as the following examples will demonstrate:

> . . . the reason why our sentient, percipient, and thinking ego is met nowhere in our world picture can easily be indicated in seven words: because it is ITSELF that world picture. It is identical with the whole and therefore cannot be contained in it as part of it.

> . . . all phenomena and their development are simply manifestations of mind, all causes and effects, from great universes to fine dust only seen in the sunlight, come into apparent existence only by means of the discriminating mind.

The first quotation is from the mathematician Schroedinger and the second one is from the mystic Surangama Sutra. Both men seek to describe the interface of subjective perception and external reality, and both rely on poetic expression to convey a sense of awe and inspiration. This parallel between the words of physicists and mystics illustrates that ASC experiences can be a profound source of insight for individuals in widely disparate disciplines. Although the translation of that experience may be in terms of mathematical logic, painting, or poetry, the subjective reports of the states are remarkably uniform. ASC experiences of such profundity are indicative of an aspect of consciousness common to all men—the collective unconscious. This universal dimension of human consciousness is a potential source of rejuvenation for people who undertake the lifelong task of individuation which inevitably elicits an ASC experience. Despite the inherent dangers of such a task, despite the infrequent occurrence of ASC experiences, these states constitute the essence of religious, creative, and scientific inspiration. For this reason alone, inquiry into them is of paramount importance, for there are existing systems of meditation that establish the minimum prerequisites for experiencing that state of consciousness.

The essential differences between psychotic, drug-induced, and meditation-induced ASC phenomena are found in preparation. For the experienced meditator, ASC experiences are consciously chosen and sought over a prolonged period of time and allowed to develop slowly within a supportive cultural context. Meditators often report that they are engulfed by experiences analogous to Perry's basic themes exhibited during a psychotic episode or during a drug-induced state (Burns 1966). Again, the critical variables seem to be preparation and timing: a psychotic episode is unpremeditated and sudden; a drug-induced experience is moderately prepared for, gradual in onset, and brief in duration; and a meditative experience constitutes lifelong dedication and extreme patience over many years. Meditators recognize the value of inner experience and seek to cultivate it while simultaneously immersing themselves in constructive social action. The necessity for continued investment in social reality is attested to by all major systems of meditation and is recognized by Jung in his own personal experiences with ASC phenomena.

> Particularly at this time, when I was working on the fantasies, I needed a point of support in "this world." . . . It was most essential for me to have a normal life in the real world as a counterpoise to that strange inner world. . . . No matter how deeply absorbed or how blown about I was, I always knew that everything I was experiencing was ultimately directed at this real life of mine (Jung 1961, p. 189).

Such an involvement is not simply a matter of preference but rather a necessary prerequisite in avoiding the abyss of degenerative psychosis. Whereas the meditator seeks to enhance his inner experience and insight into the external environment, the schizophrenic's purpose is to escape from his social environment, not realizing the potential chaos of his own inner world. Despite the fact that psychosis and drug-induced states constitute escapes from social reality, they still contain the potential for substantial insight and a higher order of individuation. Kenneth Wapnick has succinctly stated the difference between psychotic and meditative phenomena: "The mystic provides the example of the method whereby the inner and outer may be joined; the schizophrenic, the tragic result when they are separated" (1972). It is in this union of inner and outer experience that meditation can be understood as the highest form of altered-state experience and a rich source of insight; psychosis and drug-induced states are less successful attempts to experience and integrate various altered states of consciousness. What is common to all of them is the suspension of the ordinary conception of identity; this experience, according to all religious tradition, is an essential prerequisite to comprehending the true nature of the self. Whether this transcendent insight is achieved is entirely dependent on how well the various ASC phenomena are comprehended and integrated. The comprehension and integration is the task of all those who explore and expand the dimensions of mind.

THE MEDITATIVE STATE: GENERAL PRINCIPLES

Meditation is first of all a deep passivity, combined with awareness. It is not necessary to have a mystical rationale to practice meditation, but there are marked similarities in the psychological assumptions which underlie most approaches. The ego, or conscious self, is usually felt to be only a portion of the real self. The conscious, striving, busy attempts to maintain and defend myself are based on a partial and misleading concept of my vulnerability, my needs, and the deeper nature of reality. In meditation I suspend this busy activity and assume a passive attitude. What I am passive *to* is conceived in many different ways, but I need only assume that deeper resources are available when I suspend my activity. Instead of diffusing myself in a welter of thoughts and actions, I can turn back on myself and direct my attention upstream to the out-pouring, spontaneous, unpredictable flow of my experience, to the states of mind which produce all the business and thinking. It is well at this point to distinguish the practice of meditation from special experiences of mystical union or "satori." These dramatic states have probably been overemphasized in the meditation literature. Meditation may be worthwhile in itself without such states, which are unlikely to come about without prolonged practice under skilled supervision.

The position used in meditation is important. It should be such that you can let go and relax in it, yet not fall asleep. The relaxation is not the totally heavy kind you get when you lie down, but balanced and consistent with alertness. In Asia the cross-legged lotus positions are ordinarily used. If you want to try, sit on the floor and cross your legs so that your right foot rests on your left thigh and your left foot rests on the right thigh. This is very difficult to do. You might try the slightly easier procedure of only getting one foot on one thigh and crossing the other leg so that it is underneath the opposite thigh close to the buttock (the half-lotus position), or simply sit tailor fashion. In all three positions your rump should be raised by means of cushions so that knees and buttocks form a stable three-cornered base. Now see if you can let your back rest down into this base in such a way that it is a straight column which requires no strain to keep straight. The hands rest in the lap; the head is erect; the eyes should be open and directed without focusing at a point a few feet ahead of the knees. (All this is following Zen procedure most closely. Yoga practice usually omits the cushion and permits closing the eyes—which leads more easily into trances than to wakeful awareness.)

The cross-legged positions are not essential. You can meditate effectively in a straight-backed chair with your feet planted wide apart and flat on the floor, your back straight, head erect, and eyes open as before. The most comfortable height should be adjusted with cushions. A less erect posture in an ordinary easy chair can also be used.

After you get into position, sway back and forth for a while to settle in, take a few deep breaths, and begin to let go. You may find it useful to contact various parts of your body with your attention, especially your base, the legs and pelvis on which you are resting. Now you are ready to begin directing your attention according to the technique you have decided to use.

The techniques presented are fairly simple ones, classically used in the early stages of training. You may wish to experiment with more than one to find which is the most effective for you. They are all suitable for daily use for between a half hour and an hour. Although they are apparently different, they all seem to aim at increasing awareness of what is happening inside and making possible a detached look. It is extremely misleading to strive toward any particular state of mind, but all of these exercises will sometimes make possible a state of clear, relaxed awareness in which the flow of thought is reduced and an attitude of detached observation is maintained. In contrast with the usual thinking activity, which carries one off into abstractions or fantasies, this observing attitude keeps close contact with the here-and-now of experience. Thoughts are not prevented, but are allowed to pass without elaboration. It is not a blank state or trance, and it is different from sleep. It involves deep physical relaxation as well as letting go of the usual psychological busyness. Actually, one discovers very early how closely psychological and physical relaxation are related.

How you handle distractions is extremely important. Do not try to prevent them. Just patiently bring your attention back again and again to the object of your meditation. This detaching from fantasies and thoughts and outside stimuli is some of the most important work of meditation. If you attempt to prevent distractions in some other way, you may get into unproductive blank states, or get distracted by the task of preventing distractions, or become tense. If you patiently return to the meditation, gradually your attention to the object will replace the distractions, and your physical relaxation will make it possible for the flow of thoughts to decrease.

It is also very important that you not have some preconceived notion of what "should" happen in a "good" session. You may become relaxed and clear, but you may also remain tense and distracted, or you may uncover extremely painful kinds of experience. Allowing yourself to be honestly aware of whatever you experience is more constructive than the most pleasant relaxation. Accepting the session wherever it leads is essential. You may feel sleepy. Try observing the process of falling asleep itself—perhaps it is a response to some feeling you want to avoid. If sleep continues to be a problem, get up and walk around and breathe deeply for a while. You may feel bored and restless with the task. Observe and experience these feelings. In this culture you may well find yourself taking a negative attitude, beating yourself over the head, as it were, to do a good job of meditating. Try to observe this self-critical, hostile attitude in yourself. There is a kind of friendly neutrality you can bring to bear on any experience which emerges.

As the ego activity is reduced, inner material, some of it formerly outside awareness, begins to emerge. Herrigel (1953) writes:

"This exquisite state of unconcerned immersion in oneself is not, unfortunately, of long duration. It is likely to be disturbed from inside. As though sprung from nowhere, moods, feelings, desires, worries and even thoughts incontinently rise up, in a meaningless jumble. . . . The only successful way of rendering this disturbance inoperative is to . . . enter into friendly relations with whatever appears on the scene, to accustom oneself to it, to look at it equably and at last grow weary of looking."*

This is one reason why you should probably be supervised if you want to practice meditating more than an hour at a time. With more time the emerging material may become more dense and impelling, more difficult to treat as an illusory distraction. Supposedly it was a Zen student in Japan who burned down the golden pavilion on grounds it was so beautiful that all it lacked was transience. The emerging material may change form, become predominantly visual imagery in contrast to the verbal form of earlier distractions, and so on. However, it is not necessary to be *too* cautious about this material. My psychotherapy patients, when they have meditated at home, have had no special difficulty in treating their distractions as distractions. All that is required is to observe them and return to the meditation (Maupin in Tart 1969).

A particular form of meditation called Transcendental Meditation, or TM, has been employed in an increasing number of empirical investigations over the past five years. The originator of this meditative style, Maharishi Mahesh Yogi, describes TM as a natural technique of directing one's attention inward toward more subtle levels of thought, until the mind transcends the experience of the most subtle level and arrives at the "source of all thought." This source (state) is the goal of all meditative styles and is what several researchers have termed *the fourth state of consciousness*. TM differs from other meditative styles (Zen and other yogic techniques) and from various Western methods of self-actualization (psychoanalysis and Biofeedback) in that it does not demand any form of concentration, reflection, suggestion, submission, control, faith, intellectual understanding, or confidence in the efficacy of the discipline. Maharishi believes that these effort-laden systems are basically acts of will and, as such, are counterproductive in that they perpetuate the waking state of consciousness rather than facilitating the meditative one.

* E. Herrigel, *Zen in the Art of Archery* (New York: Pantheon, 1953).

THE PHYSIOLOGY OF MEDITATIVE STATES

The possibility of altering one's state of consciousness via meditation and, hence, reducing physical and mental stress levels has long been entertained. Although many of the earlier studies that attempted to establish physiological correlates of meditation states have been shown to contain equivocal results, several well-executed investigations have revealed consistently significant physiological alterations during meditation. In 1935, the French cardiologist Thèrese Brossé traveled to India and took physiological measurements (electrocardiographic) of students of varied yogic practices. Wallace (1970) observes that the initial systematic electrophysiological investigation was conducted in 1957 when M. A. Wenger, B. K. Bagchi and B. K. Anand researched varied autonomic functions of Indian yogis. The results indicated a decreased respiratory frequency, an increased skin resistance, and no consistent change of heart rate, blood pressure, and EEG during mental and physical yoga practices (Wenger, Bagchi, and Anand 1961a, 1961b). The authors concluded that (1) the direct control of so-called "involuntary" autonomic functions, such as heart rate, is most probably accomplished through intervening voluntary mechanisms; and (2) physiologically, yogic meditation is a form of deep relaxation of the autonomic nervous system without the induction of the sleep state. Wallace notes the difficulty in selecting and measuring subjects consistently in research on yogic meditation. In part, this is due to the many techniques subsumed under the general rubric of *yoga*. Wallace feels that the inconsistency of research results is intimately related to this confounding variable, and he offers the example of the conflicting results of the oxygen consumption studies. Behanam (1937), Rao (1962), and Miles (1964) reported significant increases in oxygen consumption while Hoenig (1968), Karambelkar (1968), and Rao (1968) noted a decrease in oxygen consumption during meditation.

Datey et al. (1969) report what appear to be the most clinically relevant results, in their work with hypertensive patients. Of the forty-seven patients trained in a yoga breathing exercise, ten who were not under drug treatment showed significant decreases in mean blood pressure, while nineteen who were being treated with drugs showed significant decreases in drug dosage. In addition, patients reported fewer headaches and less irritability and insomnia. Wallace cites the research of Anand, China, and Singh (1961), who investigated the EEG of four yogis and found considerable alpha-wave activity before and during meditation, with increased alpha amplitudes in the latter condition. Furthermore, when subjected to external stimuli during meditation, two of the yogis showed no blockage of alpha waves and, when not meditating, showed no habituation of the alpha-blocking response to repeated stimuli. Similar results were reported by Kasamatsu and Hirai (1966) in their EEG investigations of Zen meditators. A notable difference between the yogis and Zen monks was that alpha-blocking responses were evidenced when Zen subjects were exposed to external stimuli during meditation. The interested reader is referred to Akishige's (1970) comprehensive review of all the physiological research on Zen meditation. In summarizing this research, Akishige reports the following physiological alterations: decreased rates of respiration and oxygen consumption, a decrease in spontaneous galvanic skin response (GSR), and a slight increase in pulse rate and blood pH.

One could conceivably argue that the research mentioned above reports physiological alterations characteristic of one or more substates of the waking state. However, Wallace (1970) contends that an alternative possibility is the existence of a physiologically unique state of consciousness. In his research on students of TM, he found the following:

1. Brain-wave patterns of subjects during meditation indicated that they were awake and in a state of restful alertness. Metabolic rate was generally reduced to a level below that of deepest sleep

2. Total oxygen consumption showed a mean decrease of twenty percent, a figure that is greater than the mean decrease for an entire night's sleep

3. Cardiac output (quantity of blood pumped by the heart)

showed a mean decrease of twenty-five percent compared to the figure of about twenty percent during deep sleep

4. Galvanic skin resistance, an indicator with an inverse relationship to stress level, increased by a factor of from two to eight following several minutes of meditation; eight hours of sleep increases this indicator by a factor of approximately two

5. Lactate ion concentration was found to decrease over thirty percent during meditation. This ion in lactic acid accounts for fatigue and, in excess, for anxiety neurosis

6. Skin temperature of the forehead and throat, as measured by infrared radiation techniques, increases from 0.4°C to 1.6°C during meditation. No temperature alterations were evidenced in nonmeditators sitting with eyes closed. It has been hypothesized that if these changes in temperature affect the thyroid and pituitary glands, which are located in the throat and head respectively, they are of sufficient magnitude to trigger complex physiological and biochemical processes.

Wallace states that the physiological alterations occurring during TM are dissimilar to those that occur during wakefulness, sleep, or dreaming—the three generally accepted states of human consciousness. His assertion, therefore, is that while in meditation, the subject approaches or is in a fourth major state of consciousness—the transcendental state. Table 5, from Wallace (1970b), summarizes and compares the physiological correlates of each state of consciousness.

Kanellakos (1971) of the Stanford Research Institute supports Wallace's view and further contends that this fourth or transcendental state is as vital to general psychosomatic health as are the other states. Kanellakos diagrams the states of consciousness as four contiguous boxes, with the transcendental state seen as the direct opposite of the dream state.

Thoughts and Experiences?

		Yes	No
Self-awareness?	Yes	Waking state	Transcendental state
	No	Dream state	Deep sleep state

Table 5. Physiological Correlate of States of Human Consciousness

Correlate	Wakefulness	Deep Sleep (Stage 4)	Dreaming (Stage 1: REM)	Transcendental
Electro-encephalogram	Low voltage mixed frequency and/or alpha activity (9–11 cps). Alpha activity increase with eyes closed. A moment of tension or an attempt to solve a mental problem may disrupt it. Tiredness or drowsiness is characterized by a flattening of the alpha waves to low voltage mixed frequency waves with an increase in activity in the 2–7 cps range	There is a decrease in regular activity and an increase in sleep spindles 14–15 cps (20–40 uV). K complexes and 2–7 cps activity. When 50% of the epoch consists of waves of 2 cps or slower which have amplitudes greater than 75 uV, the EEG record is defined as Stage 4 or deep sleep	Low-amplitude (25–50 uV) variable frequency waves accompanied by episodic REMs and quiescent EMGs. Resemble that of Stage 1 of sleep except vertex sharp waves are not prominent. Saw-tooth waves frequently but not always appear in vertex and frontal regions in conjunction with a burst of a REM. Alpha activity (9–11 cps) is more prominent than during Stage 1 sleep and the frequency of the alpha waves is lower by 1 or 2 cps than that of the alpha waves of wakefulness. An absolute absence of sleep spindles and K complexes (first REM period is interspersed with spindles).	There is an increase in alpha-wave activity (usually 8–9 cps activity) which occurs in the central and frontal regions. Sometimes rhythmical theta-wave activity (5–7 cps) appears in the frontal regions
Electro-oculogram	Rapid eye movements, eye blinks, various movements	First slow eye movements (several seconds each), then rolled up and immobile	Episodic rapid eye movements	No apparent change
Electro-myogram	Can change according to the activity	Less than during wakefulness: relaxation in Stage 1 to very relaxed in Stage 4	Head and chin muscles relax. Tonic mental and submental activity reaches low level	No muscular activity recordable
Body motility	Can change according to activity	Cannot stay erect; motion uncommon (except in somnambulism). Must lie down or sit to support spine to sleep	Relaxed, although spasmodic movement of certain movement of muscle groups does occur	Sitting comfortably. Body becomes relaxed

Table 5 *(continued)*

Correlate	Wakefulness	Deep Sleep (Stage 4)	Dreaming (Stage 1: REM)	Transcendental
Total oxygen consumption	Can change according to activity	Decrease about 10 to 20%	Higher rate of oxygen consumption than sleep state	Decreases significantly. The mean decrease (17%) in 30 minutes is greater than most of values reported for the mean decrease over a full night of sleep
Body temperature	Attains highest value of circadian cycle	Attains lowest value of circadian cycle	Slight variations (increases) constituting subcycles or modulations of the circadian cycles (or rhythm)	
Cardiac output	Can change according to activity	Decrease about 20%		Decreases significantly with a mean decrease of about 25%
Blood gases	"Normal" range of arterial blood pH is 7.36 to 7.42. PCO_2 and PO_2 can change according to activity	PCO_2 significantly increases (3.6 mmHg) and pH significantly decreases (.03 pH units)		Slight but not significant decrease in pH (.01 pH units). No significant change in PO_2 and PCO_2. Base excess significantly decreases
Heart rate (counts per minute)	Can change according to activity	During deep sleep, the heart rate, respiration rate, and blood pressure fall to the lowest level of the circadian cycle; falling at sleep onset and continuing to drop until one hour before waking	Erratic. Usually about a 5% increase above deep sleep	Decreases significantly with a mean decrease of about 5 beats per minute
Blood pressure	Can change according to activity	See above (under heart rate)	Erratic and irregular (like breathing rate) superimposed on deep sleep record. Blood pressure shows a slight increase and variability	Tendency to decrease with intermediate fluctuations

Table 5 (continued)

Correlate	Wakefulness	Deep Sleep (Stage 4)	Dreaming (Stage 1: REM)	Transcendental
Respiration rate	Can change according to the activity	Shallow and even. See above (under heart rate)	Erratic and exceedingly variable, fluctuates widely above and below wakefulness, relaxed value. Average value higher by 1–2 breaths/minute over sleep	Decreases significantly with a mean decrease of 3/min. Changes from 12 to 4 breaths/minute in one individual
Skin resistance	Can change according to the activity	Two frequent patterns have been noted. In both patterns, there is an increase in skin resistance of about 50%	No significant change	Increases significantly. In some cases, there is an increase of over 500% after only ten minutes
Blood lactate concentration	Increases with stress or activity, especially in patients with anxiety neurosis			Decreases
Awareness	Can change according to the activity	It is hard to awaken the subject with the low noise or buzzer that would have aroused him earlier. Subject usually awakens slowly and may feel he has not been experiencing any mental activity	It takes a relatively loud noise to awaken subject, although a very slight noise with significance may quickly alert him	Subjects report that their attention was primarily attracted to inward processes of thought. They were, however, steadily responsive to significant or disrupting, external stimuli. Subjects also report an expanded inner awareness, both during and after the practice of transcendental meditation. They described the transcendental state as "restful alertness"

Table 5 (*continued*)

Correlate	Wakefulness	Deep Sleep (Stage 4)	Dreaming (Stage 1: REM)	Transcendental
Deprivation		Prolonged deprivation can produce sensory disorders, disorientation, and loss of efficiency in physical activity. There is an alteration in EEG activity, energy metabolism, and the hormonal and biochemical conditions of the body after 1–5 days of deprivation	Subjects become disoriented, irritable, hallucinogenic, and sometimes psychotic. In subsequent nights, subjects increase their time dreaming	Deep relaxation and rest are natural and necessary to the proper functioning of the body and mind. Transcendental meditation gives a deep state of rest with minimal effort. Deprivation of the periodic rest and rejuvenation gained through transcendental meditation is postulated to be the cause of many mental and physical diseases

SOURCE: The information given in this table is mainly from Kleitman (1963). PHS Publication No. 1389–1965, and from research given in text. When information was not available the section was left blank.

Although there is no awareness of self in the dream state, the individual does have various thoughts and experiences. In the transcendental state, however, the individual possesses an awareness of self as an existent being but has no thoughts or experiences. This existential state receives much attention in the mystic literature cross-culturally and is known as *samadhi* to the yogi and *satori* to the Zen Buddhist. In discussing individual well-being, Kanellakos suggests that all four states are essential. The waking state is clearly necessary, since it allows the individual to meet environmentally related survival needs. The sleep state is instrumental in providing the conditions for the physical/mental restoration and rejuvenation mandatory for organismic survival. It has been asserted that during the dream state, the body produces those chemicals vital to the facilitation of information transfer and interneural processing. As only several days' supply of these chemicals may be stored, the dream state is necessary to prevent mental deterioration and the manifestation of psychoticlike behavior (Hartman 1967). Finally, it is contended that the attainment of the transcendental state is a necessary and sufficient condition for the development and utilization of one's "creative intelligence," a faculty triggered by the more subtle levels of the nervous system. The well-known fact that man makes use of but a small portion of his mental potential (perhaps five to ten percent) is due to the obstruction of the deeper and more sensitive layers of the nervous system by deep-rooted stresses that accumulate over one's lifetime. These stresses may be released only when one experiences a profound state of rest, as in meditation. It has been determined that the rest obtained in deep sleep is insufficient to appreciably reduce these deep-rooted stresses.

Wallace and Benson (1972) maintain that the pattern of physiological changes occurring in the transcendental state suggests that meditation "generates an integrated response, or reflex, that is mediated by the central nervous system." They further suggest that this reflex is a counterpart of the "fight or flight" or "defense alarm" reaction described by Harvard physiologist W. B. Cannon. The latter reflex is characterized by an arousal of the sympathetic nervous system, which in turn mobilizes a number of physiological responses marked by increases in blood pressure, heart rate, oxygen consumption, and blood flow to the muscular system. This is clearly a hypermetabolic condition quite the opposite of the hypometabolic state induced by meditation. Placing both reflexes in historical, that is, evolutionary, perspective, Wallace and Benson offer the following intriguing analysis:

> During man's early history the defense-alarm reaction may well have had high survival value and thus have become strongly established in his genetic makeup. It continues to be aroused in all its visceral aspects when the individual feels threatened. Yet in the environment of our time the reaction is often an anachronism. Although the defense-alarm reaction is generally no longer appropriate, the visceral response is evoked with considerable frequency by the rapid and unsettling changes that are buffeting modern society. There is good reason to believe the changing environment's incessant stimulations of the sympathetic nervous system are largely responsible for the high incidence of hypertension and similar serious diseases that are prevalent in our society.
>
> In these circumstances the hypometabolic state, representing quiescence rather than hyperactivation of the sympathetic nervous system, may indicate a guidepost to better health. It should be well worthwhile to investigate the possibilities for clinical application of this state of wakeful rest and relaxation.

THE PSYCHOLOGY OF MEDITATIVE STATES

As Tart (1969) has noted in discussing meditation: "One would expect that such a venerable practice would have been thoroughly studied by psychology, especially because of its mental health implications, but this is far from the case. . . . Our scientific knowledge of meditation is virtually nil." Despite this lack of scientific investigation, the practice of meditation has gained considerable popularity in the West in the past decade. To varying degrees, Westerners have become cognizant of the Eastern claims regarding meditation, namely, that it is a technique employed (1) to bring about an alteration of one's perception of self and world characterized by a sense of unity of the individual with his environment, and (2) to obtain control of autonomic functioning and thereby ultimately achieve a psychological state termed *satori* or "transcendental awareness." This ASC may be characterized by experiences of timelessness, elation, heightened affect, and a sense of expanded global awareness.

Two fundamental approaches or methods have been traditionally used to attain the meditative alteration of consciousness: [(1) the focused deployment of attention on a particular object of meditation (Rinzai Zen), on a physiological process, for example, breathing (Zen Buddhism), or on a mantra (Tantric yoga, Transcendental Meditation); and (2) the expansion of attention by the meditator, whereby he attempts to attain a state of maximum receptivity to internal and external stimuli (Soto Zen). As Naranjo and Ornstein (1971) have indicated, the basic goal of both approaches is to gain control over attention deployment in an effort to "develop an awareness that allows every stimulus to enter into consciousness devoid of our normal selection process, devoid of normal tuning and input selection or model building, and devoid of the normal automatic categorizing." This goal is attainable only after the mind's usually interminable activity ceases and the meditator is able to experience a state of being more basic and distinct from both his thoughts and attention. It is this ASC that has been called variously *nirvana, satori,* or *transcendental awareness.*

To date, only two researchers, Maupin (1965) and Deikman (1963, 1966a, 1966b), have attempted to determine the psychological correlates of those physiological alterations recorded in meditation. Maupin instructed twenty-eight male college student volunteers in a *zazen,* that is, a Zen Buddhist concentration exercise, which they practiced forty-five minutes daily for a period of two to three weeks. Following each session, the students reported their experiences, and their response to *zazen* was rated as high, moderate, or low. These responses were then correlated with pre-meditation test measures of digit-span attention; concentration on a continuous additions task; scanning control; tolerance for unrealistic experience as determined from Rorschach test responses; amount of autokinetic movement reported; and capacity for adaptive regression, as assessed by the Rorschach test and by visual imagery during a free-association test. Significant correlations were found between tolerance for unrealistic experience and capacity for adaptive regression, as measured by the Rorschach test and by the subjects' responses to the meditation exercise. Those subjects who most tolerated unrealistic experience and who were most able to regress adaptively were also most responsive to the practice of meditation. Maupin concluded that transcendental awareness may be conceptualized as a psychologically adaptive regression and that the practice of meditation may be understood as a sequence of regression states, each state developing from the tolerance and skills attained in preceding states.

Deikman's (1963, 1966a, 1966b) work supports Maupin's conclusions. In this research, a contemplative meditation technique (concentration on an object) was used with subjects who had no previous exposure to meditation. As few as twelve sessions over a three-week period resulted in the subjects experiencing unusual alterations in consciousness. These changes included time contraction, transfiguration of the object, and feelings of intense pleasure and beauty. Following postmeditation interviews, Deikman concluded that meditation includes a deautomatization of perceptual and cognitive experience that frees one from mental stereotyping. He further stated that these data could not readily be explained using the concepts of suggestion, projection, autohypnosis, or sensory isolation. Deikman suggests that meditation may be viewed as a means whereby attention is withdrawn from thinking and reinvested in percepts—a reverse of the usual learning sequence. This analysis appears in accord with Maupin's emphasis on the individual's capacity for adaptive regression. In a more recent paper, Deikman offers the following:

> It may be that these benefits and changes reflect the enhancement of organizing activities in systems other than those associated with perception and cognition. In some way these other systems may be able to function more effectively or at greater speed and intensity when perception and cognitive activity is in abeyance. Such systems are probably involved in creative synthesis and the establishment of

the superordinary physiologic control and coordination reported of Yogis and Zen masters. From this point of view, we can understand why "passive volition" is needed to effect autonomic body functions. The autonomic nervous system has its own level of organization and organizing activity different from that associated with conscious control. Active willing imposes a different level of organization that interferes with the organizing pattern of autonomic functions. The admonition "let go," a cornerstone of mystic wisdom, may be interpreted as "let go of cognitive organization so that extra-cognitive organization may take place, whether it be your own activity or the organizing activity of sources outside of yourself (1970a).

Shaw and Kolb (1972) have conducted pilot studies indicating that the reaction time of meditators is significantly faster than that of nonmeditators. The meditators were found to respond thirty percent faster than the nonmeditators to a task involving a response to a cue signal, that is, pressing a key. In addition, the performance of the nonmeditators was found to decrease over time while the meditators' scores remained constant. Following this portion of the research, twenty minutes elapsed during which the meditators were asked to meditate and the nonmeditators to sit with their eyes closed and rest. After this period, both groups were tested again, with the performance of the meditators increasing by approximately fifteen percent over their previous testing and the performance of the nonmeditators decreasing by about ten percent. The authors concluded that although the twenty-minute interval may have rested the nonmeditators physically, their mental (task) performance indicated a diminished alertness. This was attributed to a lessened coordination between mind and body and a consequent increase in irritability and decrease in efficiency. The meditators, however, were thought to have been rested physically but had no decrement in mental alertness during the twenty-minute meditation.

Orme-Johnson's (1971) measurements of galvanic skin response appear to support the notion that meditators (TM) are less irritable than nonmeditators. GSR amplitude shows a marked decrease for several seconds when an individual is exposed to a sudden unexpected stress, for example, a loud noise, and then returns to the basal level. Frequent repetition of the stress, however, results in habituation. In general, individuals who are most tranquil habituate most rapidly to a repeated stress known to be innocuous. Orme-Johnson found that when both meditators and nonmeditators were subjected to repeated high-amplitude noises, the meditators ceased reacting after far fewer repetitions than did the nonmeditators. While it took the nonmeditators thirty to thirty-five repetitions to habituate to the stress and stop producing corresponding changes in GSR amplitude, the meditators took only ten to fifteen trials. In fact, this investigator found an inverse relationship between the number of trials needed for habituation and the length of time the subject had been practicing meditation. Based on this finding, Orme-Johnson offered the hypothesis that meditation has a cumulative effect with regard to stress. Another indicator of general anxiety level used in this study was the number of spontaneous changes in GSR amplitude recorded while a subject was sitting quietly without exposure to environmental stress. The researcher found that a random selection of nonmeditators produced a mean of approximately thirty-five spontaneous GSR changes over a ten-minute interval; a group of meditators, however, produced fewer than ten changes. More dramatic was Orme-Johnson's finding that when several of the subjects who had produced the greatest number of GSR alterations per unit time were instructed in the practice of meditation, their rate decreased to ten to fifteen alterations within several days.

Research has recently been done with meditators in the area of self-actualization, or, in Maslow's terms, the degree to which an individual is utilizing his full potential. Nidich, Seeman, and Banta (1971) tested thirty-five subjects on a psychological measure of self-actualization and subsequently trained fifteen of them in TM. Following a period of two months, all thirty-five were retested, with the meditators scoring significantly higher than originally in six of twelve indices of self-actualization. The nonmeditators scored about the same as they had previously. Similar results have been reported by Shelly (1971).

Empirical investigations in the area of meditation continue to abound. Although most of this research has dealt exclusively with

Transcendental Meditation to the relative exclusion of comparative studies of meditative systems, the results have been encouraging. Significant physiologic and psychologic alterations in the direction of what most researchers agree is improved functioning lead us to conclude that meditation can indeed be a potent tool in the development of the human potential.

8

Psychophysiological Substrates of Consciousness

Psychotherapeutic systems are showing a significant evolutionary trend toward increasing the involvement of the patient in his own treatment. It is evident in several emerging therapeutic disciplines that the parent-child medical model of a therapeutic relationship is giving way to a process of mutually shared responsibility between doctor and patient. This concept of shared responsibility proposes that the patient is helped to become aware of his physical and psychological distress in order that he might become a responsible partner in the curative process. Emphasis here primarily will be on this type of psychotherapy, which is represented by the European systems of autogenic training, psychosynthesis, and Jungian analytic therapy; by the Oriental systems of Morita therapy and Zen psychotherapy; and by the American systems of Gestalt therapy and Biofeedback. Jungian analytic therapy and Gestalt therapy are included in this discussion primarily to serve as comprehensive frameworks for the lesser-known and less-developed systems of psychotherapy cited above. All these therapies differ primarily in terms of degree of focus on a specific psychological or psychophysiological process as the basis of therapy, and differences between these systems are largely a matter of emphasis rather than any mutually exclusive theoretical or applied orientation. For purposes of brevity, all of them will be collectively referred to as *imagery therapies* in this presentation because of their common focus on an individual's subjective symbolic functions. Since imagery therapies tend to be unsuitable for treating gross pathology, such as chronic schizophrenia, but are potent systems for promoting individual growth and individuation, this discussion will present the imagery therapies as a major trend in psychotherapy toward the full development of human potentials rather than as remedial intervention. Last, the theories and techniques will be discussed in terms of individual therapy, although all of these psychotherapies have been employed in the entire range of mental-health settings, from inpatient wards to private practice. The overriding consideration here will be to explicate how each of the disparate imagery therapies is an integral aspect of a larger, more comprehensive system of psychotherapy that is in the process of evolution.

Underlying these seemingly divergent systems of psychotherapy are a number of implicit assumptions and explicit principles about the techniques and theoretical rationale by which the patient is to be more effectively incorporated into the therapeutic process. The first and most prominent is the emphasis on the patient's subjective imagery and the use of fantasy techniques in order to facilitate therapy. Therapeutic systems ranging from behavior modification to psychosynthesis stress the importance of the patient's use of his subjective imagery and fantasies. The second principle, which is closely related to this emphasis on fantasy techniques, is that the therapeutic systems either explicitly or implicitly prescribe a posture or series of exercises designed to induce a state of deep relaxation in order for the patient to experience his own mental imagery. Third, a technique that is subsumed under the process of deep relaxation is the attempt to induce a focused awareness on the part of the patient in order for him to sustain the conscious awareness of his own fantasies. Last, the therapeutic systems strongly advocate the presence of a skilled therapist to serve as a guide rather than as an analytic interpreter of the patient's experience of his subjective imagery. Of course, there are exceptions to each of these general principles in each imagery therapy, especially in the more complex Jungian and Gestalt psychotherapies. However, by using these basic observations, it is possible to explicate the integrating commonalities from which each system is derived.

In addition to these fundamental similarities in technique, there are two common theoretical assumptions that link the imagery therapies. One assumption is that the systems postulate the existence of a higher center of awareness or a higher self that can be attained by means of prescribed fantasy techniques (Goleman 1971). An individual functioning in accord with his higher self will manifest the traits of immediate awareness of himself and others leading to actions of controlled spontaneity. This seemingly paradoxical state of controlled spontaneity is the therapeutic goal of the imagery therapies; it will be more fully explained in chapter 9. Second, all of the above systems implicitly subscribe to a model of psychophysiological functioning that assumes a patient has access to psychological and physiological processes that normally occur out of awareness. Through a prescribed system of disciplined exercises, the patient can presumably attain a degree of control over these processes in order to facilitate therapy. These assumptions are based on a particular neuroanatomical model of the brain. Neurologically based theories of psychological processes have been simultaneously lauded as definitive and summarily dismissed as reductionistic and simplistic. Neither position is tenable; yet this recurrent debate is being revived, since all of the above therapies implicitly subscribe to a specific neuroanatomical model, which will be more fully explicated later.

For purposes of clarifying the above observations, this book will proceed in the following manner: (1) explicating and evaluating the neuroanatomical model of psychological processes in order to clarify the theoretical, experimental, and applied basis of the imagery therapies; (2) discussing imagery and fantasy techniques with emphasis on the role of the therapist in imagery therapies; (3) defining specific therapeutic techniques of each of the imagery therapies in order to identify the similarities and differences among the systems. Each system, except Jungian and Gestalt therapies, will be outlined and discussed with the references, Jungian and Gestalt systems serving as the more comprehensive frameworks for the less-developed therapies; (4) presenting a comprehensive overview of each system as it contributes to the evolution of a highly systematic therapy based on Biofeedback and imagery techniques; and (5) concluding with a delineation of the parameters and future applications of such a comprehensive therapeutic system. Throughout these discussions, emphasis will be on pragmatic procedures to be employed in the psychotherapeutic process rather than on a purely theoretical consideration of the philosophical basis of each therapy. It will become evident that, although the philosophical positions of therapeutic disciplines vary considerably and appear mutually exclusive of other systems, the actual practice and pragmatic applications of these divergent systems are strikingly congruent and complementary.

Three major issues will be considered throughout each of the above sections. One issue is that the psychotherapeutic techniques employed in each of the therapies are additive, in the sense that each technique or procedure is a specialization of one aspect of an ideal, totally comprehensive therapeutic process that will be postulated at the conclusion of this discussion. Familiarity with each of these disparate systems will give the therapist a more comprehensive knowledge of specific interventions and the theoretical justification for these procedures. This emphasis on a comprehensive overview does not preclude specialization in one technique or system, depending on the predisposition and limitations of the individual therapist. Actually, specialization in a well-developed discipline such as psychoanalysis is advocated, since it prescribes specific procedures and a rational paradigm for those interventions. If an individual therapist were to deviate from such a specialized discipline, he would need to formulate an equally rigorous technique and paradigm in order to justify a serious departure. Innovation need not and should not preclude rigorous evaluation by the individual therapist and the therapeutic community.

Second, and closely affiliated to the above consideration, is the fact that any one therapeutic system could be loosely "interpreted" to subsume all the other systems in an astonishing feat of intellectual imperialism. Such an overwrought extension of any particular theoretical system results in an endless proliferation of tenuous interpretations and rationalizations until the clarity of the original system becomes obscured. Subsuming Gestalt therapy under psychosynthesis, or vice versa, has the effect of undermining and obscuring the clarity and impact of each of the distinct theories, which are neither mutually exclusive nor mutually inclusive. Preserving the autonomy of each system while demonstrating the invaluable contributions of other psychotherapeutic systems is the intent of this discussion.

Third, numerous references will be made to the actual procedures employed in Zen-Buddhist training, since all of the imagery therapies, explicitly or implicitly, bear remarkable similarities to it. Striking correspondences between the ancient tradition of Zen Buddhism and the comparatively recent imagery therapies can be accounted for by several means. One explanation is that several psychotherapists, such as Jung (1969a), and Fromm (1960), specifically acknowledge the direct or indirect influence of Zen Buddhism on their theoretical formulations. Another is that it is possible that some psychotherapists adhere to Eastern techniques, although they purposely do not acknowledge them because it is considered to be professionally disreputable to acknowledge such esoteric inclinations. The most probable explanation is that the imagery psychotherapists arrived at Zen-like techniques autonomously, with no influence from Zen itself. If this is the case, then such an occurrence attests to the transcultural and transtemporal efficacy of these ancient psychotherapeutic techniques. Since almost all of the imagery therapies subscribe to Zen-like theories and techniques, it is edifying to clarify the similarities and differences between these innovative therapies and Zen-Buddhist meditation procedures. Assuming that the imagery therapies are evolving toward a Westernized form of Zen psychotherapy, this discussion will periodically postulate what this psychotherapeutic technique might become.

CONFLICT VERSUS CONTINUUM MODELS

It is of paramount importance to note at the outset of this section that it is not intended to be a reductionistic equation of neurological and psychological processes. Activity of the neurological system is electrical, while that of psychological processes is symbolic, and neither can be reduced or transformed into the other. With that one distinction clarified, we will proceed on the accepted convention of localizing conscious processes within the cerebral cortex and unconscious processes in the subcortical or diencephalic areas of the brain. Research and theoretical evidence will be cited that support this convention, which remains extremely useful despite the fact that researchers agree that such a one-to-one correlation is increasingly improbable.

Based on extensive research at Harvard Medical School, neurologist Walter B. Cannon first defined the neuroanatomical substrates of consciousness in 1937. According to Cannon, there are two basic anatomical parts of the brain, which are the *diencephalon,* or thalamus, and the *cerebral cortex,* or gray matter. Within the diencephalic area of the brain is localized the autonomic nervous system; until the last decade, it was thought to function autonomously of conscious control. Cannon's classic study *The Wisdom of the Body* focused primarily on the physical and chemical reactions that occur spontaneously when any animal initiates a series of "fight or flight" mechanisms: "Respiration deepens, the arterial pressure rises, the blood is shifted away from the stomach and intestines to the heart and central nervous system and the muscles, and the spleen contracts and discharges its content of concentrated corpuscles, and adrenalin is excreted from the adrenal medulla" (1963, p. 136). Such autonomic reactions would be coordinated with the voluntary reaction on the part of the animal to flee or engage in a struggle. In researching this complex process, Cannon concentrated on the unified action of the two anatomical parts and elaborated his principle of the preservation of biological homeostasis within the brain and the physiological organism. However, this exposition of the homeostatic principle overlooked the possibility of conflicting reactions between the diencephalon and the cerebral cortex that would result in physiological as well as psychological confusion and intraorganismic conflict. By failing to address this issue, Cannon contributed substantially to the preservation of a model of the brain that split the brain into a diencephalic, or thalamic, level governing crude sensations and a cortical level governing more differentiated conscious experiences. There is no difficulty in this model when the brain operates in a unified manner, but the introduction of discrepant intracerebral information raises the issue of which of the two systems will dominate the organism's reactions. Clearly, this neuroanatomical model has had extensive impact on psychological theories, as seen in the debate on unconscious drives versus cognitive control (Whyte 1962). Additionally, the autonomous unconscious is alternatively viewed as essentially negative and requiring control or as essentially positive and a potential source of liberation. This controversy is much in evidence in contemporary psychology, but it is based on an outmoded concept of neuroanatomy. There is a third alternative proposed by the more innovative imagery therapies that is based on recent neurological research.

Duality had been proposed as an integral aspect of neurological, and thus psychological, functioning, with little or no discussion of a mediating principle. However, as early as 1938, neurologist Walter Penfield noted the need for a subcortical integrating system that would mediate such conflicting information. Penfield offered neurosurgical evidence for its presence and described several features of this system, which only came to be recognized as the reticular activating system, or RAS, in the early 1950s (Starzl and Magoun 1950; Papez 1956). Structurally, the reticular activating system is a "column of cells occupying the central portions of the medulla, pons, and midbrain and extending upwards through the subthalamus into the ventro-medial parts of the thalamus" (Prince 1971). This detailed description is given simply to note that the reticular activating system crosses many conventional anatomical boundaries and is presently conceived of as a physiological unity rather than as an anatomical one. This brief digression into neuroanatomy is intended to point out that psychological theories prior to the early 1950s have either explicitly or implicitly subscribed to the model of the brain that was definitively summarized by W. B. Cannon. Supplanting this model is one based on more recent research on the functioning of the reticular activation system. The new model does not necessitate a dualistic schema of the brain or of psychological processes (Prince 1971). Rather than viewing man as either dominated or liberated by his animal or autonomic processes, it provides the basis for postulating a more harmonious integration of the subcortical and cortical processes.

Current neurological theory provides a communication model of continual information exchange between the subcortical and cortical sectors of the brain. Thus, neurological evidence suggests a dialogue between autonomic and cortical processes rather than an incessant zero-sum, or mutually exclusive, struggle between these processes vying for dominance. This information is an invaluable asset in validating and researching the evolving imagery therapies, since they are based on the assumption that a person is capable of engaging in a dialogue between his conscious and unconscious, or image-producing, processes. Logically then, the task of the imagery therapies is to enumerate the conditions under which a constructive intracerebral dialogue will occur, rather than concerning itself with a conflict theory based on mediating between man's social obligation and his animal instincts (Maddi 1968). The communication process can be demonstrated by a brief explanation of reticular activating system functioning.

Physiologically, the RAS serves two basic functions: (1) a general arousal function in which it activates the cortex to become receptive to visceral stimulation; and (2) it transmits impulses from the cortex to the musculature and the autonomic nervous system (Rothballer 1956). These two inseparable functions are termed *tonic activation* when the ascending RAS serves its arousal function and *phasic activation* when the descending RAS serves its directive function (Sharpless and Jasper 1956). According to their research, the tonic component of the "reticular system is capable only of crude differentiation between stimuli and produces long-lasting, persistent changes in the level of reactivity . . . but [is] ill adapted to the sudden and brief changes in reactivity that must occur in response to highly specific stimuli." Brief reactivity comprises phasic activation, which occurs when an individual consciously reacts to a stimulus and initiates an action. Descending, or phasic, functions have been demonstrated to be closely concerned with the psychological process of selective attention. Research by Hernandez-Peon (1963) recorded electrical activity from the cochlear nucleus of an unanesthetized cat. Prominent electrical potentials were evoked and recorded from this nucleus when the relaxed or drowsing cat was exposed to a click stimulus. However, these evoked potentials were markedly attenuated or absent when the cat's attention was distracted by mice in a beaker or by the odor of fish. In accounting for this phenomena, Hernandez-Peon hypothesized that the descending RAS determines the threshold of sensory stimulation to sensory organs. This research, in conjunction with similar investigations (Galambos 1956; Granit 1955), indicates that an RAS descending function is the narrowing and focusing of attention that results in the selective alteration of information at the first synapse, or even at the receptor organ itself. The RAS is recognized as serving an increasingly important function of selecting and screening stimuli from the autonomic nervous system prior to its registration in the cortical or more conscious areas of the brain. These stimuli are debarred from conscious consideration but are registered subliminally, or out of conscious awareness, and do affect an individual's behavior. Therefore, the communications model of the brain suggests a psychological differentiation of consciously versus unconsciously registered stimuli or information rather than a dualistic conflict model of conscious control versus unconscious impulses.

This last critical point can be restated as follows: the communications model of the brain proposes that the psychological distinction between conscious and unconscious processes is more a matter of difference in the quantity and quality of available information than an inherent conflicting duality between conscious social control and animal instincts. This concept will be more fully explicated by an examination of research on subliminal perception in the following paragraphs. It is significant to note here that this model suggests a continuum of consciousness rather than a dualistic system and defines the RAS as mediating conscious awareness along that continuum. Again, neurological evidence supports and clarifies the assumption of the imagery therapies that an individual needs to gain access to those stimuli or bits of information that are registered out of conscious awareness yet do have a profound effect on his behavior. This is not a simplistic equation of unconscious psychological processes with autonomic neurological processes—the activity of mentation is symbolic while the activity of the neurological system is electrical. However, the functioning of psychological and neurological systems are inextricably intertwined, and the insights of one discipline can lend significant insight into the other. What the precise correlation is between neurological activation and psychological processes is the essential question both the imagery therapists and the neurologists are probing in their own manner; each is invaluable to the other. Neurologists have tended to conceptualize the nervous system as a collection of more or less separate circuits, each performing a particular task. Yet, there is increasing evidence that the nervous system is an integrated totality, with the reticular activating system serving that integrative function. A noted UCLA neurosurgeon, J. D. French, has stated this finding most succinctly:

> It [the RAS] awakens the brain to consciousness and keeps it alert; it directs the traffic of messages in the nervous system; it monitors the myriad of stimuli that beat upon our senses, accepting what we need to perceive and rejecting what is irrelevant; it tempers and refines our muscular activity and bodily movements. We can even go further and say that it contributes in an important way to the highest mental processes—the focusing of attention, introspection and doubtless all forms of reasoning (1957).

Exactly what process constitutes the link between neurological and psychological processes remains a speculative area of theory, research, and application.

Another important theoretical link between neurological and psychological models of consciousness also has direct bearing on the imagery therapies. Research on subliminal perception supports the neurological observation that important stimuli that affect behavior are registered out of awareness. Of particular interest is the research demonstrating the impact of subliminal stimulation on dreams, fantasies, free associations, and spontaneous imagery, which are the fundamental material for imagery therapists. The classic study in this area was conducted in 1917 by Poetzl (Poetzl 1960): in it, he exposed pictures tachistoscopically to subjects for 1/100 of a second and had his subjects report what they had consciously perceived by verbal reports and by drawings. Then, he demonstrated that parts of the pictures that had not been consciously described or drawn appeared in the manifest content of the dreams the subjects reported the next morning. More recent research by Fisher (1954, 1957) and Luborsky and Shevrin (1956) has used much the same procedure and has confirmed this phenomenon. Additionally, research by Fisher (1956, 1957) has demonstrated that aspects of subliminally presented pictures may subsequently appear in conscious imagery, free association, and hallucinations, as well as in dreams. Drawing on these findings, it can be hypothesized that (1) a large amount of visual material is subliminally registered in extremely brief intervals, such as 1/100 or 1/200 of a second; (2) that these perceptions are largely debarred from conscious registration, yet it can be demonstrated that they have effects on psychological processes such as dreams, spontaneous imagery, and free association (Maupin 1965); and (3) that although the previously unreported elements may be reproduced with photographic accuracy, the dreams and images more often demonstrate that numerous transformations and distortions have occurred (Fisher 1957). Evidence from research in subliminal perception supports a communications model of neurological and psychological processes; findings demonstrate that information is registered out of awareness and that this unconsciously perceived information does have an effect on psychological processes. Of further interest is the fact that this subliminally perceived material may undergo marked transformations, since the task of a therapist employing imagery techniques is to acquaint his patient and himself with the symbolic transformations of physical stimuli, past perceptions, and ongoing fantasies and images.

Drawing on subliminal-perception research, Klein (1959) suggests that the data warrant a distinction between *registration* and *conscious perception,* where *registration* denotes the general sensitivity of all incoming stimuli by one aspect of the nervous system, and conscious perception denotes those stimuli that gain dominance over less immediately important stimuli and enter into conscious awareness. Similar distinctions are in use by neurologists in order to differentiate between the tonic and phasic functions of the reticular activating system. Again, this convergence of neurological and psychological theory supports a communications model of the brain where all internal and external information is potentially available for conscious scrutiny but is attended to differentially, either in terms of RAS activation in neurology or attention in psychology. In this model, it is assumed that an individual processes psychological and physiological stimuli in a manner in which some stimuli are processed consciously and other stimuli processed out of awareness, or unconsciously.

COMMUNICATIONS MODELS OF THE BRAIN

To date, only two theorists, John Lilly and A. T. W. Simeons, have proposed substantially innovative models of neurological and psychological functioning that can serve as the basis for further understanding and development of the imagery therapies. John Lilly has proposed such a model in his book *Programming and Metaprogramming in the Human Biocomputer,* where the concept of innate biological instincts is replaced by that of those influences on behavior most inaccessible to conscious mentation (Lilly 1968; Pelletier, 1974b). Therefore, conflict between conscious and unconscious processes or between social and instinctual processes is conceptualized as difficulty in gaining access to the unconscious influences on behavior. Although this reformulation of intraindividual and interindividual conflict is moderate, it provides the basis for a model of psychological functioning stressing that unconscious processes are simply held out of immediate awareness rather than emphasizing a qualitative, categorical, dualistic distinction between conscious-unconscious and voluntary-autonomic. Metaphorically, it is quite different to think of a person as sorting out conflicting information rather than as attempting to subordinate a bestial animal to conform to the external demands of a social order.

This latter model remains prominent as a tacit assumption in psychological theory according to Arthur Koestler, who summarizes the neurological basis of such a position in *Ghost in the Machine:* "Evolution superimposed a new superior structure over the old one, with partly overlapping functions and without providing the new with a clear cut hierarchic control over the old, thus inviting confusion and conflict" (1967, p. 281). Although Koestler does not refer to neurological or psychological evidence of a mechanism by which this inevitable conflict might be mediated, he does theorize about the possibility of such a psychological process: "It seems that between the primary process and the so-called secondary process, governed by the so-called reality principle, we must interpolate several layers of mental activity which are not just mixtures of primary and secondary, but are cognitive systems in their own right" (1967, p. 117). Unfortunately, he concludes his analysis of the dualistic model of the brain by advocating the development of a drug that would have the effect of creating "a state of dynamic equilibrium in which thought and emotion are reunited and hierarchic order restored" (1968, p. 336). By proposing a biochemical solution to this problem, he has overlooked the possibility of a constructive dialogue between the conscious and unconscious processes and opted for the "hierarchic order" of conscious processes over unconscious processes. This solution is unsatisfactory, since it is dependent on externally administered drugs rather than on placing more responsibility on individuals to formulate an internal psychological solution. Also, it supports rather than challenges a dualistic model of the brain and of human behavior. This digression is intended to point out the persistence of the intracerebral conflict model in the theoretical positions of those who have sought alternative models of psychological functioning.

In 1961, neuropsychiatrist A. T. W. Simeons proposed a communications model of psychosomatic disease based on thirty years of research. Drawing evidence from neurology, paleontology, and anthropology, Simeons asserted that the cortex of the brain had evolved to the point where it now asserted excessive control over sub-cortical, diencephalic processes. He pointed out that modern man was increasingly subject to moral precepts that had no biological basis, and that these moral sanctions were purely cortical, that is, consciously formulated, and arose solely out of the cultural environment man created. Despite the stresses of contemporary society, man has imposed conscious censorship over his more biologically based reactions to those stresses. This censorship is interpreted as a process of misinterpreted communications between cortical and diencephalic brain functions rather than as an inherent, irremedial conflict between conscious and unconscious processes. Briefly, the basic contention of Simeons is as follows:

> Modern man's cortex, having censored the diencephalic reactions at the level of consciousness, is unable to interpret the bodily preparations for flight correctly. His cortex cannot understand that his primitive diencephalon still reacts in the old way to threats which the cortex no longer accepts as such. When these once normal and vitally important reactions to fear do not reach his conscious awareness, he interprets them as something abnormal and regards them as afflictions. He speaks of indigestion when apprehensiveness kills his appetite, and insomnia when fright keeps him awake at night. . . . The increased heart-beat becomes palpitation, the sudden elimination of waste matter he calls diarrhea, the clenching of his back muscles he calls lumbago, and so forth. It is man's civilization which prevents him from realizing that such bodily reactions may be merely the normal results of diencephalic alarm and the mobilization of those marvelous flight mechanisms to which he owes his existence as a species (1960, p. 52).

These normal diencephalic reactions are interpreted in the cortex as signs of disease; this, in turn, increases the individual's anxiety. In essence, this cycle is the means by which psychosomatic disease becomes established. While the basic instincts of sex, hunger, sleep, and fear are diencephalic, the wide range of human emotions, such as pity, shame, hope, and guilt, are considered to be "cortical elaborations" of the more basic instincts. Actually, this last observation has served as the basis of a theory of emotional states by psychologist

Stanley Schachter, who writes: "Given a state of physiological arousal for which an individual has no immediate explanation, he will 'label' this state and describe his feelings in terms of cognitions available to him. . . . One might anticipate that precisely the same state of physiological arousal could be labeled 'joy' or 'fury' or any of a great number of emotional labels, depending on the cognitive aspects of the situation" (Schachter, 1964). Schachter's theory emphasizes an individual's behavior in a social situation and is not concerned specifically with psychosomatic disease, but it is based on much the same evidence cited by Simeons. Neurologically, Schachter's theory stresses the process of *tonic activation,* or generalized state of subcortical arousal, which is cognitively labeled. However, by neglecting to consider *phasic activation,* Schachter's theory cannot allow for a two-way communication between cortical and subcortical processes in order to mediate between conflicting information. Thus, he has written several books in which he interprets diseases such as ulcers, arteriosclerosis, diabetes, obesity, and psychological disorders such as guilt and depression in terms of his communications theory and offers innovative treatments. There is no need to pursue his specific diagnoses of these disorders, for the major point here is that an individual's physiology is ill suited to cope with the extended duration of stress and anxiety of contemporary society from which no physical escape takes place. While the diencephalon reacts to stress by preparing for fight or flight, the individual consciously restrains himself. Immobility is interpreted by the diencephalon as insufficient preparation for fight or flight, and the individual experiences mounting tension in a highly destructive cycle.

Termination of this cycle is the key to alleviating psychosomatic disorders. Throughout his research, Simeons suggests specific interventions, but they are predominantly chemotherapeutic. With the development of the imagery therapies and Biofeedback techniques, it may be possible to alleviate many of the disorders cited by Simeons without the use of drugs. In essence, Simeons and Lilly recognized a communications model of the brain but did not offer a means of therapeutic intervention based on their observations. Now it is possible to use their insights as the foundation for understanding the processes on which the imagery therapies operate and to guide further research and applications. There are several conclusions that provide the basis for exploring the imagery therapies as the means by which cortical and subcortical processes may become more harmoniously integrated into a symbiotic relationship. These conclusions are: (1) neurological and psychological research supports a communications model of the brain rather than a conflict model; (2) information is unconsciously registered in the brain; this fact gives rise to a distinction between *conscious* and *unconscious* based on information processing rather than on inherent duality of instincts and cognition; (3) unconsciously registered information and purely physiological autonomic processes do have an effect on an individual's behavior; (4) most important, it is difficult but not impossible to consciously alter and control both unconscious information and autonomic processes; and (5) the means by which this last end can be accomplished as through the use of a combination of imagery therapies and deep-relaxation techniques. This concludes the specific discussion of the neurological substrates of consciousness and defines the essential problem of the newly emerging therapies, which is to formulate the "language" by which conscious-unconscious and voluntary-autonomic might be mediated.

THE HYPNOTIC STATE

In 1924, Berger made the initial physiological measurements distinguishing the differential activities of the human brain during the major states of consciousness. Five years later, he discovered the generation of electrical activity by the brain in state-specific patterns, that is, electroencephalograms, or EEGs. Berger's descriptions of the sleeping and waking states were followed in 1935 by Loomis and Harvey, who defined various substates of sleep via EEG records and also measured oxygen consumption, heart rate, and body temperature.

Wallace (1970) notes that a major discovery in the field was made by Aserinsky and Kleitman in 1953, when they observed that dreaming was accompanied by the presence of active electrooculogram activity, that is, rapid eye movement, or REM. This activity, which takes place during one of the defined EEG stages of sleep—stage 1 REM—has been called *paradoxical sleep* because the EEG pattern resembles that of the waking state, in spite of the fact that the individual is behaviorially asleep. Following more extensive physiological findings, as well as the correlation of EEG patterns with the subjective experience of dreaming, both psychologists and physiologists began to deal with three major states of consciousness, which were well defined physiologically and biochemically: waking, sleeping, and dreaming (Kleitman 1963).

Varied applications of the neurophysiological descriptions of the three states of consciousness began to appear in the research literature. The state-specific EEG patterns, in particular, enabled "researchers to better understand the systemic and neurophysiological processes which underlie these states" (Wallace 1970). In addition, investigations focusing on the relationship between the cyclic occurrence and duration of the major states and mental and physical wellbeing were now undertaken. In 1894, de Maneceine discovered that the deprivation of sleep in animals, that is, prolonged wakefulness, resulted in lethal brain deterioration. Wallace makes the point that similar deprivation in humans has been causally linked to visual and tactile sensory disorders and disorientation, loss of physical efficiency, reduction of alpha-wave activity in EEG, altered energy metabolism (decreased production of adenosine triphosphate), and altered hormonal and biochemical functioning (elevation of stress hormone ACTH and incidence of indole, structurally related to serotonin and LSD-25, which has been also found in states of artificial stress).

He further observes that deprivation of stage 1 REM (dreaming) has resulted in irritability, disorientation, and psychoticlike behavior and ideation, including hallucinations. The necessity of dream-state activity to human functioning is indicated by the marked increase in dreaming time following deprivation. These findings suggest that abbreviations in the usual time spent dreaming and/or sleeping induce physiological and biochemical alterations that may result in behavioral and mental abnormalities.

Thus, one may conclude that such state-specific physiological descriptions appear to have considerable clinical import. Certainly, there is ample support for the contention that more sensitive investigation is needed in the study of human consciousness. The former reluctance of much of the Occidental scientific community to consider investigations in altered-state phenomena may be due, in part, to the fact that

> within Western culture we have strong negative attitudes towards ASCs: there is the normal (good) state of consciousness and there are pathological changes in consciousness. Most people make no further distinctions. We have available a great deal of scientific and clinical material on ASCs associated with psychopathological states, such as schizophrenia: by comparison, our scientific knowledge about ASCs which could be considered "desirable" is extremely limited and generally unknown to scientists. . . . [There exist ASCs which] have positive qualities in that they are ASCs that many people will go to considerable trouble and effort to induce in themselves because they feel that experiencing a particular ASC is rewarding. Our understanding of mental processes has been greatly facilitated by focusing on psychopathology, but it cannot be complete without looking at the other side of the coin. Further, we need to drop the "good" or "bad" judgments about various ASCs and concentrate on the question: What are the characteristics of a given ASC and what consequences do these characteristics have on behavior in various settings?
>
> A normal state of consciousness can be considered a resultant of living in a particular environment, both physical and psychosocial. Thus the normal state of consciousness for any individual is one that has adaptive value within his particular culture and environment; we would expect the normal state of consciousness to show qualitatively and/or quantitatively different aspects from one culture to another. But one of the most common cognitive errors made is what Carl Jung has called the fallacy of the psychologist projecting his own psychology upon the patient, that is, we almost always make the implicit assumption that everybody else thinks and experiences about the same way as we do, with the exception of "crazy" people (Tart 1969).

One additional introductory point should be made: that is, we are acutely aware of the logical paradox inherent in any attempt to communicate the nature of human consciousness and its alteration through a linguistic medium. The mass-communications theorists (for example, McLuhan and Carpenter) have persuasively dealt with the point "that learning to speak a language means learning to think in a language—that is, learning to think in terms of abstract verbal concepts and grammatical categories" (White 1972). To continue with White's thesis, language is by nature symbolic, and, hence, thinking in a particular language is symbol thinking. As symbols are, by definition, less than the realities they represent, any linguistic medium must necessarily constrict consciousness and delimit understanding. Hence, we are presently endeavoring to explain the nature of human consciousness through a linguistic medium that, by definition, restricts consciousness. The way to escape this paradox is extremely difficult and perhaps impossible to comprehend for most of Western civilization. As the anthropologists and philosophers, among others, have indicated, our escape is to transcend words and other symbols to a direct, unmediated perception that has not been filtered through a linguistic mental screen.

It is generally acknowledged that hypnosis was "discovered" by the Viennese physician Franz Anton Mesmer, who ascribed it to the effect of the "animal magnetism" of one individual on another. Alexander (1965) notes that "it was not generally known until John Dos Passos' historica and biographic study [*The Men Who Made the Nation*] that the Marquis de Lafayette was a pupil of Mesmer, and that it was he who presented the first paper on the subject in the United States before the American Philosophical Society in Philadelphia in 1784." It was Mesmer's contention that the human body resembled a magnet and that disease was attributable to an improper distribution of magnetic fluid. In 1842, James Braid, a surgeon in Manchester, England, recognized the physical and psychological effects of *mesmerism* as subjective in nature, and it was Braid who originated the term *hypnotism,* derived from the Greek *hypnos,* meaning "sleep." In the late nineteenth century, J. M. Charcot and H. Bernheim used hypnosis in the treatment of nervous mental diseases. Both were central figures in the controversies over whether hypnotism was basically physiologic or psychologic and pathologic or normal. Perhaps of greatest significance at this time was the use of hypnosis by Breuer and Freud. Moss (1965), in discussing the debt owed by psychoanalysis and psychiatry to hypnotism, states that

> Through the employment of hypnosis, Breuer and Freud were able to demonstrate convincingly the causal connection between hysterical symptoms and unfortunate childhood experiences ("the hysteric suffers mostly from reminiscences"). Symptoms were found to have a specific meaning which became transparently clear when the etiology was known ("one cannot attribute too much meaning to them"). To their repeated surprise they found that symptoms disappeared if they caused recall of a traumatic memory with sufficient vividness ("traumatic experiences must be repeatedly recalled until the emotional elements are exhausted"). They also observed that the memories which caused the hysterical phenomena are preserved with remarkable fidelity but were not available to voluntary conscious recall. Forgetting in these instances was apparently not a passive process but an active one in which the painful memory is repressed or pushed out of conscious awareness.

As Alexander (1965) has observed, the dynamic quality of symptoms, which was originally discovered through the use of hypnosis, became the point of departure of psychoanalysis. In 1897, Renterghen incorporated this notion into hypnotic psychotherapy when he "formulated suggestions in terms of the dynamic meaning of the symptom" rather than the more overt but less substantial manifestations. It is precisely this approach that has been expanded on by Erikson (1943) and Wolberg (1948) and that constitutes the basis for modern clinical hypnotherapy.

The Physiology of Hypnotic States

A number of theoretical formulations regard hypnosis as a product of physiological alterations in various sectors of the brain. Moss (1965) notes that other theories include viewing hypnosis as (1) reducing conduction at synaptic nerve junctures through the alteration of biochemical substances in the neural system, (2) shifting nervous energy from the central nervous system to the vasomotor system, or (3) a state that results in an inhibition of the ganglion cells of the brain. Perhaps the most obvious similarity underlying these contentions is the common and still widespread assumption that hypnosis is a physiological state of the organism.

The primary focus of physiological studies of hypnosis has been on the relationship between the hypnotic and sleep states; the implicit assumption in these investigations has been to regard hypnosis as a form of incomplete sleep. It was the belief of the renowned Russian neurophysiologist I. Pavlov that hypnosis resembled sleep in that both states involved a spread of cortical inhibition. As an extension of his experimentation on classical conditioning, Pavlov maintained that hypnosis was a complex conditioned reflex learned by the subject. Moss observes that it was Pavlov's contention that words become conditioned to both internal and external stimuli and the words used in hypnotic induction become stimuli that release physiologically related conditioned reflexes. The implication of this view—namely, that almost any supposedly involuntary response can be conditioned through appropriate training—has received further validation as a result of recent research in the area of the voluntary control of internal states, for example, through Biofeedback.

Hoskovec (1967) notes that the Pavlovian perspective, which has been well integrated in Soviet literature on hypnosis, centers about what has been termed the two "excitation-inhibition propositions of hypnosis"—namely, that (1) hypnosis is incomplete sleep (sleep accompanied by partial wakefulness). This proposition is explained as follows:

> Suggestion causes a concentration of excitation in part of the cortex, while other areas are inhibited by negative induction. This diminishes the effect of influences which would otherwise tend to counteract the suggestion. Pavlov's theory implies that some degree of inhibition should be present following a period of suggestion, and that the amount of inhibition will to some extent determine the response to suggestion. Pavlov stated that, just as we learn to go to sleep when we close our eyes, so too an individual may be taught to enter into

an hypnotic state as a conditioned reflex to appropriate stimuli, and also pointed out the influence of repetition. Suggestion is defined as concentrated excitation in a limited point or area of the brain, induced by a word, as a conditioned-reflex stimulus in the framework of the second signal system or explained as a physiological factor (Hoskovec 1967).

(2) The dissociation of cerebral functions is held to be an important characteristic of the hypnotic state. This proposition may be understood as follows:

> . . . there is a subdivision of the cerebral hemispheres into sleeping and waking parts, and there also exists a "watch zone," a more or less confined center of concentrated excitation isolated from the remaining regions of the cortex by negative induction. According to the Pavlovian school, this "watch zone" represents the physiological foundation of hypnotic rapport. For Pavlovians, hypnotic rapport is the special faculty of a hypnotized subject to perceive, selectively and exclusively, the words of the hypnotist without maintaining any contact with the rest of the external world. Pavlovians point out that this is not an exclusive property of the hypnotic state and that it is sometimes also observed in normal sleep (Hoskovec, 1967).

Hoskovec uses the following diagrams to illustrate (a) wakefulness; (b) sleep; (c) what Hoskovec maintains is a common misinterpretation of the Pavlovian position, which is most notably found in Hull (1933); and (d) the Pavlovian conceptualization. He notes that the shading represents inhibition, while the white areas represent excitation.

a. Wakefulness   *b*. Sleep   *c*. Partial inhibition   *d*. Dissociated
                                    view of hypnosis   excitation-inhibition
                                                         view of hypnosis

The Hullian misinterpretation appears to point to the necessity of distinguishing between the concept of incomplete irradiation of inhibition encompassing the whole cortex (*c*) and that of dissociated sectors of excitation encircled by irradiated areas of total inhibition.

The conditioning theory of hypnosis is given further support by Salter (1944), who asserts that "hypnosis is based on associative reflexes that use words as the triggers of automatic reactions." Through repeated associations starting in infancy, a word, for example, *sleep,* acts as a signal for and elicits many of those reactions normally elicited by the actual internal and external stimuli. Chertok and Kramarz (1959), however, make a strong case for the repudiation of the Pavlovian conceptualization of hypnosis (incomplete sleep) on two grounds. (1) As Pavlov himself conceded, there are implicit difficulties in applying the results of animal experimentation to man. The authors further contend that these difficulties are most manifest in the fact that one cannot possibly compare language with a physical stimulus. (2) The hypothesized similarities between the hypnotic and sleep states have received no electroencephalographic confirmation. These counterarguments do not preclude the possibility that some functional relationship exists between the two states of consciousness that has yet to be physiologically objectified. Psychoanalytic theorists such as Bellak (1955) and Brenman (1951) have affirmed the existence of this type of relationship but claim that it is intrinsically psychological in nature.

Moss notes the work of Kubie and Margolin, who maintain that hypnosis results from the creation of a focal point of central excitation surrounded by areas of inhibition. "According to this description, the onset of the hypnotic state can be defined as a condition of partial sleep, in which one or more open channels of sensorimotor communication are maintained between the subject and the outside world" (Kubie and Margolin 1944). This conceptualization incorporates a psychological component as well. During induction, the hypnotist is seen as the sole element in the subject's external world. Following the attainment of the hypnotic state, the subject (1) reinstates normal time and space boundaries and (2) retains the hypnotist, in conscience, as an "experimentally induced superego figure."

Whatever similarities exist between hypnosis and sleep appear to stem largely from the fact that both ASC represent a reorganization of brain mechanisms toward allowing lower cortical centers to assume a dominant function in behavioral organization. Disimilarities appear related to the fact that only in hypnosis is sensorimotor communication maintained during the abolition of the subject's analytic and integrative activity. A distinct type of reorganization of brain mechanisms occurs as a result of (1) the continuation of prior levels of sensorimotor communication, and (2) the presence of a significant other—that is, the alter ego—to serve as a frame of reference. The inhibition of the cortical field associated with waking-state behavioral organization does not occur as in sleep. Reyher (1964), in addressing this point, says of the waking-state cortical field: ". . . it becomes a subsystem to another cortical field which is not capable of integrating highly adaptive, self-directed commerce with the environment. This cortical field can be activated or suppressed by suggestion. EEG records during hypnosis are like those of the waking state, but suggested symptoms of sleep produce EEG records like those of natural sleep." Reyher also makes the point that suggestions devised for the purpose of waking-state simulation often result in behavior indistinguishable from that occurring during the waking state. He concludes that since both waking- and sleep-state behavior can be elicited through suggestion, like any other response, it would appear that hypnosis is qualitatively different from both these major states of consciousness.

Chertok (1968) notes that another line of physiological research on the nature of hypnosis is being taken in animal hypnosis, in which there have been occurrences of shamming death, catalepsy, and akinesis. He points out that while some researchers are reluctant to postulate any identity between animal hypnosis and the human variety, others, such as Schilder and Kauders (1956), have attempted to establish such a connection. In speaking to this point, Chertok (1967) maintained that

There exists, in any case, in both forms of hypnosis, a common factor, i.e., motor inhibition, which is constant in animals and frequent in man. In the absence of physiological signs characteristic of hypnosis, this specific manifestation is certainly deserving of study in the perspective of basic research. Might it not be possible here to adopt the same approach as in the case of dreaming sleep (REM) —another phenomenon common to man and animals, where the difficulty of transposition does not prevent the extensive use of observations made on animals?

The Psychology of Hypnotic States

Orne (1959), in attempting to metatheorize about the psychology of hypnotic states, notes that "the most meaningful present-day theories of hypnosis interpret hypnotic phenomena along three major lines: (a) desire on the part of the subject to play the role of a hypnotized subject (Sarbin 1950; White 1941a), (b) increase in suggestibility (Hull 1933), and (c) a further less well-defined category that is called by White 'an altered state of consciousness. . . . .' " It is this third interpretation of hypnosis, that is, as an altered state of consciousness, that has proven to be the major focus of researchers in the decade or more following Orne's analysis. After factors such as increased motivation and role playing are accounted for, factors that Orne contends are artifacts, there remains a residual aspect felt to be the "essence" of hypnosis. It is this essence, or the need to invoke the use of the concept ASC in order to fully explain hypnotic phenomena, that serves as a focal point in this section of our book.

Historically, it is clear that varied social-psychological explanations of hypnosis have contributed much to the current body of scientific knowledge. The traditional psychoanalytic stance, for instance, has been to regard hypnosis as a variety of the transference phenomenon. A number of analytic theorists, starting with Freud, predictably chose to highlight the erotic aspects of the hypnotic relationship. Moss notes that Ferenczi offered the hypothesis that hypnosis involves a resurgence of the original parent-child relationship. It was Ferenczi's belief that there exists a "mother hypnosis" and a "father hypnosis" corresponding to the persuasive and authoritarian modes of hypnotic induction.

White (1941) proposed the thesis that "hypnotic behavior be regarded as a meaningful, goal-directed striving, its most general goal being to behave like a hypnotized person as this is continuously defined by the operator and understood by the subject." The essence of White's conceptualization extends beyond the interpersonal realm when he avows that hypnosis cannot be understood merely in terms of motivation. He chooses to refer to hypnosis as an "altered state of the person" and compares this ASC with light sleep or drowsiness. White continued to stress the multidimensional nature of hypnotic phenomena in his analysis of subject motivation (White 1941b). Moss notes that in this investigation, White found a positive correlation between susceptibility and need for deference (the tendency to willingly yield to the dictates of a superior individual) and a negative correlation between susceptibility and need for autonomy. In addition to the motivational dimension, White also posits the existence of an essential "unspecified aptitude or innate peculiarity as the decisive determinant of hypnotizability" (Moss 1965).

Moss continues with an explication of White's motivational hypothesis, which has served as the basis for Sarbin's (1950) non-physiological social-psychological interpretation of hypnotic phenomena. It is Sarbin's belief that hypnotic behavior is merely a subset of the general class of behaviors falling under the rubric of *role playing*. It is also his contention that in hypnosis, the subject endeavors to assume the role of the hypnotized person in accord with his general understanding of that role. A situational parallelism is presented between hypnosis and drama, where conduct that is also overtly automatized, discontinuous with so-called normal behavior, and of wide individual variation, is elicited through the use of simple verbal instructions. In considering Sarbin's parallelism as well as his theory, it appears vital to note that

> The introspective accounts of actors often are indistinguishable from the accounts of hypnotic subjects and that the stage director stands in much the same relationship to the actor as does the hypnotist to

the subject. . . . Both the actor and the hypnotic subject must possess a role-taking aptitude if a role is to be portrayed completely and convincingly, and there is some modest experimental evidence to this effect. Thus, hypnosis is only a word for a special type of culturally defined influence situation and, according to Sarbin, there is no need to postulate a special state or trance. A frequently voiced criticism of this position is that it taxes credibility that any subject, regardless of his skill as an actor, could avoid falling out of role when subjected to situations such as major surgery without chemoanesthesia. Sarbin's response is that people manifest wide differential sensitivity to pain and too little is known about the use of inattention in the inhibition of pain experiences (Moss 1965).

After a long-term and thorough review of the English-language research literature on hypnosis, we have found it to be clear that the proliferation of experimental investigations during the past fifteen years (1959–1974) has exceeded in quantity all the material published since the time of Mesmer (circa 1780). This rapid increment in the quantity of experimental research has resulted in fundamental theoretical revisions of the prevailing conceptualizations of hypnosis. The reader may refer to the following for comprehensive reviews of the more recent work in the area of experimental hypnosis: Hilgard (1964, 1965a), Orne (1966), Evans (1968), McPeake (1968) and Barber (1969b). An examination of these reviews has left us in accord with Spanos and Chaves's (1970) conclusion that "contemporary research and theory pertaining to the topic of hypnotism can be summarized in terms of two divergent conceptualizations. One of these conceptualizations . . . we shall call *hypnotic state theory*. . . . In recent years, an alternative conceptualization of hypnotism has evolved . . . [and] has reached maturity largely through the work of T. X. Barber."

It has been pointed out by Spanos and Chaves that the three pivotal assumptions supporting hypnotic-state theory are: (1) given a susceptible subject, procedures of hypnotic induction can evoke an ASC known as a hypnotic or trance state; (2) when in this ASC, an individual is subject to the possibility of varied behavioral alterations as well as powerful modifications of subjective experience; (3) although an individual's subjective experience, as in the hypnotic state, is necessarily a private affair, its existence may be inferred from its behavioral consequences.

Barber's work, which has primary roots in the aforementioned theories of White and Sarbin, rests mainly on two fundamental assumptions: (1) any scientific theory that endeavors to explicate the phenomenon of hypnosis must necessarily deal with and explain those overt behavioral manifestations and self-reported data that traditionally have been subsumed under the term *hypnotism,* for example, catalepsy, hallucination, analgesia, age regression, and amnesia; (2) in order to satisfy the aim of the previous assumption, one must first establish lawful relations between the behaviors under consideration and antecedent variables present in the context. These lawful relations must be incorporated into a theoretical structure under a smaller number of fundamental principles using concepts that adhere closely to empirical data.

Spanos and Chaves (1970) further assert, and rightfully so, that "These divergent conceptualizations are sufficiently distinct to be regarded as independent scientific paradigms. 'The term paradigm, in the present context, is used to refer to a set of implicit and explicit assumptions which have methodological and theoretical significance' (Kuhn 1962)."

These authors' attempt to differentiate hypnotic-state theory from Barber's conceptualization in a paradigmatic and, more specifically, a Kuhnian sense, is both valuable and commendable. Such an approach to the evaluation of theory and the formulation of metatheory may be instrumental in avoiding the confusion that often accompanies the evaluation and comparison of social-science theories.

Hypnotic-State Theory

The major proponents and most prolific investigators in hypnotic-state theory have been M. T. Orne and E. R. Hilgard. It is our intention to review, briefly but systematically, the formulations of both theorists before considering the alternative conceptualization of T. X. Barber. This overview essentially will condense the extensive reviews noted earlier, that is, Hilgard (1964, 1965a), Orne (1966) and Barber (1969b).

M. T. ORNE. Orne et al. have maintained that behavioral altera-tions manifested subsequent to hypnotic induction are a result of both the ASC and the "demand characteristics" associated with the context in which hypnotic induction occurs. The term *demand char-acteristics* is used to describe the set of all intra- and extra-experi-mental cues that aid the subject in the determination of (1) the general intent of the experiment, and (2) his specific role or roles within the experiment. Orne has particularly stressed that class of behavior called compliance resulting from the operation of demand characteristics (Orne 1966, 1967). Spanos and Chaves note that Orne identifies a confounding variable in many investigations as the mistaken equation of compliance with responses produced by the essential features of the hypnotic state. The central thrust of Orne's work has been to delineate these essential features.

In his attempt to extract that subclass of behaviors that are a function of the hypnotic state from the larger class of behaviors manifested during the hypnotic situation, Orne has developed the following experimental design:

> This design involves the administration of a hypnotic induction procedure to both a control and an experimental group. The control group consists of "poor hypnotic subjects who have previously shown that they are unresponsive to hypnotic suggestions. Prior to receiving the hypnotic induction, these "poor" subjects are told to simulate hypnosis. The experimental group consists of "good" or suggestible subjects who are not told to simulate hypnosis. These "good" subjects are presumed to enter a trance state when they are administered an hypnotic induction procedure (Spanos and Chaves 1970).

Orne outlines the assumptions inherent in his simulation experiments as follows: (1) when the control and experimental groups are sub-jected to identical induction procedures, both groups are equally exposed to the demand characteristics of the situation; that is, both groups develop the same expectations about the general aims of the experiment and the specific role or roles to be assumed by the individual; (2) consequently, those differences between the control and experimental subjects that cannot be accounted for by the "faking" situation may be viewed as characteristic of hypnosis; that is, the variable assumed to be causally related to the behavior of the experimental subjects, the hypnotic state, can be eliminated in the control situation. Thus, if such behavior still occurs, it can then be satisfactorily accounted for by the demand characteristics of the situation.

E. R. HILGARD. In commenting on the work of Hilgard, Spanos and Chaves note that "Hilgard's theoretical and experimental interests have covered the spectrum of hypnosis research. His most important experimental work can be subsumed under four topic areas: (a) developmental correlates of hypnotic susceptibility, (b) the relationship between hypnosis and suggestibility, (c) the effects of hypnosis on pain, and (d) the development of instruments for measuring hypnotic susceptibility."

Developmental Correlates of Hypnotic Susceptibility. Spanos and Chaves note that the fundamental hypothesis presented in Hilgard (1965b) is that, while the potential for deep hypnotic susceptibility and profound hypnotic experience is universally inherent in normal infants, it can only be realized if the frequency of positive childhood experience is of sufficient magnitude. This potential is particularly influenced by aspects of the parent-child relationship such as parental attitudes, childhood identifications, temperamental similarities between the child and his parents, and parental hypnotizability. Perhaps Hilgard's most fascinating notion is his postulation of "multiple pathways" through which the adult may enter the hypnotic state. These pathways are thought to be the resultants of various modes of childhood experience, such as the child's ability to freely engage in fantasy or in his easy acceptance of an adventurous orientation.

Primarily on the basis of extensive quasi-structured pre-hypnotic interviews, Hilgard (1962, 1965b) has proposed a comprehensive developmental-interactive theory of hypnotic susceptibility. Spanos and Chaves observe that this theory has generated a number of hypotheses regarding the relationship between (a) personality and developmental characteristics which predispose an individual toward hypnotic susceptibility (Hilgard 1964, 1965a, 1965b; Hilgard and Hilgard 1962), (b) the relationship between subjects' hypnotic susceptibility and their temperamental resemblance to their parents (Hilgard 1964), (c) the relationship between subjects' hypnotic susceptibility and the hypnotic susceptibility of their parents (Hilgard 1964, 1965a), and (d) the relationship between subjects' attitudes and self-predictions concerning hypnosis and their hypnotic susceptibility (Melei and Hilgard 1964).

Hypnosis and Suggestibility. The most central and controversial of Hilgard's contentions in this area is that hypnotic induction results in a heightened level of suggestibility above and beyond that evidenced as a result of other motivational procedures. This is clearly in conflict with Barber's research, which concludes that short, task-motivating instructions result in increases in suggestibility that approximate those obtained with standard hypnotic induction procedures. Spanos and Chaves point to the fact that Hilgard and Tart (1966) and Edmonston and Robertson (1967) claim to have localized Barber's inability to find significant differences between hypnotic and task-motivated subjects in his use of a random multigroup experimental design. If Barber randomly assigned subjects to different treatments and his intersubject variability was high, his design may have been lacking in the sensitivity required to detect minimal but significant differences between treatments.

Hypnosis and Pain. Hilgard et al. have also focused much attention on the problems of hypnotic analgesia (Hilgard 1967, 1969; Hilgard, Cooper, Lenox, Morgan, and Voevodsky 1967). Spanos and Chaves note that these investigations have centered about the following dual focus: (1) the determination of how one measures pain, and (2) pain reduction through hypnotic suggestion. The experimental procedure has been one in which pain is induced either by placing the subject's arm and forearm in cold water or by an ischemic technique whereby the subject exerts pressure on a dynamometer following the placement of a tourniquet above the elbow. While still exposed to the nociceptive stimuli, the subjects assess their experienced pain on a subjective rating scale. In addition, a variety of physiological measures are taken (for example, systolic blood pressure). In his attempt to study hypnotic analgesia, Hilgard has compared the magnitude of experienced pain in the following experimental conditions:

1. Waking state with no special instructions to subjects
2. Hypnotic state without suggestions of analgesia
3. Hypnotic state with suggestions of analgesia
4. A simulation condition in which "poor" hypnotic subjects first fake hypnosis and then undergo a hypnotic induction with suggestions of analgesia

Hilgard (1969) has reported that the increment rate of both ischemic and cold pressor pain was the same in conditions (1) and (2). In addition, the increment rate of both ischemic and cold pressor pain was found to be decreased significantly in condition (3) when compared to any of the other conditions, and this decrease was greater for subjects of high hypnotic suggestibility.

Measurement of Hypnotic Susceptibility. A substantial portion of Hilgard's earlier work (for example, Weitzenhoffer and Hilgard 1959, 1962, 1963) was directed at the development and standardization of hypnotic-susceptibility scales. The initial measure assessing this construct is called the Stanford Hypnotic Susceptibility Scale (SHS), which consists of three forms—A, B, and C—and attempts to assess both motor and cognitive aspects of hypnotic performance. Weitzenhoffer and Hilgard (1963) devised another scale called the Stanford Profile Scale of Hypnotic Susceptibility (SPS), which purports to measure specific abilities related to individual differences in hypnotic performance. Our search of the research literature confirmed the Spanos and Chaves (1970) assertion that the "Stanford Scales have been widely employed by investigators of varying theoretical persuasion."

T. X. BARBER. "The central focus of Barber's paradigm involves the delineation and measurement of the behaviors traditionally subsumed under the rubric of hypnotism and the delineation of objective antecedent variables which are instrumental in eliciting these behaviors" (Spanos and Chaves 1970). Explicit in Barber's formulation is the delineation of three categories of behavior generally encompassed by the label *hypnotism*. These categories are: (1) responses to direct suggestions of amnesia, analgesia, age regression, catalepsy, and hallucination; (2) verbal self-reported data as to whether or not the subject felt he was or was not hypnotized; (3) behavior, such as psychomotor retardation, limpness, and diminished spontaneity, generally termed *hypnotic appearance*. Barber has developed instrumental measures for the assessment of these hypothetically discrete categories of behavior.

Undoubtedly, a core feature of Barber's position is his criticism of the scientific utility of the hypnotic-state construct. The apparently logical basis for this criticism is Barber's contention that "the trance state construct is usually employed in a tautological fashion. That is, the presence of a 'trance state' is commonly inferred on the basis of the subjects' responsiveness to test suggestion; then, in a circular fashion, the 'trance state' is used to 'explain' the responsiveness from which it was initialy inferred" (Spanos and Chaves 1970). Furthermore, Barber (1964) and Barber and Calverly (1969) develop two additional points—namely, that (1) both the subjects' verbal self-reports and "hypnotic appearance" are invalid when used as confirmation of the existence of a hypnotic state; Barber notes that both criteria are variably independent of subjects' response to test suggestion; (2) "all three of the above classes of behaviors (labeled hypnotic) can be lawfully related to objective antecedent variables that need not be conceptualized under the penumbra of the hypnotic state" (Spanos and Chaves 1970).

Barber's impressive array of published material in the area of experimental hypnosis is admittedly geared toward the eventual development of an empirically grounded theory of hypnotic behavior (Barber 1969*a*). Barber (1969*b*) offers seventy empirical generalizations summarizing his findings related to hypnotic behavior. The purpose of making explicit this substantial number of generalizations is to establish a sufficient number of lawful relationships that can collectively account for the considerable variance in hypnotic phenomena—that can functionally relate the main antecedent and consequent variables. Barber (1969b) briefly outlines his future research plans in relating his intention to integrate these empirically determined antecedent-consequent relationships under a more parsimonious structure, consisting of fewer and more general principles. As Spanos and Chaves have noted, Barber's main efforts have focused on three experimental problems: (1) the delineation of objective antecedent variables instrumental in eliciting hypnotic behaviors, (2) the delineation of antecedent variables instrumental in eliciting subjects' testimony concerning personal experience during the hypnotic situation, and (3) the development of reliable assessment techniques for measuring hypnotic behavior. To recapitulate, Barber's efforts appear to indicate that, given the proper research design and experimental manipulations, most, if not all, hypnotic behaviors (dependent variables), that is, muscular rigidity, analgesia, visual and auditory hallucinations, age regression, deafness, color blindness, "physiological" effects, amnesia, postexperimental (posthypnotic) responses, appearance of hypnosis, and subjective reports, can be elicited from nonhypnotized, independent control groups. Barber has gone to great lengths to bolster his "theory" of hypnotic behavior. The utilization of factorial designs (Barber and Calverley 1965a, 1965b) permits the experimenter to determine which combination of variables most effectively produces behavioral alteration. For example, Barber and Calverley (1965a) found that the combination of defining the situation as hypnosis and suggesting relaxation, drowsiness, and sleep and the combination of motivational instructions and suggestions of easiness of response were equally effective in eliciting responses to the Barber Suggestibility Scale. These two combinations of variables were more effective than individual variables alone.

As a result of this painstaking research, Barber totally rejects the concepts of *trance* and *hypnosis*. In fact, in all his work, these terms are enclosed by quotation marks to indicate their nonexistence and the inherent circularity in their utilization (for example, subjects are hypnotized by responding to suggestion; we know they are hypnotized when and if they respond to suggestions!). The focus of consideration must then be whether Barber has really proven that hypnosis does not exist. Does equivalence in performance between independent groups necessarily imply equivalence in essence (Gordon 1967)? Surely, failure to find treatment differences in a placebo and drug psychopharmacological study is not tantamount to the assumption that the drug and placebo are the same, though, in the long run, their effect might be quite similar. Rather, we would contend that the substantial import of Barber's efforts lies primarily in his ability to determine those independent manipulations that are powerful enough to equal the effects of hypnosis. Even if the addition of hypnosis to these variables does not enhance behavioral effects, the logical implication is not that hypnosis does not exist. In addition to these logical difficulties, the use of randomly assigned subjects to independent control and experimental groups, although partially controlling for expectancy effects, still, according to Hilgard, presents difficulties in answering major questions in hypnosis research.

Hypnosis research has revealed that, while it seems that a hypnotic state of consciousness does exist, this state in itself is not responsible for much of the behavior associated with hypnosis. Experimenter bias, demand characteristics, and the experimental situation as a whole are factors influencing the behavior of the hypnotic subject. In addition to these variables, there are other elements in hypnosis experimentation that have been shown to be important in the production of behavioral alteration; they are: motivational instruction, "suggestions," attitudes and expectations of the subject, qualities of the experimenter, and the relationship between the hypnotist and the subject. One immediate application of this finding is the use of hypnosis as a prototypic interpersonal situation in which various social-influence processes may be studied. Although verbal conditioning is more easily manipulated than hypnosis, the latter does have the added quality of at least appearing to the subject to be closer to the "reality" of psychotherapy.

A truly significant contribution of hypnosis research is the demonstration that motivation, expectancies, suggestions, and interpersonal relationships are social-influence variables that do produce behavior change. Interestingly, these elements seem to be common to the placebo effect. In a classic historical review, Shapiro (1960) pointed out that until very recently in the history of medicine, medicine itself was the placebo, since, on a biochemical level, the prescribed medicines probably did more harm than good. However, the reality of the situation was that people did get better, as evidenced by the fact that physicians continued to be respected and revered public figures. Frank (1961) provides further crosscultural evidence addressing this point. The primary medical techniques were suggestion, encouragement, attention, emotional arousal, warm solicitude, and confident application of treatment coupled with high patient expectancy of relief and implicit trust. These various social-influence methods were undoubtedly applied somewhat unsystematically. One can only begin to wonder what carefully controlled experimentation and systematic application of placebo elements might yield.

9

Altered States and Psychotherapy

Underlying all the imagery therapies are three comprehensive issues that require clarification. Before delineating the specific techniques and theories of the individual systems, we will point out the aspects that are common to all of them: (1) an orientation toward goals that involve a value judgment by the therapist concerning the patient's subjective images and fantasies; (2) the role of the therapist as that of a guide rather than of an analyst—this has profound implications for all systems of psychotherapy; and (3) use of relaxation or awareness techniques designed to induce in the patient a state of controlled involvement in his immediate images and fantasies. *Psychotherapy* is broadly defined to include meditation as it is used in China and Japan as a system of therapy. One broad definition by Jerome Frank is most useful:

> Attempts to enhance a person's feeling of well being are usually labelled treatment, and every society trains some of its members to apply this form of influence. Treatment always involves a personal relationship between healer and sufferer. Certain types of therapy rely primarily on the healer's ability to mobilize healing forces in the sufferer by psychological means. These forms of treatment may be generically termed psychotherapy (1961, p. 1).

Psychotherapy and each of the above points will be considered in order to define the common basis from which the various discrete systems are derived.

THERAPEUTIC GOALS

One immediate observation that can be made about the imagery therapies is that they emphasize the individual's experience of his own symbolic processes. Despite this focus on symbolic production, few theorists have considered the question of why the unconscious functions in that mode. An implicit assumption of imagery therapists is that the unconscious symbolic processes are a source of wisdom for the individual and a means of inspiration and rejuvenation. Following a lengthy discussion of this issue, psychologist Wilson Van Dusen concludes: "Symbolic thinking shows the internal connections in this world in which all things are related. These inner processes of mind tend to be symbolic because they stem from a world in which all things are understood as related. . . . Hence we are puzzled by glimpses of this inner world and have to laboriously work at new connections and associations of ideas" (1972, p. 181). This position proposes that unconscious symbolic processes provide an individual with an alternative mode of perception significantly different from its ordinary mode of conscious, analytic, and reality-oriented functioning. In the very process of experiencing or attempting to analyze these symbolic processes, one is potentially capable of discovering new connections, perspectives, and insights into his usual stance toward himself and others. Actually, Erich Fromm has acknowledged this assumption as fundamental to psychoanalysis: "Whatever criticism may be made of the contents of Freud's unconscious, the fact remains that by emphasizing free association as against logical thought, he transcended in an essential point the conventional rationalistic mode of thinking of the Western world, and moved in a direction which had been developed much farther and more radically in the thought of the East" (Fromm 1960, p. 83). In psychoanalysis, free association evolved into a means of analysis rather than of experience whereas in the imagery therapies, an attempt has been made to preserve symbolic processes as a source of real experience. Neither the discrete, analytic mode of conscious perception nor the syncretic, holistic mode of symbolic processes is sufficient in and of itself. What is most important is that these modes of functioning contrast each other and in that contrast offer the possibility for an individual to increase his appreciation and insight into each mode of perception. Rather than dismissing or subordinating symbolic processes to more cognitive processes, imagery therapies view the two modes of functioning as equally real and valuable. Dreams, hypnagogic images, and fantasies are viewed as real experiences with intrinsic value rather than as symptoms of neurosis or as compensation for the defenses of repression and suppression. For this reason, imagery therapies advocate the deliberate cultivation of symbolic processes in essentially stable personalities in order to promote individual growth.

Commitment to the deliberate induction of symbolic processes is the most important principle of the imagery therapies. Their orientation is most aptly summarized by Claudio Naranjo: "In contrast to the psychoanalytic and related schools, there has been a growing concern for the noninterpretive aspects in insight psychotherapy (typically in Gestalt therapy) and, in general, for the importance of sensing and feeling, rather than the intellectual understanding of reality" (1969a, p. 106). Fantasies are to be experienced as alternative realities rather than as unusual occurrences to be interpreted. Yet, experience does not preclude intellectual interpretation, and analytic commentary is not neglected in the imagery therapies, although it is not emphasized. Following an extensive review of imagery techniques, Jerome L. Singer observes that

> The Europeans . . . take the fantasy-life symbolism and imagery much more seriously. It really seems there for most of them, not just as a reflection of conflicts but a fundamental part of the personality that requires treatment and modification as much as the sexual or social adaptation functions of the individual. . . . These images are fundamental human symbols held in common through man's evolutionary development. The images seem to have an independent existence and their organization is part of the total personality structure; one might almost say they represent the fate of the particular patient (1971, p. 32).

Although Singer does not share the enthusiasm of the imagery therapies for fantasy production, he does acknowledge that such processes
represent an important dimension of psychological functioning,
which is invaluable to explore as a distinct reality rather than as
simple compensation (Desoille 1961; Donnars 1970). Ultimately,
the goal of the imagery therapies is to demonstrate to the individual
patient that he is neither his social role nor his subjective fantasies
but that his real identity or true *self* in Jung's terminology (Jung
1969*b*; Naranjo 1969*a*) lies between those two extremes.

As Erich Fromm observed (Fromm, Suzuki, and De Martino
1960), this last assumption of the European imagery therapists has
been most fully explicated by the Eastern cultures. To assert that an
individual's true identity lies between his social role and subjective
fantasies requires a modification of the concept of neurosis and of
the goal of psychotherapy. First of all, it should be noted that all
Eastern methods of psychotherapy assert that ordinary ego consciousness is a limited and impoverished consciousness that represents a
social construct (Watts 1961). Neurosis arises when an individual
either confuses and merges his social role with his true identity or
recognizes that the two are distinct but becomes confused about that
realization. This ancient concept of neurosis is the essence of R. D.
Laing's distinction between the *real self* and *false self* that results in
the conflict leading to the onset of schizophrenia (Laing 1965*a*,
1967). According to Eastern disciplines of psychotherapy, neurotic
behavior arises from *maya* (Suzuki 1956), which is literally translated as "illusion." Illusion refers to the arbitrary definition of an
individual's identity that a given social context assigns to that person
(Naranjo and Ornstein 1971). Thus the goal of psychotherapy is not
to adjust the individual to accept that illusion or to destroy it but
rather to recognize that social constructions of identity are arbitrary
and to achieve a degree of calm detachment from one's ego identity.
In order to achieve this end, one is encouraged to experience the
alternative modes of functioning that are available to him through
his subjective images and fantasies. Both the Eastern disciplines of
psychotherapy and the imagery therapies share this goal and technique in common. However, Western psychotherapists have tended

to equate calm detachment with indifference or noninvolvement—
but this is a misconception. Detachment is intended to allow the
individual to step back from his daily activity for contemplation, not
escape, and is therefore consistent with the most fundamental method
of psychotherapy, which is self-examination. This distinction between
detachment and indifference is noted by D. T. Suzuki when he
writes, "Not caring is the parody of serenity, just as worrying is the
parody of concern" (Watts 1961, p. 33). Affirming this state as
the goal of psychotherapy is C. G. Jung, who was the first Western
psychotherapist to recognize the assets of Eastern systems of psychotherapy: "One must be able to let things happen. I have learnt
from the East what is meant by the phrase, 'Wu-wei': namely, 'not
doing, letting be,' which is quite different from doing nothing. . . .
A way is only the way when one finds it and follows it oneself.
There is no general prescription for how one should do it" (1969*b*,
p. 31). Despite Jung's observation that there is no general description of how to achieve that state, there are a substantial number of
Eastern and Western imagery therapies that have undertaken that
task. Eastern and Western systems of psychotherapy differ in that
Eastern systems advocate that one should remain in a paradoxical
state of involved detachment whereas Western systems of psychotherapy tend to advocate that state as a temporary means to solve a
personal difficulty. There is no need for excessive references to the
esoteric language of Eastern disciplines of meditation in order to note
the convergence of those systems and the imagery therapies. Eastern
disciplines can be thought of as advocating one final goal—immediate awareness—that is a common goal of the imagery therapies, as
attested to by Claudio Naranjo: "This trend represents a movement
in the direction of the Eastern approach that regards sensing-feeling
as closer to 'reality,' and our interpretation thereof as removed from
and a substitute for real knowledge. . . . The Eastern disciplines
place great weight in the act of simple awareness and attention to the
immediacy of experience" (1969*a*, p. 107). Immediate awareness is
most analogous to the paradoxical quality of controlled spontaneity
exhibited by highly trained musicians, dancers, or actors and requires
diligent effort to achieve. Both therapists and theoreticians have

come to recognize the importance of addressing themselves to symbolic processes as sources of insight rather than as symptoms of neurosis. Additionally, it has been hypothesized that purposeful involvement in these symbolic processes is a means of achieving and maintaining a state of immediate awareness. Attainment of this state will be clarified in the following section by more fully defining the role of the therapist in the imagery therapies.

IMAGERY THERAPIST AS GUIDE

Practitioners of the imagery therapies use the symbolic processes of their patients for diagnostic purposes but also recognize that the very experience of the symbolic realm of images and fantasies is intrinsically therapeutic. Working from this premise, imagery therapists function primarily as guides for the patient and secondarily as analytic interpreters of the patient's experience. Guiding the patient is an active process that places the therapist in the role of suggesting specific fantasy experiences. This section will define the specific type of activity involved in techniques of active imagination. Essentially, the role of the therapist is to allow an individual to act on his fantasy in a certain consistent direction until he is able to experience the logical conclusion of that fantasy.

It has been demonstrated that the major therapeutic element of these therapies involves the active exploration of the patient's imagery and the working through of blocks in that process (Singer 1971). While therapists frequently engage in traditional dialogues with the patients, the major emphasis is on the imaginary journey induced during the therapeutic session. These induced symbolic journeys are referred to as "active imagination" in Jung's system of analytical therapy, and that term will be used to refer to all such procedures used in the imagery therapies. Strictly speaking, active imagination is not considered a technique for inducing fantasies but rather a method of elaborating on the content of a spontaneously occurring fantasy, such as in a dream. Usually, a patient recounts a dream or fantasy and is then asked to focus on a particular feature and allow his imagination to drift and to describe the elaborations and transformations of the imagery. However, this concept has been expanded by later analysts to include spontaneous and induced symbolic journeys, and that is the definition of active imagination to be used in this presentation.

Among the earliest therapists to employ active imagination were Desoille (1938) and Jacobson (1938). Both of these therapists subscribed to a concept of collective human symbolic process analogous to Jung's collective unconscious and based their therapeutic techniques on allowing the patient to experience this aspect of his psychological composition. One basic assumption of these therapists was that patients had a limited repertory of actual life experiences but that they entertained fantasies of alternative life experiences without ever having the opportunity to live out and test those fantasies. Therefore, one of the primary functions of an imagery therapist is to allow the individual patient to act on his fantasies in a prescribed manner in order to pursue them to their conclusion and gain insight because of that experience. In this connection, Virel (1968) has demonstrated that collective or mythic fantasies such as "slaying dragons," "flying to mythic lands," and "becoming a king" have considerable impact on disorders ranging from obsessional neuroses to psychosomatic disorders. Since the therapeutic techniques involving imagery range from analytical psychology to behavior modification, discussion of specific cases and research will be undertaken in chapter 10, which deals with specific therapeutic interventions. One important psychodynamic assumption underlies all of these imagery techniques involving active imagination. As long as an individual fantasizes an alternative mode of action to his actual actions, he is not fully committed to any one course of action. This leads to indecision, indecisiveness, and neurotic anxiety as he vacillates between two or more alternatives. Without acting, he is unable to assess the consequences of his fantasies; this process becomes increasingly autistic until no action is possible and fantasy reigns, as in acute psychosis. In order for a patient to constructively experience his unconscious fantasies, the imagery therapists provide an environment in which the outcome of those fantasies can be experienced and evaluated.

In order to accomplish this end, the imagery therapist creates a situation in which the patient assumes an active rather than a passive role in the healing process (Perls 1969). One extremely useful means of examining this process is offered by Jay Haley's analysis of psychotherapy in terms of a communications model. Communication models of psychotherapy are based on Gregory Bateson's double-bind theory, where an individual is called on to take two mutually exclusive courses of action and at the same time is prevented from being able to comment on the paradox (Bateson 1972). An individual can only resolve this impasse by withdrawing from the double-bind situation, but in order to withdraw he must make it appear that he is not withdrawing of his own volition, since a voluntary withdrawal would constitute a commentary on the dilemma. Therefore, the individual must make it appear as though the withdrawal is happening beyond his control and that he has no choice in becoming psychotic (Laing 1961, 1965, 1969). Based on this model, Jay Haley has conceptualized psychotherapy as a constructive variation on the double-bind theory. Haley's formulation is useful in examining the imagery therapists for several reasons, since they do employ double-bind situations and also make extensive use of symbolic processes as a means of intraindividual and interindividual communication.

According to Haley's theory, symptoms are the strategic means by which a patient controls others without accepting responsibility for doing so (1959). They become the means of justifying an individual's withdrawal from a double bind, in much the same way as a headache serves as the means to avoid a boring social engagement. However, the symptom must appear to be involuntary and spontaneous or else it cannot serve the function of allowing one to deny responsibility. In other words, the patient must produce spontaneous symptoms. Haley asserts that the root contradiction of all double binds is, "You must be spontaneous" (Haley 1959). Controlled spontaneity is a logical contradiction, yet it is a state achieved by musicians, dancers, actors, and bicycle riders—but not without extensive training. Pathology results when a patient fails to achieve controlled spontaneity. However, there is great potential for one to achieve a positive state of controlled spontaneity through a therapeutic situation in which he is trained to achieve that state. As was pointed out in chapter 7, all the imagery therapies attempt, as the goal of therapy, to induce a state of immediate awareness leading to controlled spontaneity. How this is to be achieved is largely a function of the role of the therapist in the process.

On entering therapy, a patient is engaged in a deliberate, constructive double bind. By refusing to be responsible for the patient's actions, the therapist creates a situation in which the patient must assume responsibility and initiative. However, the patient will characteristically attempt to place the burden of external control on the therapist, who must frustrate that attempt in order to elicit the patient's independence. While the patient demands direction, the therapist remains supportive but nondirective; these two mutually exclusive positions constitute the therapeutic double bind for all psychotherapeutic systems (Haley 1959). Eventually, the patient recognizes this double bind, which can be fully resolved only when the patient elects to change his behavior of seeking external directives. This process is common to almost all systems of psychotherapy, but the imagery therapists maintain that encouraging a patient to experience rather than verbalize his fantasies is a more effective means of achieving that end. It is always clear that the patient is responsible for his fantasy productions and that, in that way, he is rehearsing responsibility for his later actions outside of the therapy situation. Experience rather than explanation is the means by which therapeutic change is elicited in the imagery therapies. As the fantasy experiences take place, the patient discovers that all his attempts at blocking, projection, and self-concealment are futile and that he is locked in a situation from which the only exit is to be what he is without restraint (Perls 1969). Patients experience that there is nothing they can do that is other than what they are. Once that realization is experienced, they must either alter their behavior or resign themselves to accept who they are. In either case, the imagery therapists maintain that the experience of that self-acceptance will allow the individual to cease his neurotic vacillation between fantasied alternatives and to begin to act with controlled spontaneity.

Imagery therapists encourage patients to fantasize the logical conclusion of illogical premises and to experience the results. Therefore,
the primary function of the therapist is to suggest specific fantasies
that will enable the patient to undergo therapeutic experiences. Most
important, the therapist selects certain symbols and suggests specific
fantasies that have been demonstrated to have specific results. One
of the earliest psychotherapeutic systems to employ specific fantasies
was that of Robert Desoille (1938). In this system, the therapist
begins by inducing a state of deep relaxation and then suggests that
the patient imagine a scene that is extremely important or pleasant.
Frequently, this suggestion invokes an image of lying on the grass in
an open meadow (Singer 1971). Then, the patient is told he can
fly and is encouraged to soar higher and higher, describing what he
sees. Inevitably, the patient encounters moments of hesitation, or
frightening images appear that threaten to stop the patient's journey.
When these situations arise, the therapist will suggest a course of
action for the patient to take in overcoming that obstacle in order to
continue his journey. On arriving at a specific goal, such as the top
of a mountain, the patient is asked to return to the therapy room,
and the fantasy may or may not be discussed. At approximately the
same time, German psychiatrist Carl Happich developed a more
comprehensive system of imagery therapy that was to serve as the
model for all the later European systems of imagery therapy. Happich (1932) also induced a state of deep relaxation and suggested
the first psychological exercise, which he termed *meadow meditation*.
A patient is told to visualize a meadow and to feel comfortable in
his environment as he describes it in great detail. Following that
fantasy, he is told to walk out into the country and slowly climb a
mountain in an exercise termed *mountain meditation*. In climbing
the mountain, the patient usually encounters an obstacle that must
be overcome, preferably by his own ingenuity or by the therapist
suggesting a means. After overcoming these obstacles, which are
considered to be symbolic of the patient's own fears and anxieties,
the patient is instructed to sit alone on a bench at the top of the
mountain and to listen to the murmur of a flowing stream. These
early, simplistic attempts to explore an individual's subjective fan-

tasies were the basis of the later and more sophisticated systems of autogenic training, Gestalt therapy, and psychosynthesis, which will be examined in greater detail later in this chapter.

Clearly, both Desoille and Happich defined the role of the imagery therapist as that of a guide. Interestingly enough, Joseph Hart concludes his most recent book, *New Directions in Client-Centered Therapy,* with the following: "The psychotherapist or counselor should be at the forefront of this cultural development (i.e., a synthesis of Eastern and Western psychotherapy). By going beyond psychotherapy the therapist becomes a psychopomp, a 'soul guide' " (Hart 1970, p. 591). Although Hart's pronouncement may sound rather "pompous," it does point out the persistence of the concept of therapist as a guide rather than as a strictly verbal analyst. This tradition of the therapist as a guide predates the advent of the earliest European imagery therapies and finds its roots in the tradition of Zen Buddhism. Examining the role of the Zen teacher as therapist, psychologist Edward W. Maupin notes that "while the Zen master does not attempt to interpret the emerging material, he is apparently active in guarding the student against acting out, unconscious projection, and loss of awareness of its subjective origin. . . . All of these are considered blind alleys. Such dangers must be taken into account in any proposed application of Zen or its procedures" (1965, p. 67).

In this ancient tradition as well as in the most current positions of the imagery therapists, emphasis is on gaining great insight by controlled attention to one's inner fantasies under controlled conditions. Additionally, the Zen masters who were the first to develop imagery therapies recognized the use of the double bind as a therapeutic agent and as a means to terminate an individual's tendency to verbalize rather than experience his inner psychological processes. After training a student to achieve a state of deep relaxation, the student is given a *koan* to solve. Masters instruct the students to concentrate on the koan, since it is a problem that requires a solution. Unknown to the student is the fact that the koan is logically insoluble. Examples of traditional koans are "What is the sound of one hand clapping?" or "Show me your face before you were born." Time after time, the student formulates an intellectual solution that is rejected by the Zen master, just as a purely intellectual solution to a patient's difficulty is ineffectual and must be rejected. In the course of meditating on this paradoxical, double-binding koan, the student becomes immersed in his own subjective fantasies and often experiences great despair (Kondo 1952; Herrigel 1956). Finally, the student, like the patient, experiences the insolubility of his situation and must act rather than think and fantasize about acting. In essence, the student has come to recognize that there is no answer to an irrational question, in much the same way that a patient is guided to recognize that there is no solution to his problem that is based on irrational fears and anxieties (Maupin 1965). What is demanded of the Zen student and of the patient in the imagery therapies is to act in a completely spontaneous manner in accord with his deepest convictions. Controlled spontaneity based on extensive introspection is the projected outcome of the Zen discipline and of the imagery therapies.

Entertaining and fantasizing possible outcomes of an impossible situation is the essential task of the patient in imagery therapies; constructing and suggesting fantasies to facilitate that process is the task of the imagery therapist. Specific means are offered by the specific systems of imagery therapy, based on psychological insight extending back into ancient history. Before defining the specific details of these systems, one last major commonality that they all share will be discussed—the induction of a state of deep relaxation in order to promote the onset of active imagination.

THEORETICAL BACKGROUND OF
DEEP-RELAXATION TECHNIQUES

Prototypic of all methods of deep-relaxation techniques is the ancient discipline of meditation. Techniques of meditation are far too numerous to elaborate here, but the goal for each technique is essentially the same. Meditation consists of concentrated attention on some particular object, word, or physiological process in order to induce a state of deep relaxation. While he is in this state of deep relaxation, the meditator achieves a state of detached observation from the thoughts and fantasies that occupy his mind (Naranjo and Ornstein 1971). This state of attention is analogous to "passive concentration" (Schultz and Luthe 1959) and is the necessary prerequisite to entering into and exploring subjective symbolism and fantasies. There is no need to elaborate at this point. We wish simply to point out the longevity of these techniques that are beginning to exert such a profound influence on Western psychotherapies.

Present techniques of deep relaxation derive from two main sources: (1) Jacobson's "progressive relaxation" (1938) and (2) Schultz's "autogenic training" (Schultz and Luthe 1959). Each system of imagery therapy subscribes to an implicit or explicit method of deep relaxation. Their assumption that such a state is a prerequisite for the induction of active imagination should be explored. Additionally, information concerning such techniques is of particular significance for all systems of psychotherapy that seek to comprehend subjective psychological processes.

Jacobson's procedures focus the patient's attention on his muscular tension by having him contract large muscle groups in successively smaller degrees until he is aware of even small amounts of tension. Following this contraction, the patient is then instructed to relax the same muscles in small increments until he feels completely relaxed (Jacobson 1938). This training is designed to enable the patient to use the minimum muscular tensions required for an act by learning to pay attention to that process. Progressive relaxation was used primarily as a means of physical therapy and was later expanded into a psychophysiological system by Schultz and Luthe (1959). Based on hypnotic techniques, their method instructs the patient to sit or lie down and assume a relaxed state of mind. Through a series of directives, such as "my right arm is heavy," the patient enters a state of deep relaxation and is asked to report his fantasies out loud to the therapist. There are numerous articles reporting increased free association and increased accessibility to primary-process fantasies by patients in this state (Schade et al. 1952; Schultz and Luthe 1959). Investigators have found that deep relaxation alleviated symptoms of hypertension and frequently promoted insights into psychosomatic illnesses.

Most notable among the effects of deep relaxation is the spontaneous emergence of thoughts or emotions that were previously unconscious. One possible explanation for such phenomena is offered by Fenichel: "The physical effects of the state of being dammed up emotionally are readily reflected in the muscular system. Pathogenic defenses generally aim at barring the warded off impulses from motility (the barring from consciousness is only a means of achieving this); thus pathogenic defense always means the blocking of certain movements" (1945, p. 246). Relaxation of these muscle tensions is accompanied by a release of the associated conflict. In a series of papers, Braaty (1942, 1952, 1954) discussed the specific musculature constrictions associated with hypertension. Hypertensives characteristically exert tension in the maxillary, respiratory, and abdominal muscles. This observation leads Braaty to hypothesize that shallow breathing is one sign to pay attention to while a patient is engaged in active imagination because it may be indicative of an unconscious conflict. By combining deep relaxation with active imagination, therapists have noted several beneficial results: (1) quicker and more restful sleep (Haverland 1953), (2) feelings of increased energy and endurance (Neufeld 1951), and (3) less susceptibility to emotional outbursts and a greater sense of self-control (Schultz and Luthe 1959). Impressive as these studies are, the most significant fact seems to be that the effectiveness of deep-relaxation therapy is totally dependent on one's commitment to diligent practice in applying exercises. This factor reinforces the concept of the patient as an active participant in the therapeutic process.

Most research concerning deep-relaxation therapy has been conducted on psychosomatic disorders. The range of disorders that have been treated, by a variety of methods, is far too expensive to cover here, but it is significant to note that the most effective therapeutic interventions always involved a combination of deep-relaxation techniques and active imagination (Maupin 1969). Most recently, this combination of techniques has given rise to the use of Biofeedback as a scientifically based system of monitoring the interaction of subjective and physiological states. Research and applications of Biofeedback indicate that this synthesis is a highly effective means of treating physiological disorders, ranging from hypertension and migraine to cardiac arrhythmia as well as psychological disorders, ranging from depression to free-floating anxiety. Methods of deep relaxation accompanied by active imagination evolved before the neurological discoveries of the functioning of the reticular activating system and of communications models of the brain. Prior to these recent insights, therapists and researchers had developed imagery psychotherapies based on the assumption that an individual was capable of regulating unconscious psychological processes and autonomic physiological processes by means of specific exercises. Recent theory and research have confirmed those early insights and offer the possibility of even more effective therapeutic methods.

Imagery therapies have been demonstrated to share several common attributes: (1) patients assume an active role in the therapeutic process, which ostensibly enables them to achieve a state of immediate awareness and controlled spontaneity; (2) therapists engage in the deliberate evocation of unconscious fantasies and function as guides while patients experience the course and consequences of their fantasies and symbolic processes; and (3) various forms of deep-relaxation exercises are used to facilitate the patients' ability to gain access to their unconscious fantasies. This observation can be summarized as follows: "In many forms of meditation the body is kept in a state of relaxation, and when the mind is allowed to wander, it naturally leads to the unresolved conflict-laden areas that press for attention. Thus, what happens in the course of time is that fantasies and reminiscences are contemplated in a state of lucidity, and the person's reactions toward them change" (Naranjo 1969, p. 65). These fantasies are effective means by which the patient may familiarize himself with the information that has been subliminally registered through the autonomic nervous system. Mediating between conscious and unconscious, voluntary and autonomic, is the language of symbolism and fantasy, which the patient must learn to interpret in his own manner. After learning this language, the patient is assumed to be more capable of functioning in a manner consistent with both his conscious and unconscious processes and also more capable of achieving controlled spontaneity.

The use of deep-relaxation techniques leads to immediate advantages that facilitate this self-exploration. Frequently, on entering therapy, patients exhibit a state of anxiety accompanied by some feeling of helplessness. Relaxation techniques are a means of alleviating neurotic anxiety without the use of drugs. There are two effects of this procedure: (1) patients exhibit a marked reduction in anxiety, and the therapist avoids the difficulty of sorting out symptoms from drug side effects; and (2) most important, the patient is given immediate evidence of his personal efficacy in controlling his anxiety. By using phenothiazines, the therapist reinforces the patient's dependence on external influences on his behavior and fosters dependence in the therapeutic process. Relaxation and meditation techniques offer the double gain of avoiding the use of drugs and of offering the patient the immediate experience of self-control and efficacy.

Proceeding from these basic observations, we will next explain specific systems and techniques of several of the major imagery therapies. Each system emphasizes particular aspects of the general attributes discussed up to this point. These similarities and differences will be viewed as the emphasis of a particular system rather than as qualitative and mutually exclusive distinctions.

HYPNOSIS AND PSYCHOTHERAPY

The reluctance of psychoanalysis to consider the use of hypnosis as a psychotherapeutic agent originates in part with Freud. However, in Western cultures, negativistic attitudes toward all ASC have been evident for many hundreds of years. Only within the past twenty-five years has hypnosis been used successfully in the treatment of a wide range of psychopathology—for example, psychotic and neurotic disorders, psychosomatic conditions, and drug and alcohol abuse. Beginning with the pioneer work of Milton Erickson, the modern-day hypnotherapist utilizes such glamorous-sounding techniques as free and directed associations, age regression, abreaction through revivification, automatic writing and drawing, experimentally implanted conflicts, symptom substitution and transformation, visual and auditory hallucinations, scene visualization through crystal gazing, time distortion, suggested dreams, relaxation through autohypnosis, and even simulated electroshock. These techniques are used to directly reduce or eliminate annoying symptoms, promote catharsis or abreaction (release of the emotions believed to support neurotic symptom formation), desensitize or recondition a patient. to a traumatic experience, and to uncover the meaning behind his symptoms (insight) (Moss 1965).

In the sections to follow, it will be seen that hypnosis has been utilized by psychotherapists of varied theoretical persuasions. Research has revealed unexplained favorable, as well as unfavorable, results of the utilization of hypnotherapy. Nevertheless, Frank (1961), in referring to the therapeutic use of hypnosis, notes that "if its advocates are hard pressed to prove the special efficacy of their techniques, and to many the value seems self evident, they can at least take some measure of consolation in the fact that there is little experimental evidence that one form of psychotherapy is superior to any other or, for that matter, that psychotherapy works at all."

THE HYPNOTHERAPY OF MILTON ERICKSON

Beahrs (1971) summarized the following features of Erickson's approach to psychotherapy:

1. Always pay close attention to the patient's verbal and nonverbal communications in order to comprehend both conscious *and unconscious* messages
2. Meet the patient at his own level
3. Achieve control by modification of the patient's behavior
4. *Manipulate* the patient so that his behavior changes *from within* to one more acceptable to himself and others
5. New mental patterns should be such as to exclude or displace

earlier unstable ones, and the former *must* be compatible with the patient's personality structure

6. The unconscious is extremely important, not as a cauldron of seething impulses, but as a potent constructive force for life and growth

7. The major goal of therapy is not abreaction or uncovering but rather *coordination between conscious and unconscious functioning.*

Embedded within this fundamental theoretical and procedural context is Erickson's psychotherapeutic use of hypnosis. Erickson defines hypnosis in a communicational sense: "Induction of hypnotic states and phenomena is primarily a matter of communication of ideas and the elicitation of trains of thought and associations within the subject and consequent behavior responses" (1964*b*). Beahrs divides Erickson's use of hypnotic induction into three categories: (1) standard inductions, (2) interspersal techniques, and (3) surprise techniques. Standard inductions include posthypnotic suggestion, hand levitation, progressive relaxation with eye closure, and the elicitation of unconscious responses. Erickson uses these standard inductions in a basically experiential orientation. "Every effort is made to direct the subject's attention to processes within himself, to his own bodily sensations, his memories, emotions, thoughts, feelings, ideas, past learnings, past experiences, past conditions, as well as to elicit current conditionings, understandings, ideas" (1964*b*). He proceeds with characteristic indirectness during induction and minimizes direct suggestions. Erickson contends that the therapist must maintain a basic flexibility in adapting standard induction techniques to the personality of the patient.

Interspersal techniques are based on the practice of diluting standard hypnotic suggestions with unrelated conversation in order to camouflage the induction procedure. This form of induction is used to overcome defensive resistances and, in general, is more readily acceptable to the resistant patient than direct suggestion. Standard induction may be interspersed with irrelevant dialogue or with conversation related to the patient's presenting behavior, including the patient's own verbalizations. In addition, Erickson has developed interspersal techniques for particular categories of patients. For example, the obsessive-compulsive intellectualizer is asked to attend to the "logic" of a systematic mass of confusing logic, non sequiturs, contradictions, and absurdities interspersed with consistent hypnotic suggestions. Erickson has found that "the patient's unconscious desperately grasps at these coherent thoughts without realizing it, and before long a somnambulistic trance ensues" (Beahrs 1971).

Erickson (1964a) describes the surprise technique as effective when the patient is in a confused or bewildered state and, hence, most receptive to any suggestions that might clarify things. This technique is characterized by swift, unanticipated suggestions, which may result in a vivid hypnotic hallucination facilitating other altered-state phenomena. Beahrs notes that this technique was employed successfully with a woman who was desperately seeking therapy and who had invested in twenty hours of hypnosis without attaining a trance state. Following a greeting, she was authoritatively instructed to "Shut your mouth, sit down all the way into that chair, relax, and go into a deep trance NOW!!"

These induction procedures have been employed by Erickson within the scope of three psychotherapeutic strategies: behavior therapy, uncovering therapy, and displacement of cathexis. The similarities between Erickson's induction procedures and behavior therapy, that is, in the areas of conditioning and desensitization, appear obvious. In cases where Erickson operates from a strictly behavioral orientation, there usually exists a well-defined symptomatology without a complex matrix of related psychopathology. The focus of these behavioral techniques is the assignment to the patient of tasks that facilitate the modification of his behavior from within rather than by the constraint of external regulation.

In speaking of his use of uncovering therapy, Erickson (1954) states: "It is essential that the therapist understand the patient's past, as fully as possible, without compelling him (the patient) to achieve the same degree of special erudition." Beahrs has observed that uncovering is limited primarily to complex phobias, deeply rooted fetishes, and those neurotic and psychotic conditions not amenable to behavior therapy or displacement of cathexis. Erickson has found that the identification of these cases is often difficult and poorly defined. Concerning the emergence of unconscious material in uncovering therapy, Erickson asserts:

> Many psychotherapists regard as almost axiomatic that therapy is contingent upon making the Unconscious conscious. When thought is given to the immeasurable role that the Unconscious plays in the total experiential life of the person from infancy on, whether awake or asleep, there can be little expectation of doing more than making some small parts of it conscious. Furthermore, the Unconscious *as such, not as transformed into the conscious*, constitutes an essential part of psychological functioning. Hence, it seems more reasonable to assume that a legitimate goal in therapy lies in *promoting an integrated functioning* in complementary and supplementary relationships (as occurs daily in well adjusted living) in contrast to the inadequate disordered and contradictory manifestations of neurotic behavior (1953).

Several features of Erickson's uncovering techniques indicate marked divergences from the mainstream of depth hypnotherapy. In particular is Erickson's de-emphasis of (1) regression to the time of the traumatic event and (2) direct questioning under deep hypnosis. These de-emphases are a product of Erickson's concern with an excessively rapid emergence of repressed material into consciousness. The application of total amnesia for the trance as well as the investment of considerable time in waking therapy are deemed necessary to maximize the patient's integration of his insights.

Beahrs (1971) reports the following imaginative use of uncovering hypnotherapy by Erickson:

> One of the most dramatic is a highly disturbed catatonic schizophrenic who alternated between violence and unresponsiveness, from whom several psychiatrists had tried unsuccessfully to take a history or even elicit a response over the course of three years. He was easily hypnotized, and by elaborate questioning with answers by head nodding or shaking, it was found that he wanted to discuss his difficulties but did not know how. An uncovering technique was employed which also encompassed the principles of gradual desensitization, *Repetitive Dreaming* (Erickson, 1967).
> Under hypnosis, the patient was asked to "dream informatively

about his problem, about the reason why he was in a mental hospital." (A dream could be acceptable, since it is an inner experience, and direct communication is not.) The dream was a horrifying nightmare, with a flood of unrecognizable symbolic material. He was later asked several times to dream "the same dream with the same emotions, but with a different cast of characters." Gradually, ward staff noted a decrease in disturbed behavior. Later he was asked to dream again, but "with less pain, less discomfort, and to dream more clearly—to see the characters more plainly." Then it was to be "nearer, clearer, more understandable, but not too understandable," at the same time the emotional charge continued to be desensitized until it could be suggested that "you've progressed well. . . . it won't scare you . . . I'll be here. If things get too rough I can stop everything." Originally the patient had been able to dream only a cauldron of stabbing knives coming at him. Eventually he told of a horrible childhood of immigrating to this country, racial persecution, the distraught parents taking out their frustration by verbally and physically abusing their children, a family history including cancer, alcoholism, and suicide. Most important, the patient had never had the opportunity of learning to communicate, and was forced to shelve all of this past deep into his Unconscious, where it continued to dominate his behavior without his awareness. Following the successful uncovering and desensitization, the patient made a satisfactory life adjustment, married, and never returned to a mental hospital. This example shows more than just uncovering, although this was highly successful. It also involves desensitization, and displacement of cathexis (to a profoundly significant relationship with the therapist). Most important, it shows how hypnosis can be used to learn how to communicate.

Erickson's creative bent is clearly manifested in his use of the technique of automatic writing or drawing in uncovering therapy. In this procedure, the patient is instructed while under hypnosis to give the meaning of a particular neurotic symptom through the use of automatic writing. Beahrs comments that the product is similar to those phenomena characteristic of regressed thinking and dreamwork, that is, it reveals condensation, displacement, and so on. A joint enterprise is then undertaken in which the patient and therapist, in the contexts of both waking and hypnotic therapy, endeavor to unravel the production. This technique(s) is apparently quite similar to the

use of free association in psychoanalysis in that both elicit spontaneous unconscious material that must then be analyzed and interpreted.
The advantages of the hypnotherapeutic technique appear to lie in
diminished interference from ego defenses, reduced filtering through
a linguistic medium, and greater access of unconscious material.
Beahrs offers a case of Erickson's (1954) in which a variant of the
above technique was used in the treatment of a compulsive nympho-
maniac who would sleep "with anyone" but was frigid. After induction of the hypnotic state, the woman was asked to underline the
letters on a randomly selected typewritten page which would spell out
the basis of her problem. The letters underlined spelled "fuckfau-
thor" (sic); this aided "in the uncovering of her well-defended
incestuous drives and subsequent favorable sexual adjustment."

The major portion of Erickson's published case material deals
with the application of his technique known as "displacement of
cathexis." Beahrs briefly summarizes this technique as one in which
"the patient is merely given something new upon which to displace
psychic energy from the original symptoms or conflicts. The conflict
may remain in principle, but it is *de-cathected;* if it is not charged
with energy, it can do no harm." After reading a large number of
case reports in which this technique was implemented, it appears
evident that considerable skill is required to achieve that manipulation of the patient that will result in the positive reinvestment of
substantial psychic energy. Beahrs is correct when he states that the
criticism frequently directed at the seemingly magical nature of these
cures is apparently a product of the extreme subtlety required in
determining the most advantageous energy displacements. A thorough explication of the myriad strategies subsumed under the label
displacement of cathexis is assuredly beyond our scope. Thus, we will
adopt Beahrs's categorization in order to briefly summarize several
of the more prominent techniques.

Symptom Substitution

This technique is frequently used in cases involving highly resistant
symptoms. Erickson chooses not to assume that uncovering therapy

is indicated but, instead, endeavors to alleviate stress by accepting the patient's need for a symptom. This basic acceptance is followed by the substitution of a less painful symptom for the original one, that is, cathexis is displaced to the advantage of the patient.

Symptom Transformation

Erickson often attempts to alter the underlying anxiety from the symptom to a more "natural and healthy object of concern." Certainly, there is much reason to doubt that any fundamental psychodynamic has been dealt with, but in Erickson's terms, "it is often sufficient that the patient see for himself in a convincing manner that things can be different in order to allow extensive displacement of cathexis to occur from within." Beahrs illustrates Erickson's use of symptom transformation in the following interaction with a terminal patient in severe pain. The patient asked, "What can mere words do to get rid of real pain?" Erickson's reply, given authoritatively while gesturing emphatically toward an open door was, "Imagine as vividly as you can a man-eating tiger licking his chops coming through that door to get you—now how much pain do you feel?" Amazingly, the patient's reply, "None," was followed by a feasible hypnotic analgesia. In Erickson's terms, the patient had discovered that his dismal state of affairs could be altered.

Spontaneous Cures

Erickson (1965) reports that one of the most dramatic cases of marked improvement without direct suggestion or uncovering was that of a young psychotic man who had been in a state hospital for nine years without even being able to give a coherent history.

All of his verbal productions were an unintelligible word salad. Erickson introduced himself to the patient, who responded with a flood of word salad. Erickson then responded *in kind*, with unintelligible word salad of his own, timed to match that of the patient. The patient first appeared bewildered, but continued the exchange of word salad much as a normal conversation. In *four hours* (Note: He had not talked intelligibly for *nine years*) he asked, "Don't you think we should talk some sense?" In continuing therapy, coherent phrases were responded to in kind, and word salad in kind, but speech became more and more coherent. Within five months the patient was out of the hospital and gainfully employed! (Beahrs 1971)

Erickson attributes the patient's profound improvement to a thorough displacement of cathexis. The patient had been communicated with at his own level, that is, on his own terms, and a relationship had been established that facilitated the de-cathexis of underlying conflicts and the reinvestment of energy into the encounter with a significant other.

Time Falsification

Beahrs (1971) contends that "the most radical and imaginative of Erickson's displacement techniques are those involving subjective falsification of the patient's experience of time." Following hypnotic induction, the patient receives suggestions that deliberately distort or falsify either his past or future in an attempt to facilitate the transfer of substantial psychic energies into these new constructs. Again, energy is shifted from the underlying conflicts and reinvested to the advantage of the patient. Beahrs observes that (1) Erickson makes certain that total amnesia for the suggestions occurs, thus preventing the constructs from ever reaching consciousness, and (2) such suggestions are effective only as they are in accord with the patient's conscious and unconscious needs. The following case illustration uses the technique of time falsification:

Falsification of the past (Unpublished case report). A young married woman sought therapy because she wanted to have children but at the same time abhorred them. Examination showed that she not only had a deep underlying hatred of children, but that she hated all people in general, including herself. The only positive feeling towards anyone was towards her father and her husband, but even here was severe ambivalence. The problem was too extensive a life-long pattern for an uncovering approach, so it was necessary to find a way to build her capacity for meaningful interpersonal relationships, a formidable task.

Knowing a small child's love of fairy-tale figures, Santa Claus and the like, a hypnotic technique was devised. She was regressed to early childhood, and instructed that she would see the therapist as "The February Man" (February was the month of her birthday). He presented himself in a manner so as to be most pleasing to a small child, and quickly established superb rapport in the regressed state. She was then awakened with total amnesia for the experience, but showed enough improved rapport with the therapist for her to continue in therapy. At the next session, she was regressed to a slightly older childhood state, again saw the therapist as the "February Man," "remembered" her "earlier experience," and again achieved pleasant, satisfying rapport. This process was repeated many times, each regression being an older age and the therapist's manner adjusting accordingly, until by a process of extrapolation the falsification was extended all the way to the present. The patient now had a *new* element in her "past history," a warm and genuine interpersonal relationship which she had never experienced before. No *further therapy or specific therapeutic suggestions were given.* Care was taken to insure complete amnesia for the falsification, so that the "February Man" remained in the patient's Unconscious forever.

The patient rapidly developed increasing ability to enter into more and more meaningful relationships after termination. She eventually raised several children. This case can be seen as a very dramatic example of displaced cathexis, with psychic energy being re-directed into the hypothetical relationship with the "February Man." Something additional happened, whose mechanism needs further investigation; the patient *progressed in a continuous growth into greater mental health.* Possibly the unconscious construct guided her behavior like an internal hypnotic suggestion, just as our normal waking life is guided by unconscious processes. Perhaps the fact that it involved the actuality of a happy, meaningful relationship gave the implicit guiding suggestion that such relationships were possible in real life, and helped to shape further behavior along those lines. Maybe it involved just seeing in her Unconscious that things could be different. At any rate, once a number of meaningful *real* interpersonal relationships had been established, *these* could provide the new focus for cathexis. Once the artificial construct had served its purpose, it was able to become spontaneously and gradually de-cathected, to simply "fade away." This remarkable case, if any single factor needs emphasizing, shows that the most effective direction of displacement of cathexis is into the *formation of trusting interpersonal relationships*. It is this very capacity which is deficient in most people seeking psychiatric help (Beahrs 1971).

THERAPY OF PSYCHOSES

Erickson's ingenuity and high level of clinical expertise are clearly manifested in his approach to the treatment of the borderline patient or the psychotic in remission. In Beahrs's terms, this diagnostic category includes those individuals whose impulses are terrifying. Erickson vehemently repudiates the claim that in such cases a gentle "covering-over" approach to therapy is indicated. He offers the following protocol of his own:

1. Attempt to determine some aspect of the patient that is strong and to fortify it to act as protection against later frightening procedures
2. Locate a facet of the patient's problem that is least threatening and attempt to uncover and work it through
3. Repeat this procedure with progressively more difficult problems in a way that resembles desensitization
4. *Hypnosis, wherever possible, is indicated.*

This is in marked contrast to the usual psychotherapeutic perspective on the use of hypnosis in therapy with psychotics. Erickson contends that the use of hypnotic experience with psychotics should be as varied as possible. His reasons are twofold: (1) hypnosis aids in the establishment of an interpersonally authentic relationship, which is so totally lacking for the psychotic, and (2) a wide variety of hypnotic phenomena *superficially resembling psychotic phenomena* (for example, hallucinations, time distortions, reality distortions, and depersonalization) are experienced in a manner that insures full control. This control of psychoticlike phenomena tends to diminish the likelihood of their recurrence in full-blown psychosis (Beahrs 1971).

The following case illustration is an example of Erickson's work with a prepsychotic:

A good example of this approach (unpublished) is a young Negro registered nurse who was referred to Erickson by several residents who feared she was on the verge of a major psychotic break. Erickson concurred, and felt that her first symptoms would be hallucinations. His first move was to hypnotize her and have her actually hallucinate. This placed the capacity for hallucination under full control and made it non-threatening. She had a history of severe racial oppression, but had nevertheless succeeded in becoming a competent nurse. This strength was reinforced *indirectly* (characteristic of Erickson) by having her enjoy hallucinating a vividly colorful Polish wedding ceremony (identification with another oppressed people who have risen above their degraded status). As it turned out, uncovering was unnecessary. She was trained extensively as a hypnotic subject, and was able to give a lecture on hypnosis to a group of hostile physicians *while in the trance state*. She was able to displace cathexis onto the therapist, then to other meaningful relationships, and onto her extensive autohypnotic skills. She has done well; the psychosis was averted; and she now has considerable status in her nursing profession (Beahrs 1971).

It should not be construed from the comparatively lengthy presentation of Milton Erickson's use of hypnosis in psychotherapy that his are the only worthwhile applications. Much has been written of Erickson's work, and it is difficult to dispute his claim to the title "Father of Hypnotherapy." However, outside of Erickson's approach, we were unable to locate a single systematic overview of the various other attempts to incorporate hypnosis into the psychotherapeutic process. The sections that follow constitute just such an overview, albeit a brief one as, in many cases, very few articles are available in print. The approaches to be introduced include:

1. Hypnosis and short-term psychotherapy
2. Hypnosis and group psychotherapy
3. Hypnosis and Gestalt therapy
4. Hypnosynthesis
5. Hypnodelic therapy
6. Hypnosis and autogenic training

HYPNOSIS AND SHORT-TERM PSYCHOTHERAPY

Hypnosis is often seen as an invaluable adjunct to short-term psychotherapy. The fact that the patient has undergone a fundamental alteration in consciousness facilitates the establishment of a unique kind of relationship between therapist and patient. This relationship is of a supportive but persuasive nature and has been found to be most helpful with patients characterized by high levels of anxiety and frustration. Its proponents claim that through the intensification of rapport, hypnosis often rapidly activates an effective therapeutic relationship.

> Reproduced for the average patient in the trance is the protective child-parent alliance, where needs are gratified and fears become allayed. The sicker the patient the more he reaches for those comforting bounties. This contingency is, of course, an aspect of every helping process; but whereas in the usual interviewing situation considerable time may be needed to register change in the relationship, in hypnosis one may observe a transformation almost immediately. Quickly the patient will respond with hope, trust and a quieting of inner tension. In this soil plantings of therapy can take root, greatly advantageous in short-term therapy (Wolberg 1965).

Wolberg goes on to note that those conditions that appear to respond best to the use of hypnosis in short-term psychotherapy are "anxiety and tension states, certain hysterical conversion symptoms, some obsessive-compulsive reactions, and habit disorders, like insomnia, enuresis, over-eating, nail biting and smoking."

Wolberg and others have noted additional effects of hypnosis on the short-term therapeutic process.

1. The patient's ability to withstand explosive affect is greater during the hypnotic state than during the waking state. In addition, a positive effect on emotional catharsis may continue posthypnotically
2. Hypnosis is seen as a valuable aid in dealing with unconscious conflict.

The influence of hypnosis on repressive processes, facilitating the return to awareness of repudiated psychic aspects, is of great benefit in dealing with unconscious conflict. Hypnosis is particularly valuable in handling resistance, both by detecting it in early stages and by promoting its resolution. In the trance state, dreams may be stimulated, revived and explored, and memories that have been shunted from consciousness may sometimes be restored. In employing hypnoanalytic techniques, such as regression, one may remove amnesia in stress reactions, and lift repressions in conversion and dissociative reactions (Wolberg 1965).

3. The patient's ability to resolve communicational blocks is enhanced under hypnosis. An increased willingness to verbalize may result from the resolution of such resistances
4. Often, a comparatively rapid resolution of transference is possible through the utilization of hypnosis. By catalyzing the transference, hypnosis enables the patient and therapist to focus directly on the reality aspects and interpretation of this phenomenon
5. Since the nature of short-term therapy precludes the possibility of working through well-conditioned patterns, self-hypnosis is often used to aid the patient in mastering those anxieties that accompany the reconditioning of his behavior, allowing him to better convert insight into action.

HYPNOSIS AND GROUP PSYCHOTHERAPY

Perline (1968) notes that "there is no reason to believe that the success reported in the literature derived from individual hypnotherapeutic sessions cannot be had with group hypnotherapeutic sessions." Our review of the research in this area appears to lend at least minimal support to this contention. Peberdy (1960) made use of group hypnotherapy in treating outpatients suffering from morbid tension. The primary hypnotic suggestions were aimed at instilling confidence and relaxation "given with indications of post-hypnotic continuance and reinforcement." Although Peberdy noted an absence of spontaneous abreaction and attributed this to the restraining influence of the group milieu, he concluded that in 25 percent of the cases, morbid tension was much improved, in 25 percent of the cases, it was reasonably improved, and the remaining 50 percent were not aided by group hypnotherapy. While these results are far from extraordinary, they are congruent with the success rates reported for other psychotherapeutic modalities with similar populations.

Some of the most promising work in this area has been Moreno and Enneis's use of hypnodrama as a therapeutic agent. Perline notes that these authors have found that

> In psychodrama the achievement of a state of spontaneous action is dependent upon stimulation of the patient by internal and external processes manipulated between the patient, director, and auxiliary egos. In hypnodrama the hypnosis acts as a psychological starter for the warming-up process in that it frees the patient from many of his inhibiting barriers, and places him in a condition of readiness to rise to a state of greater spontaneity. It is made possible for the patient to warm-up with a minimum of interference from the self. . . .
>
> . . . Hypnodrama has the advantage of showing the patient's deeper personality structure early in the course of therapy. He responds verbally and kinesthetically to a situation and carries through the action on his own terms, involving the major portion of the personality. There is a minimum of defensive and evasive behavior. This enables the therapist to make a good estimate of the situation in terms of the patient's present functioning, and to base his plan of therapy more directly on the patient's needs. As the patient is treated in interaction with his social atom, the therapeutic results will be reflected in his extra-therapeutic life in a relatively short time (Moreno and Enneis 1950).

Moreno concludes with the following:

> Hypnodrama has been found useful in cases where the patient is unable to express himself, through other techniques, sufficiently well to gain catharsis and therapeutic success. It has special value in conversion hysteria and psychopathic states. It has been found to have some success with schizoid personalities. . . . When used in conjunction with psychodrama, it speeds up the therapeutic process without loss of values attributed to therapy given on conscious levels (Moreno and Enneis 1950).

Supple (1962) has found, in using Moreno's hypnodrama techniques, that withholding is largely overcome and that patients appear highly motivated to reveal "their innermost and subconscious thoughts" for both personal and group benefit. He also reported that patients gain access to much deeper psychic levels than is possible with ordinary psychodrama. Supple agrees with Moreno that the major principles of psychodrama are applicable to hypnodrama as well. In addition, they contend that any substantive differences lie in the realm of the patient's behavioral manifestations.

Perline observes that an extremely vital, though less promising, area is the use of group hypnotherapy as a method of treatment for the psychoses. Ilovsky (1962) treated eighty women who had been diagnosed as chronically schizophrenic and whose mean length of hospitalization was six to eight years. They were hypnotized twice weekly for six months, and direct therapeutic suggestions were given at each session. Ilovsky found that this technique was most beneficial in the treatment of paranoid schizophrenics, "whose push of hostility could be controlled and directed through hypnosis to both socially and individually satisfactory channels" (Perline 1968). The results of Ilovsky's year-long investigation revealed that 60 percent of the patients treated were released from the hospital, and the remainder were considered to be better adjusted. Since successful adjustment apparently was equated with increased investment of energy in menial labor and more effective repression of aggressive and hostile impulses, perhaps this "success" may be attributed to Ilovsky's existentially countertherapeutic acceptance of the value orientation of that institution. However, it is difficult to quarrel with a rate of release such as Ilovsky's, particularly in view of the apparently improved functioning of those released.

HYPNOSIS AND GESTALT THERAPY

Although very little has been written on this intriguing subject, there are apparent commonalities underlying hypnotherapy and Gestalt therapy. In essence, we feel that a systematic synergistic relationship between the two approaches may prove to be an extremely valuable approach in psychotherapy. Obvious similarities between the techniques used in the two therapies include the "induction" of "experimental" conflict, the intensification and powerful expression of emotions, and ultimately the awareness of the total affect present in a given situation. The Gestalt therapist attempts to heighten awareness through the use of varied experiential techniques; the hypnotherapist appears to have a distinct advantage, however, as he is able to focus the patient's attention to a particular idea or affect and facilitate a sharp awareness. The hypnotic state may be conceptualized in terms of the Gestalt background principle, in which the idea or affect becomes a clearly defined *gestalt* while the remainder of the perceptual field assumes the character of a ground. Both therapies strive to enable the individual to directly confront his resistances in order to have a greater awareness of them. The Gestalt-like nature of the hypnotherapeutic attempt to allow the individual to confront those realities functionally related to his resistances appears evident. This confrontation, however, occurs while the person is in the hypnotic state and allows him to experience his anxieties in fantasy while in an emotionally secure and supportive milieu.

A fundamental difference between the two approaches lies in Gestalt therapy's relegation of the unconscious to a position of almost absolute unimportance. This clearly appears to be a reaction to the varied depth therapies, especially psychoanalysis, and it also, unfortunately, excludes those techniques that are unique to hypnotherapy. For instance, hypnotic revivification allows the individual to gain conscious awareness of a past occurrence and also to reexperience the original affect associated with that occurrence. Hence, the union of the past event with the affect of the "here and now," seen to be of paramount importance in Gestalt therapy, is often readily accomplished in hypnotherapy. It is through this more direct access to the unconscious obtained through the hypnotic alteration of consciousness that the union, rather than the fragmentation, of the cognitive and affective realms of the individual may be achieved.

HYPNOSYNTHESIS

Conn (1968) maintains that the origin of hypnosynthesis stems from the question, "Why must there be a therapeutic effect if the patient searches deeply into the past?" In answering this query, Conn quotes Progoff (1956):

> . . . for Freud it was something that he took for granted, as though it were a self-evident fact. He was completely committed to the belief that the understanding obtained by tracing events to their antecedents, that is, by reducing "effects" to their "causes," would have a healing result. . . . It was simply a preconception of his, an unconscious habit of his mind, inclining him to regard analytical reasoning not merely as an intellectual mode of procedure but as a "higher" principle, a principle with curative and life-renewing power. . . . This analytical attitude carried strong emotional overtones, so strong in fact that he often applied it with the fervor of a man with a religious dedication.

Hoch (1955) and Conn (1957) accept this critique of reductionistic fervor and attempt to utilize the hypnotic relationship as a present-centered, dynamic experience rather than as an effort to reconstruct the past. In addition, Conn (1952) states the following: "It would appear, therefore, that the common factor in all 'psychogenic' cures is the fostering of self-esteem and active participation both of which are achieved by collaboration in the therapeutic 'learning' situation; thus it is the effective working relationship which is the basis of every therapeutic success." A basic position of hypnosynthesis is that no control or manipulation of the unconscious is possible, and, consequently, the patient cannot be coerced into improved functioning by any systematized approach predetermined by the therapist. The individual must discover his own path toward optimum functioning—that curative insight comes from within and is not so much a matter of offering something to the patient as it is "a matter of making the patient give up or lose something" (Zilboorg 1952).

Conn (1968) notes that the theory of hypnosynthesis is not at all in accord with Barber's (1964) contention that the term *hypnosis* is devoid of meaning. Rather, *hypnosis* is accepted and defined as one of a variety of ASC. More comprehensively, however, it is viewed "as a state to which multi-dimensional processes have contributed (Weitzenhoffer 1961) and a dynamic relationship, in which the subject is always aware of and in contact with the operator, so that questions can be asked concerning meaning and motivation at any time and at all levels" (Conn 1952). Specifically, hypnosis can be conceptualized as an alteration in reality testing that includes the subject's "conviction that the world is as suggested by the hypnotist rather than a pseudoperception of the suggested world" (Sutliffe 1961).

Hypnosynthesis makes use of biographic data as offered and does "not persist in seeking something behind and beyond experiences" (Lidz 1966). Conn notes that the basis of this orientation, as well as of hypnosynthesis as a theory, lies in Adolph Meyer's concept of psychobiology. Meyer's position is in opposition to any dichotomization, whether it be love-hate, masculine-feminine, masochism-sadism, or activity-passivity (Muncie 1951) and, as a result, hypnosynthesis speaks in terms of "more or less consciousness." In addition, hypnosynthesis has tended to reject the notion of "psychic energy" and is, in general, critical of the formulation of psychopathology in terms of an "undischarged libido." Conn (1968) mentions several other basic features of hypnosynthesis:

1. The individual is seen as an indivisible unit motivated by values and purposes as well as by drives
2. Only when the patient feels secure in therapy will he be able to reveal what is meaningful to him
3. When a patient becomes uncommunicative, the invocation of the concept of unconscious resistance is inadvisable. The silence is accepted as either a need to assert oneself or the searching for a behavioral cue by a passive-dependent individual. The therapist reacts with acceptance and approval in an attempt to facilitate patient expression. As Meyer con-

tended, "He who thinks that man will not act unless he is prompted by pain and conflict maligns nature"

4. The quest to uncover infantile traumas is replaced by the deployment of attention to the meaning of a repetitive pattern in order to allow the patient to learn to accept responsibility for his contribution to his stressful life situation (Whitehorn 1947)

5. A premium is placed on patient spontaneity, and he is instructed from the outset not to please the therapist

6. Stress is placed on the notion that "the patient is the active factor in his own recovery and that the relationship with the therapist is only a source of emotional stabilization, helping the patient to liberate his own natural forces of recovery and development" (Solovey and Milechnin 1958).

As far as the actual implementation of hypnosis is concerned, no mention of the word is made during the initial interview. In addition, no discussion of the topic is undertaken except to mention that the patient will not be asleep and will hear all that is said to him. The number of hypnotic sessions is determined by the patient while he is in the hypnotic state. Conn (1968), in discussing the altered-state aspects of hypnosynthesis, states that

The patient is never "challenged" while under hypnosis. Hypnosynthesis is opposed to the traditional concept of hypnosis as being a passive, physician-centered technique which does not fit in with the data derived from clinical practice and the change in patient-physician relations which has taken place in our culture during the past 50 years. The hypnotic condition more closely approximates the waking state than it does physiological sleep. The defenses are not obliterated, the capacity to reflect and synthesize remains unimpaired and an analysis of transference and resistance is possible in the hypnotic state (Wolberg 1945). The patient, while in the trance state, is very much aware of whether he is being investigated (physician-centered goal) or being treated in accordance with his basic characterologic needs. If the hypnotic situation is utilized as a present experience rather than a futile attempt to relive the past, the patient is freed from the compulsion to produce psychological contents which fit nicely into the postulation system of the therapist.

HYPNODELIC THERAPY

The word *hypnodelic* represents a condensation of the words *hypnosis* and *psychedelic* and was first coined by Ludwig and Levine (1965). The incorporation of hypnosis into what is basically a form of psychedelic therapy was seen as valuable in that it served to modulate and modify the character and course of the LSD reaction. Hypnodelic therapy was initially used in a pilot study with narcotic drug-addicted patients (Levine, Ludwig, and Lyle 1963), many of whom made powerful claims of therapeutic benefit including improved functioning, marked symptom relief, and a radically altered *Weltanschauung*. Following this study, a controlled investigation was designed and carried out in which seventy addicts were randomly assigned to five brief treatment techniques employing LSD, psychotherapy, and hypnosis. The results indicated that those patients treated with the hypnodelic technique (LSD, hypnosis, and psychotherapy) for a single session showed more improvement than those treated with (1) LSD and psychotherapy, (2) LSD alone, (3) psychotherapy, and (4) hypnotherapy, when evaluated both two weeks and two months following treatment (Ludwig and Levine 1965).

In utilizing hypnodelic therapy, the initial interview consists of an exploration of the patient's history and the presentation of problems. In addition, however, the patient is trained in the induction of the hypnotic trance by the use of high fixation of eyes. The actual administration of LSD in therapy occurs ten days later, employing a dose of 125 to 200 micrograms. A hypnotic trance is induced during the latency period (thirty to sixty minutes) after the drug is ingested. Gubel (1962) noted that many of the experiential aspects of LSD phenomenology were similar in nature to those of the hypnotic state, and, thus, there appeared to be a relatively smooth fusion of the effects of LSD and hypnosis. Intensive psychotherapy, which the investigators described as closest to the "insight-interpretative" therapy depicted by Ellis (1955), is then carried out while the patient is in this jointly altered state of consciousness. The therapist encourages the patient to examine particular problem areas, makes direct interpretations to the patient, and endeavors to foster abreaction. Following this two-and-a-half- to three-hour session, the patient receives posthypnotic suggestions to remember all that transpired during therapy and to continue thinking about the problems discussed.

Concerning the seemingly magico-mystical nature of the substantial therapeutic change occurring in a single session, Levine and Ludwig (1966) state:

> There are, in fact, numerous reports by investigators using hypnosis (Brenman and Gill 1947), narcotherapy (Kalinowsky and Hoch 1961; Sargant and Slater 1944), psychotherapy (Harris, Firestone and Wagner 1955; Laidlaw 1950; Rosenbaum 1964; Saul 1951) and "psychedelic therapy" (Blewett and Chivelos; Chivelos, Blewett, Smith and Hoffer 1959; Osmond 1957; Sherwood, Stoloroff and Harman 1962; van Rhijn 1960) that these changes occur. Schmiege (1963) has pointed out that many accept the fact that certain traumatic incidents occurring early in a person's life may produce serious psychological consequences, but for some reason there are only a few who are willing to entertain the hypothesis that one or several profound therapeutic experiences can produce marked and lasting improvement in patients.

It is interesting to note that following the hypnodelic session, the patients continued thinking about and exploring their experiences and difficulties, and "it was during this time that many began to feel the pieces of the puzzle were fitting together." Throughout the two-month evaluation period, the treatment experience remained mentally vivid and appeared to induce a period of introspection and attempts at personal problem solving. Levine and Ludwig (1955) offer the fascinating conjecture that "during hypnodelic therapy a significantly greater 'alteration' is produced in patients compared to any of the other techniques used. Whether there is a causal relationship between the degree of alteration in consciousness and amount of therapeutic change is an intriguing hypothesis."

HYPNOSIS AND AUTOGENIC TRAINING

A basically autohypnotic training regimen called *Autogenic Training* has been developed during the past half century by the German psychiatrist J. H. Schultz in 1932. The lack of published material in this country on Autogenic Training is evidenced by the fact that recently only ten of 604 papers published in the area originated in the United States. The definitive text on Autogenic Training is Schultz's (1953) *Das Autogene Training: Konzentrative Selbst-Entspannung,* which is literally translated as *Autogenic Training: Self-Relaxation through Concentration.* The following definition of this method is offered by Schultz: "[Autogenic Training] is a method of rational physiologic exercises designed to produce a general psychobiologic reorganization (*Umschaltung*) in the subject which enables him to manifest all the phenomena otherwise obtainable through hypnosis." Schultz views Autogenic Training as a graduated series of mental exercises geared to improving functioning and to helping decrease or remove maladaptive behavior, that is, neurotic and psychosomatic symptoms. These exercises are seen as capable of enhancing one's ability to heighten inner relaxation, to effect psychophysiologic alterations, and to increase one's capacity for introspection and insight.

Schultz began his work in 1920 by asking hypnotic subjects to report on the experience of entering the trance state. Following an analysis of their protocols, Schultz found that certain bodily sensations, such as an abnormally "heavy" feeling and an unusual sensation of "radiating warmth," were reported as an integral part of the trance experience. He concluded that "a specific suggestive alteration of somato-psychic functioning" (*Umstellung*) took place during the hypnotic alteration of consciousness, and, subsequently, he developed his method of Autogenic Training "to enable an individual himself to produce these specific manifestations of altered somatopsychic functioning manifested spontaneously during and after the induction of hetero-hypnosis" (Gorton 1958). Analyses of this spontaneous, hypnosis-related somatopsychic alteration led to the conclusion that the sensation of heaviness was intimately related to muscular relaxation and to the subsequent postulation that this relaxation was an integral part of the organismic reorganization that occurs with the induction of the hypnotic ASC. Schultz further reasoned that a similar reorganization could be effected via systematic training in self-relaxation. Gorton notes that a vital part of this training is Schultz's formulation of the "paradox of self-induced passivity," a concept quite similar to the notion of "passive volition" currently in vogue in the research literature on Biofeedback. In short, the individual must learn to abandon himself to a continuing organismic process rather than to employ consciously any exercise of "will." Just as a "willing" of sleep cannot help but perpetuate the waking state, so does an analogous situation occur in the psychosomatic reorganizational concomitants of the induction of the hypnotic ASC.

Schultz maintains that the following factors are necessary if the spontaneous psychobiologic reorganization of hypnosis is to be duplicated in Autogenic Training:

1. High motivation and cooperation of the subject
2. Reasonable degree of subject self-direction and self-control
3. A particular bodily posture is necessary
4. Reduction of external stimuli to a minimum and mental focusing on endopsychic processes to the exclusion of the external environment
5. Presence of a monotonous input into the various sensory receptors
6. Concentrated deployment of attention on the somatic processes in order to effect an inward focusing of consciousness. This is seen as a primal mode of experience, in which a de-cathecting of external stimuli is accomplished by attention deployment on bodily sensations. The result is a vegetative-passive level of functioning merging into a deeply focused meditative alteration of consciousness
7. Given these conditions, an overpowering, reflexlike psychic reorganization occurs
8. Dissociative and autonomous mental processes can then occur,

leading to alteration of ego functioning and a dissolution of ego boundaries. The inner experiential and conceptual life assumes a plasticity of imagery, and a dreamlike state of consciousness results (Gorton 1958)

Schultz recapitulates the above as follows: "In a motivated, cooperating subject who has some measure of autonomous control, a diminution of external stimuli, the assumption of a suitable bodily posture, and a monotonous sensory input aided by attention to somatic processes, leads to a focusing of concentration or narrowing of consciousness which makes possible dissociative and automatic phenomena with an alteration of organismic and endopsychic functioning." Schultz's contention is that any "normal" individual can undergo this psychobiologic reorganization, or *Umschaltung,* and can thus be hypnotized or trained autogenically, given the requisite conditions. This contention has been corroborated by extensive experience with "normal" subjects. The fundamental element involved in all cases is viewed as "a decrease in biologic tonus or waking consciousness," and the fundamental purpose is seen as the teaching of the subject to attain the basic *Umschaltung* himself through the above procedures. The interested reader is referred to Wolfgang Luthe's English translation of Schultz's definitive text for a detailed description of the psychophysiologic procedures employed.

Following the completion of Autogenic Training, the subject is able to instantaneously induce "feelings of heaviness and warmth that are both subjectively and objectively well generalized" (Gorton 1958). In addition, Gorton lists the following self-regulated functions resulting from the basic *Umschaltung,* which have been extensively verified:

1. The independent regulation and quieting of heart action
2. Profound respiratory alterations, such as apnea or hyperventilation
3. Self-regulatory suffusion of the abdomen by intense sensations of warmth. This is seen as instrumental in the process of relaxation

4. Substantial cooling of the forehead at will
5. Attaining considerable relaxation at will—that is, calming oneself and dampening the influence of disturbing emotions
6. Self-induced catalepsy, making possible dynamic effort and the mobilization of active energy when necessary
7. Sensory alteration—that is, increasing or decreasing receptivity to external or internal stimuli. The induction of anesthesias or heightened sensory experience may thus be accomplished
8. Vasomotor regulation—that is, objectively measurable changes in skin temperature of 1°C
9. Facilitation of memory
10. Introspection—that is, access to the dynamics of the unconscious in the relaxed state of concentration
11. Nirvana therapy—that is, the induction of a euphoric state of exaltation

ADVANCED STAGES IN AUTOGENIC TRAINING

Once the subject is able to attain rapidly this state of somatopsychic reorganization or *Umschaltung,* "so that the body is experienced as a heavy, warm, reposing mass suffused by a regular pulse and a quietly flowing breath . . . the cool head somehow 'floats above' the formless, warm body. The facial expression . . . is calm as in deep sleep, there is complete relaxation of all skeletal muscles, the body skin is warm and the forehead noticeably cool. . . ." He may then be prepared to pursue certain advanced techniques in Autogenic Training. Gorton (1958) summarizes these advanced techniques as follows:

A first step in the advanced technique is the *voluntary rotation of the eyeballs upward and inward*—"looking at the center of the forehead." This maneuver is an ancient tradition of hypnotic and meditative practice. It frequently triggers a sudden, over-powering intensification of the autogenic "Umschaltung," and a definite facilitation and intensification of accomplishment of the training is brought about. Good subjects are capable of remarkable feats by means of this convergence-reinforcement. Anesthesia for a third degree burn produced by a lighted cigarette placed on the back of the hand for one and one half minutes can be obtained.

If an *intensification of psychic experience* is desired, the following series of procedures is employed:

To develop the subject's ability to *experience endopsychic phenomena visually* he is encouraged to discover his "personal color" by asking him to visualize any color he likes. The ability to conceptualize different colors at will is then developed systematically. As control over endopsychically visualized colors is gained there is usually an intensification of the experiential reality of these inner visual experiences. The trainee's ability to control his color experiences adequately may be tested by disrupting them through variations in environmental illumination or the introduction of disturbing sounds. The task of visualizing various objects is taken up next. This involves the recapitulation of the visual experiences that occur during heterohypnosis. Attempt is made to visualize abstract subjects, and this often produces material reminiscent of automatic drawing or abstract art. Such material can be used psychotherapeutically and analyzed like dreams or fantasies. Well integrated subjects can often work through unconscious conflicts, achieve extensive emotional catharsis, and gain valuable personality insights at this stage. Frequently they are unaware that what they report spontaneously represents well-known psychodynamic mechanisms.

The subject may then be asked to "see" *a picture expressive of his basic emotional needs.* Static or dynamic hallucinations of complete subjective reality may then be experienced, dealing with archaic psychic motifs and mythological material, and these are sometimes felt to be ego-alien and threatening.

The subject may then be asked to hallucinate the image of a certain person and to absorb himself fully in this experience. As in dreams, it is easier to hallucinate persons toward whom one is indifferent than those for whom one has positive feelings. Careful analysis and examination of one's feelings toward the individual in question is possible in the autogenic trance. "Questioning the unconscious" can be carried out by the subject or by the training supervisor and the resulting inner experiences noted. This exercise leads to the expression and representation of innermost personality experiences and attitudes; serious psychotherapeutic work is thereby made possible. These inner experiences of extraordinary subjective reality can lead to the *analysis of complexes, nuclear personal experiences*, and to the consideration of questions of fundamental existential value.

Finally, the subject may be led to develop a *personal formula of self-understanding* to help him achieve the *goal of self-actualization*. This phase of training deals with extremely subtle, sensitive, and affectively charged psychic material. Only a great deal of caution, judgment and empathy towards the subject, as well as psychiatric training on the part of the supervisor, allow for its successful completion.

FURTHER APPLICATIONS OF AUTOGENIC TRAINING

In Europe, Autogenic Training has also been used extensively for the treatment of (1) psychophysiologic or psychosomatic disorders such as bronchial asthma, cardiospasm, hyperventilation syndrome, and functional gastrointestinal disturbances and (2) psychoneurotic disturbances, particularly those involving alterations in the action of the autonomic nervous system. As an adjunct to or as a replacement for traditional methods of psychotherapy, Autogenic Training has been successful in heightening the organism's total capacity for functional adaptation, including an increased resistance to dysfunctional anxiety. Gorton also makes the point that unconscious material becomes more readily accessible during the process of Autogenic Training, a fact that is seen as accelerating progress in most therapeutic systems. A more obvious advantage is the diminished time commitment for the patient—the exercises require a total of ten to twenty minutes per day.

HYPNOSIS AND CREATIVITY

It should be noted that the transcendence of culturally imposed imprints and of societal conditioning always has been a goal for creative persons. Hypnosis . . . when used properly, enable[s] artists to stand apart from their culture, at least for a brief period of time. In so doing, they sometimes make an artistic statement that encompasses all cultures, a statement which in time may become a classic painting or poem. For all these reasons, the hypnotic trance . . . and other forms of altered consciousness are worthy of serious study if the act of human creation is to be better understood, guided, and encouraged (Krippner 1969*b*).

We included this brief mention of hypnosis and creativity as a metatherapeutic issue. It should be clear to any psychotherapist, no matter how rationalistic his bent, that real insight is most often intuitive and, hence, creative. To the extent that hypnosis can foster this creative process and allow the individual greater access to growth-enhancing insight, it constitutes an invaluable adjunct to psychotherapy.

Krippner (1965, 1969*b*) has persuasively made the point that ASC may be instrumental in fostering creativity because creativity is itself fundamentally preverbal and unconscious in origin. In attempting to construct a relationship between ASC and the creative act, he notes Vinacke's belief in the importance of penetrating the culturally imposed linguistic structure in order to allow for the emergence of the creative act: "For creative thought to occur, it is essential that the individual be able to manipulate his perceptions and past experiences and to recognize and use his emotional and artistic responses. That is, there must be some degree of freedom in mental activity, an ability to reorganize experience with relative independence of external restraints" (Vinacke 1952). In Krippner's conceptualization, hypnosis is seen as a relatively safe and adaptable mode of consciousness alteration capable of focusing attention with such intensity that subliminal stimuli are perceived. Thus, hypnosis may assist in the vital penetration of the preverbal realm constituting the domain of origin of the creative act.

Krippner (1965, 1969*b*) cites numerous examples of individual creative efforts accomplished under varied alterations of waking-state consciousness. Certainly this is a fertile area for investigation, especially in the face of prevailing rationalistic ideologies that all too often implicitly assume an equation of creativity and conscious thought. Huxley (1963) supports this notion when he states that "the field of the psychiatrist and the psychologist today is nothing less than the comprehensive study of hypnosis, drugs, education, mysticism, and the subconscious, of mental disease and mental health, of the relation between . . . all the psychological forces operating in man's life—emotional, imaginative, intellectual and moral—in such a way to minimize conflict and to maximize creativity."

— 10 —

Toward a Transpersonal Psychotherapy

If one were given the problem of formulating an ideal imagery therapy, each of the imagery therapies to be discussed here would offer a significant contribution. Although each system claims to be complete, each one can be considered as a component in an ideally comprehensive system including deep relaxation exercises and the experience of prescribed fantasies leading to a state of controlled spontaneity. Clearly, no such system exists, but the constantly evolving imagery therapies do seem to offer the possibility of a comprehensive psychotherapy. In approaching this problem, this chapter will deal with the specific techniques of the following imagery therapies: (1) Autogenic Therapy, (2) Psychosynthesis, (3) Zen and Morita psychotherapy, (4) Jungian analytical therapy, and (5) Gestalt therapy. Jungian and Gestalt therapy will not be specifically summarized because such a task is an obvious impossibility. References to each of those systems will be used to clarify and expand upon the principles of the lesser-known and less well-developed imagery therapies. Thus, we can point out the means by which the lesser-known systems can lend significant contributions to the more highly developed Jungian and Gestalt psychotherapies. Detailed examinations of these systems will demonstrate that the imagery therapies in conjunction with Biofeedback techniques can create the foundation for a comprehensive system of psychotherapy.

AUTOGENIC THERAPY

When Autogenic Training was first formulated by Schultz, it was not intended as a method of therapy but rather as a simple method of relaxation. These relaxation techniques were based on the research on hypnosis conducted by brain physiologist Oskar Vogt during the period from 1890 to 1900. While experimenting with hypnosis, Vogt observed that certain patients were able to place themselves in a hypnotic state for self-determined periods of time; this gave rise to the concept of autohypnosis. Vogt noted that these patients were capable of reducing fatigue and tension in this autohypnotic state and that psychosomatic disorders such as headaches were greatly reduced in occurrence and potency (Luthe 1962). Combining Vogt's concept of autohypnosis with a series of specific exercises, J. H. Schultz formulated the basis for Autogenic therapy, the general purpose of which is to integrate mental and bodily functions, to achieve inner relaxation, to produce psychophysiologic changes, and to improve the capacity for introspection and insight (Gorton 1958). Each of these factors of autogenic therapy has been demonstrated to have specific clinical applications, especially in alleviating psychosomatic disorders.

Training exercises devised by Schultz were based on the fact that most hypnotic subjects experience two types of sensations: (1) an abnormally heavy sensation in the body and (2) a sensation of radiating warmth. Autogenic Training provides a systematic series of exercises that enables an individual to self-induce those sensations and the accompanying psychological state of "passive concentration" (Luthe 1962). Training proceeds in three discrete stages (although the Autogenic literature does not actually refer to stages of progress). The three stages are: (1) learning a posture and a series of exercises designed to induce a meditative state of deep relaxation, (2) experiencing subjective fantasies and controlling physiological functions, and (3) engaging in prescribed exercises intended to elicit specific unconscious fantasies. In stage one, the patient sits comfortably in a chair with his eyes closed; he is instructed to concentrate on the phrase, "I am quite still." Once a quiescent state has been achieved, the patient is instructed to concentrate on the phrase, "My right (left) arm is very heavy." According to evidence from electromyography, there is significant relaxation in the muscles of the patient's forearm when this phrase is concentrated on. Generalization of this sensation of heaviness occurs in most patients; they experience a sensation of increased body weight. Additional instructions are given in the following sequence, at varying intervals depending on the individual's responsiveness: quiet the beating of the heart, bring the breathing to a smooth and slow rhythm, experience a feeling of warmth exuding from the abdomen, and, last, concentrate on a cooling breeze blowing over the forehead (Gorton 1958). Adequate mastery of this state of deep relaxation requires twelve to eighteen weeks of practicing approximately a half hour per day. According to objective and subjective evidence, the state obtained during this initial stage of Autogenic Training is similar to states achieved through various systems of Eastern meditation.

Following the completion of this stage, the patient enters stage two, which involves the ability to enter into the stage-one state of deep relaxation with increasing ease and rapidity. One goal of stage two is to "increase or decrease the receptivity to external or internal stimuli" (Gorton 1958). Once an individual is capable of sustaining the stage-one state of passive concentration, he is capable of controlling various physiological functions through autosuggestion. Schultz reports that patients are capable of blocking out the pain of inserting three large dental fillings as well as of warming their feet by raising the skin temperature as much as 3°F. Additional research reports that hypertensive patients are capable of producing a significant drop of the systolic (ten to twenty-five percent) and the diastolic (five to fifteen percent) blood pressure (Luthe 1962). Electroencephalographic recordings indicate that this stage of Autogenic Training is characterized by an increase in alpha activity (eight to twelve Hz, or cycles per second); this increase is associated with mental relaxation (Kamiya 1968). At the present time, this control of autonomic functions remains unsolved, but psychiatrist Wolfgang Luthe

has offered one explanation that is consistent with the current neurological theories presented at the beginning of this book: "Autogenic
Training involves self-induced (autogenic) modifications of cortico-
diencephalic interrelations, which enables natural forces to regain
their otherwise restricted capacity for self-regulatory normalization.
. . . the function of the entire neurohumoral axis (cortex, thalamus,
reticular system, hypothalamus) is directly involved and . . . the therapeutic mechanism is not unilaterally restricted to either bodily or
mental functions" (Luthe 1962). During the stage-two state of passive concentration, individuals are capable of controlling various
autonomic functions through autosuggestion. However, patients
report that these various physiological alterations are not induced by
means of verbal directives but rather by learning to concentrate on
various sensations, such as warmth, or by concentrating on a mental
image that they learn to associate with the desired physiological
response (Luthe 1962). As impressive as the medical applications
seem to be, the main goal of Autogenic Training is to allow the
patient to obtain this state of physiological quiescence in order to
become more attuned to his unconscious symbolic processes and
fantasies.

Having achieved a state of deep relaxation and a degree of autonomic control after three or four months of practice, the patient
enters into stage three. One directive is the key to stage three—the
"voluntary rotation of the eyeballs upward and inward—looking at
the center of the forehead" (Schultz and Luthe 1959). This procedure is advocated by all systems of meditation and has been
recently demonstrated to increase the production of alpha rhythms
in the brain (Kamiya 1969). This stage of training is intended to
produce an "intensification of psychic experience by increasing an
individual's ability to visually experience endopsychic phenomena"
(Gorton 1958). First, the individual is instructed to visualize and
discover his "personal color" and then to experience any color at will.
Next, he is asked to visualize various objects in order to concretize
the experience of his subjective states. Third, the patient is asked to
"see a picture expressive of his basic emotional needs" (Gorton
1958). In this exercise, frequently, static or dynamic fantasies occur

that are of an archaic or mythic variety. Autogenic therapy relies primarily on spontaneous, as opposed to induced, fantasies (Beck 1970) and permits the patient to simply experience his fantasies with a minimum of analytic interpretation. Last, the patient is instructed to visualize the image of a person and to concentrate on the strengths and shortcomings of that person. At this point, the Autogenic therapist engages in "questioning the unconscious" (Gorton 1958) by involving the fantasied person in a dialogue; in it, the patient can express his ideals and fears by referring to the fantasied person. Literature on Autogenic therapy does not offer specific directives concerning either the contents or procedures by which this questioning of the unconscious might be made optimally productive. However, descriptions of the therapist's activities do not seem to differ from standard therapeutic practice, with the exception of the fact that the patient has been trained to experience his fantasies more vividly than is usually the case in traditional psychotherapies.

Although Autogenic therapy employs extensive hypnotic techniques, practitioners insist on one critical factor in distinguishing Autogenic Training from classical hypnosis. That factor is that the patient is trained over a long period of time to enter into a meditative state, and the initial use of hypnosis by the therapist is a means of instructing and familiarizing the patient with his ability to enter into that state of his own volition (Schultz and Luthe 1959; Gorton 1958; Luthe 1962). Most significantly, Autogenic Training prescribes a specific technique by which a patient is allowed to experience his subjective fantasies with increasing vividness and then to examine them in a mode of "passive concentration." All psychotherapeutic systems that depend largely on exploring the subjective processes of individual patients could facilitate that process by means of the explicit directives offered by this therapy.

Autogenic Training is an adequate system of preparing a patient to experience his symbolic fantasies, but it does not provide an adequate means of interpreting and analyzing the contents of those fantasies. For this reason it can be considered an introduction to a more comprehensive therapy. Whereas Autogenic Training does not provide a system of interpreting the contents of patients' fantasies, the second imagery therapy, Psychosynthesis, does not offer explicit directives of deep relaxation but does provide a highly developed system of prescribed fantasies and an interpretive theory.

PSYCHOSYNTHESIS

Beginning with his doctoral dissertation in 1910, psychiatrist Roberto Assagioli developed an extensive imagery therapy termed *Psychosynthesis*. It is based on the induction of daydreams and meditation experiences concerning specific sets of symbolic images. Standard hypnosis is occasionally used in order to facilitate the patient's experience, but the procedure of Psychosynthesis is simply to instruct the patient to focus on inner images. It is assumed that such focusing creates hypnoidal states since "ideosensory conditioning is a classical attribute of hypnotic inductions" (Aaronson 1968). Activity on the part of the therapist is a function of how much support and guidance the patient requires in the course of his fantasy. Generally, therapists advocate that interventions should be kept to a minimum and that the patient should be encouraged to deal with the situations that arise on his own. According to Assagioli, "the patient's unconscious is a wiser source of guidance and direction for the patient's life than the conscious mind of the therapist" (Assagioli 1965, p. 7). In this respect, there are many similarities between Psychosynthesis and Jungian therapy; the main difference is that Psychosynthesis prescribes specific fantasies to achieve certain ends in probing the unconscious. Briefly, the goal of Assagioli's system can be stated as follows: "The goal is not analysis; it is much more. It is synthesis, namely an integration, a wholeness, a unity, a harmonious use of all our functions . . . in learning theory terms . . . the substitution of healthy response tendencies for previously neurotic responses of fear and avoidance" (Gerard 1964, p. 16) It is assumed that an individual is capable of contacting an inner self that is a source of intelligence, wisdom, inner direction, and purpose. This self is analogous to Jung's "Self," Maslow's "Self-Actualized Person," and Fromm's individual who functions with a "Productive Orientation"

(Maddi 1968, p. 496). An individual must strive to achieve access to this source, and it is the role of the therapist to facilitate this process.

There are two fundamental stages of Psychosynthesis that must be experienced by means of specific fantasies: (1) personal Psychosynthesis and (2) spiritual Psychosynthesis. Personal Psychosynthesis occurs in four stages: (1) a thorough knowledge of one's personality, using free association and general techniques of psychotherapy; (2) focusing on the control of various elements of the personality—in this stage, the individual confronts the "shadow" (Jung 1969*a*), or negative aspects, of the personality; (3) the realization of one's true self or the discovery of a unifying center; and (4) the formation or reconstruction of a personality around and consistent with this center (Gerard 1964). Each of these stages involves experiencing prescribed fantasies that are the means of progressing toward the goal of personal integration.

Symbolic visualization (active imagination) is the means by which the patient learns to develop and control his imagination and fantasies. Assagioli contends that it is possible to speak to the unconscious in its own language of images and, therefore, to affect unconscious processes that, in turn, influence conscious behavior. Initially, the therapist suggests the controlled visualization of dynamic symbols and, later, the controlled visualization of symbolic scenes. As in Autogenic Training, the patient is instructed to maintain a consistent image of an object or symbol in order to begin to acquire control over his imaginative faculties. For example, patients are instructed to visualize a symbol of "harmonious human relations," such as two clasped hands or to visualize the transformation of a "worm to a chrysalis to a butterfly" (Assagioli 1965). Symbolic productions are considered to be means of psychodiagnostics as well as psychotherapeutic tools. One visualization exercise commonly used for diagnostics is the envisioning of the unfolding of a rose. Clinical inferences are: a patient with repressed hostility may envision a rose with many thorns, a withdrawn patient may express difficulty in allowing the rose to unfold, and an impatient person may be unwilling to allow the rose to unfold slowly (Gerard 1964).

Following the controlled visualization of dynamic symbols, the patient is instructed to visualize symbolic scenes that may be suggested either by the therapist or by the patient. This technique is the essential method used to guide a patient through the three last stages of personal Psychosynthesis. Several major fantasies are suggested to the individual in order that he might experience the transformation of his personality; one example is that he restore a neglected garden and report each detail of the restoration aloud to the therapist. Another series of exercises is intended to allow the patient the experience of finding a place of solace, or unifying center, within himself. Examples of these fantasies are: reaching the safety of a lighthouse after a dangerous swim in treacherous waters, or climbing a precarious mountain just in time to witness the sun rising (Assagioli 1965). It is significant that therapists can often elicit threatening or anxiety-inducing images by encouraging patients to move downward into tunnels or caves. In contrast, they can induce feelings of exhilaration and pleasure by suggesting upward movements over obstacles. What seems to be emerging is a body of research and theoretical literature indicating that certain fantasies elicit dynamic psychological processes leading to profound personal transformations. Six basic situations have been demonstrated to elicit marked personality changes (Desoille 1966):

1. Obtaining a sword, or similar symbol, for men and a bowl, or similar symbol, for women
2. Voyage to the bottom of the sea
3. A visit to the cave of the witch
4. A visit to the cave of the wizard
5. A visit to the cave of the mythical beast
6. A visit to Sleeping Beauty

Similar exercises have been advocated by Luner (1966), who cites three effective fantasies: (1) a visit to a meadow, (2) climbing up a mountain, and (3) following the course of a stream. In reporting the images and fantasies that occurred spontaneously during psychedelic-drug experiences, Masters and Houston (1966) noted strikingly similar categories of fantasied journeys. In all of the above fantasies, the essential characteristic of therapeutic intervention is to help the patient confront threatening characters or situations that arise.

Throughout the entire course of personal Psychosynthesis, the therapist uses standard psychotherapeutic techniques following the fantasy production in order to help the patient integrate the unconscious contents with his conscious perceptions. Frequently, therapists have noted profound changes in patients undergoing the final stages of Psychosynthesis fantasies, since the content and tone of the experiences are often religious in nature: "As the dreamer moves within himself away from the world of transient phenomena, he seems to be caught up in a world of myth and then in a world of exernal confrontations, a world of religious experience" (Aaronson 1968). Mythic episodes during the final stages of depth analysis have been well documented by Jungian analyst Ira Progoff (1963) as well as by psychiatrist Stanislav Grof, who notes: "We had transcended the psychotherapeutic framework and entered a mystical and religious one, or at least were observing phenomena that had previously been described in mystical and religious scriptures" (1972). Such occurrences are frequent in the final periods of personal Psychosynthesis; they led Assagioli to propose a second stage of personality integration, which he termed "spiritual psychosynthesis" (Assagioli 1965). Spiritual Psychosynthesis is based on Assagioli's hypothesis that an individual has a superconscious component, in addition to the conscious and unconscious components of conventional analysis. By experiencing this superconscious component, or higher self, the patient is potentially capable of self-actualization. Many of the same techniques of meditation, active imagination, and physical exercise are employed in this second stage of Psychosynthesis, but the content and focus of these activities change.

Rather than concentrate on individual, subjective fantasies, the patient is guided through a reenactment of mythic journeys such as the quest for the Holy Grail or Dante's *Divine Comedy*. Assagioli asserts that these exercises allow the patient to successively disidentify himself from his body, his emotions, his desires, and his intellect until he experiences himself as a center of pure consciousness and will (Aaronson 1968). This goal is the major one advocated by all systems of meditation. It is possible to conceptualize Psychosynthesis as a Western psychotherapeutic system designed to induce a transcendent experience similar to Maslow's "peak experiences" (Maslow 1962*a*). One graphic example is offered by Robert Gerard, who instructed a patient to enter a flaming sphere while they were reenacting the mythic journey of Dante in the Inferno. As the patient immersed himself in the flames, he experienced a part of himself that remained stable and unchanging amidst the flames, and he found himself transformed into a shining light (Gerard 1964). Permitting the patient to experience an inner strength, or unchanging center, has been demonstrated to have profound beneficial effects on all aspects of his psychological functioning—and these effects persist. Perhaps the experiences offer patients solace in the realization that there is a part of themselves that is stable and persevering in the midst of an unstable and often chaotic personal and social environment. It is significant that such experiences can be elicited under proper circumstances and seem to give patients a sense of efficacy that enables them to solve their personal difficulties without specific directives from the therapist (Gerard 1964; Aaronson 1968). By some unknown process, the very act of engaging and overcoming threatening situations with actions rather than with intellectual solutions provides the patient with an experience of controlled spontaneity that carries over into his everyday life.

Psychosynthesis is the most highly developed system of prescribed fantasy techniques among all the imagery therapies and, as such, is an invaluable adjunct to each system. In terms of constructing an ideal imagery therapy, the combination of Autogenic Training for deep relaxation with Psychosynthesis for interpreting the ensuing fantasies provides an excellent base for future research and therapeutic applications. Fantasy interpretation with prescribed interventions is much more highly developed in Western psychotherapy than in Eastern psychotherapy, and, in that respect, it has a great deal to offer the Eastern systems. One area of psychotherapy that is more highly developed in Eastern systems is the use of meditation, rather than hypnotic techniques, for inducing deep relaxation. Additionally, Eastern systems of psychotherapy that are little known in the United

States were being developed in Japan at the same time that psycho-analysis was founded in Europe. Emerging systems of imagery therapy and Biofeedback are moving toward treatment of specific disorders and beyond adjustment into the experience of transcendent states. An examination of two systems of Oriental psychotherapy will serve as an invaluable adjunct to the preceding discussions because the Oriental methods are now the dominant modes of treatment in Eastern psychotherapy.

ZEN AND MORITA PSYCHOTHERAPY

Zen psychotherapy is a rubric contrived by psychiatrist Ilza Veith of the University of California Medical Center in San Francisco. As a medical historian, Veith (1972) has recognized the convergence of Eastern and Western techniques of psychotherapy and has suggested the term *Zen psychotherapy* to describe this phenomenon. Despite the fact that imagery therapies emphasizé the same values as and use techniques similar to Zen meditation, very few theorists or practitioners have recognized that these evolving therapeutic methods are indicative of several profound alterations in viewing the patient and the therapeutic process. By examining briefly Zen meditation and Morita therapy—which is based on Zen—it is possible to see these evolving alterations more graphically, since they are already more highly developed in the Eastern systems.

There are three explicit and fundamental concepts that underlie Eastern systems of psychotherapy and seem to be implicit in the evolving imagery therapies. These concepts are: (1) self-contradiction rather than deviation from the cultural norm is the basis of mental disorder; the major form of self-contradiction is a division of experience into subject and object, thinker and thought, feeler and feeling (Watts 1953); (2) emphasis on present awareness and fantasies rather than on past influences; rather than assuming that knowledge of the past explains the present, Eastern systems contend that the past has no real existence and is simply an inference from the individual's immediate experience; and (3) the goal of therapy is controlled spontaneity, which is termed *mushin* (*mu* = "no," *shin* = "mind") (Suzuki 1949*b*). In this state, "there is an integration of conscious and unconscious, preparatory to a type of living, thinking and acting which Zen Buddhism calls *mushin*. It is the art of making the appropriate responses to life without the interruption of that wobbling and indecisive state which we call choosing" (Watts 1953). Imagery therapies such as Autogenic Training and Psychosynthesis adhere to these assumptions, although they do not explicitly acknowledge them. Among the imagery therapies, the influence of Eastern disciplines is most fully acknowledged and utilized in Gestalt therapy. In order to preface the lesser-known Eastern psychotherapies, it is useful to point out the influence of those disciplines on the more well-known Western system of Gestalt therapy.

Berkeley psychiatrist Claudio Naranjo is among the first therapists to attempt to bridge the gap between Eastern and Western systems of psychotherapy, especially with regard to Gestalt therapy and meditation. Essentially, Naranjo agrees with Watts's observation that the Western insistence on self-object differentiation is the cause of self-contradiction and anxiety:

> Most of us have the sensation that "I myself" is a separate center of feeling and action, living inside and bounded by the physical body— a center which "confronts" an "external" world of people and things, making contact through the senses with a universe both alien and strange. The first result of this illusion is that our attitude to the world "outside" us is largely hostile. We are forever "conquering" nature, space, mountains, deserts, bacteria, and insects instead of learning to cooperate with them in a harmonious order (Watts 1967, p. 112).

Accepting this Eastern explanation of self-contradiction as the root of neurosis, Naranjo recognizes the value of the Eastern remedy for that malady, which is to cultivate an awareness that transcends the self-object duality yet preserves the integrity of ego consciousness. Naranjo defines the similarities between Zen and Gestalt therapies as follows:

> Gestalt therapists, still more aware of the screening function of conceptual thinking, substitute free association thinking for the

exercise of "staying in the continuum of awareness," a concept much like that of sustained attention in meditation. In both meditation and Gestalt therapy, there is a place for the resource of suppressing thinking and imagining in favor of sensing and feeling, which are generally overshadowed by the former (Naranjo 1969a, p. 71).

It is clear from this statement that Gestalt therapy adheres to the first two concepts of Eastern psychotherapy and formulates the overcoming of duality as remaining within immediate awareness. The founder of Gestalt therapy, Fritz Perls, summarizes this assumption most succinctly as: "Now = experience = awareness = reality" (Fagan 1970, p. 14). In other words, self-reflexive awareness is contrasted to awareness by recognizing that "every attempt to be aware of being aware is an infinite regress, a vicious circle" (Watts 1953). This recognition that self-reflection is at least one step removed from experience is the basis for Perls's insisting on immediate awareness as the remedy for excessive intellectual distancing from experiences and emotion.

Examination of the three basic injunctions of Gestalt therapy reveals that it also adheres to the Eastern concept of controlled spontaneity, or *mushin*, as its goal. In Gestalt therapy, the state of *mushin* is termed responsibility or *response-ability* (Perls 1969), and it represents the culmination of the three basic tenets:

1. Valuation of actuality: temporal (present versus past or future), spatial (present versus absent), and substantial (act versus symbol)
2. Valuation of awareness and the acceptance of experience
3. Valuation of wholeness, or responsibility (Naranjo 1970)

The last state of responsibility is a double-bind prescription similar to Haley's "You must be spontaneous" (Haley 1959) and also similar to the Zen koan that demands action rather than mentation. For an imagery therapist to elicit this state of responsibility, he must be able to allow the patient to experience that the patient has no choice other than responsibility. Gestalt therapists allow patients to experience the logical outcome of remaining in the continuum of their awareness as they follow their fantasies and projections to the point of satiation and realize that "responsibility, for instance, is not a must, but an unavoidable fact: we are the responsible doers of whatever we do. Our only alternatives are to acknowledge such responsibility or deny it" (Naranjo 1970).

Once a patient has experienced his fantasies to their fullest extent, he becomes aware that all his attempts at concealment are unsuccessful and that he must either accept his deficiencies or change, for fantasizing about change has been demonstrated to be futile. The moment of that realization is the point when the patient is potentially capable of escaping the double bind; he must be responsible and spontaneous by acting in that manner. If the patient elects to adhere conscientiously to that paradoxical prescription, he achieves responsibility, controlled spontaneity, and *mushin*.

Recognizing that you cannot be other than totally responsible for your actions in Gestalt therapy is analogous to reconciling opposites or integrating the shadow in Jungian therapy. Jung's prescription that a patient needs to experience the resolution of opposition and to accept and assimilate the shadow, or the dark and repressed aspect of one's nature, is consistent with the concept of a double-binding paradoxical prescription that can induce the state of responsibility. In referring to the assimilation of the shadow in Jungian therapy, Allan Watts notes the double bind: "The problem is always that acceptance of oneself can never be a deliberate act; it is as paradoxical as kissing one's own lips. But the counter-game challenges the actual possibility of rejecting oneself, and in the end does not construct but reveals the wholeness of man as an inescapable fact" (Watts 1961, p. 183). Acceptance of disowned or denied aspects of the self is usually undertaken by adopting a stance that Jung terms "active passivity" (Jung 1969a), which is analogous to passive concentration (Luthe 1962) in Autogenic Training and to *mushin* in Zen Buddhism. An essential aspect of therapy stressed in the Jungian system is that the patient actively participates in experiencing, assimilating, and comprehending the emerging contents of his dreams and fantasies. Where the Jungian and Gestalt systems do diverge quite markedly is in defining the specific therapeutic techniques to facilitate this process. Whereas Gestalt therapy has an extensive literature concerning techniques, the Jungian therapy has only one article (Adler 1967) that addresses itself to methods of treatment. It is precisely because of this difference that the two systems have a great deal to offer to each other. If a Gestalt therapist uses his techniques to allow a patient to stay in the continuum of awareness, the patient will soon experience the mythic aspects of his consciousness, which the Jungians can interpret most adeptly. Both Gestalt and Jungian analysts would benefit from a more extensive exchange of techniques and insights. Actually, one of the main approaches of Gestalt therapy, which is termed "re-assimilating the unknown" (Naranjo 1969a), was recognized by Jung. In Gestalt therapy, the patient is instructed to become an object or character in a dream or fantasy in order to reassimilate that projection. By becoming that object or character, the patient experiences that the object or person is symbolic of disowned or projected aspects of himself. According to Claudio Naranjo: "By 'becoming' them and giving them a voice, we may find that we are only becoming what we already are: somebody wanting to do all that, choosing to do so, and finding some satisfaction in it, rather than remaining a passive 'victim' of such occurrences" (Naranjo 1969a, p. 49). This exercise of experiencing distant aspects of a dream or fantasy as parts of the self was termed by Jung the *subjective* level of dream interpretation, as opposed to the *objective* level. At the subjective level of dream interpretation, the dream images are regarded as "tendencies or components of the subject" (Jung, 1969a). On the objective level, "every interpretation equates the dream images with real objects" (Jung 1969a). Although Jung does not propose becoming the images in subjective interpretation, it does seem as though the Gestalt technique would be a powerful one for assimilating those disparate aspects of the self. In the Jungian system, patients are encouraged to concentrate on and amplify a dream image or to enter into a discussion with a dream or fantasy figure, but not to become that projection (Adler 1967). Despite these subtle differences, it is likely that this theoretical distinction is blurred or absent in actual practice. What is most important to recognize is that both the Jungian and Gestalt systems rely heavily on the experiencing of dream and fantasy material while the patient remains in a state of "active passivity" as a prelude to rejecting or accepting responsibility for his actions and acting with controlled spontaneity.

This lengthy introduction to Zen psychotherapy is intended to point out the tendency of Western imagery therapies to strive toward the same goals as the Eastern systems of psychotherapy. Eastern systems explicitly acknowledge three concepts that are beginning to be accepted by imagery therapists: (1) self-contradiction as the basis of mental disorder, (2) emphasis on present-time awareness, and (3) attainment of a state of *mushin,* or controlled spontaneity. One system of Eastern psychotherapy has recognized and integrated these components into Morita therapy, which is based on Zen meditation exercises. This system provides insights into the possible evolution of the Western imagery therapies.

Morita therapy was developed by psychiatrist Shoma Morita of Jikeikai Medical School, Tokyo, in approximately 1915. Following Morita's death in 1938, the therapy was further developed by psychiatrist Takehisa Kora, and it is now recognized in Japan as one of the most effective therapies for the treatment of neurosis. When Morita therapy was first developed, Dr. Morita based it on the principles of Zen but did not use the Zen Buddhist technique of *zazen,* or meditation. Actual use of *zazen* in one stage of Morita therapy is a recent innovation of psychiatrists Akikisa Kondo (1953) and Koji Sato (1958). There are only two fundamental theoretical principles that are the basis of Morita therapy: (1) all neurosis derives from *shinkeishitsusho,* or "antagonistic action of the mind" (Kora 1965); and (2) the alleviation of neurosis is achieved by *arugamama* or "leaving the symptoms as they are and leading the life as it is" (Kora 1965). Such a degree of simplicity is partially due to the fact that the Japanese words *shinkeishitsusho* and *arugamama* both describe highly complex phenomena that are described in Western psychotherapy in varied ways. Economy of theory and applications is one of the most outstanding and admirable aspects of Morita therapy.

Shinkeishitsusho is a state of self-contradiction, or a state of intrapsychic antagonism. Both the process leading to this state and the state itself can be summarized as follows:

> There is a reciprocal action between attention and sensation, colored with anxiety, to some phenomena of our mind or body; we experience this phenomena more clearly and sharply. This makes us direct our attention to it all the more. The whole procedure will end up in a vicious circle. . . . since it is not possible to negate a disquietude which occurs in a person as something natural, the attempt to negate these feelings develops into a mental conflict when the patient tries to make possible something that is impossible. This is *shinkeishitsusho* (Kora 1965, p. 6).

Evidently, this state is a double-bind situation in which a patient's insistence that his symptoms disappear is the very thing that aggravates and prolongs the neurosis. Clinically, three diagnostic categories are subsumed under *shinkeishitsusho:* (1) neurasthenia, (2) obsessive-phobic, and (3) paroxysmal neurosis characterized by acute anxiety on a hypochondriacal basis (Jacobson and Berenberg 1952). Neurotics usually establish unrealistic goals and then entertain equally unrealistic fantasies about how those goals might be achieved; they then feel increasingly frustrated and anxiety ridden when fantasies fail and also when they inhibit real in-the-world actions. What is required to alleviate this cycle is that the patient must be allowed to experience the outcome of his illogical premises as a prelude to a decision to continue the cycle or modify his premises and his behavior.

Arugamama, or "leaving the symptoms as they are and leading life as it is" (Kora 1965), is the means to achieve that end. It is assumed that neurotic individuals do not want to face anxiety directly and wish to have happiness without effort. Even their entrance into therapy is assumed to be a neurotic attempt to secure happiness from the doctor. Suppressing or denying fear and anxiety creates the inevitable psychological phenomenon of a futile battle in which the patient seeks in vain to make something possible that is impossible —that is, to gain freedom by denying bondage. In the state of *arugamama,* the patient is encouraged to acknowledge the anxieties and recognize that everyone in a comparable situation feels anxious; but he is also encouraged to act in spite of the anxiety, and that act will serve to dispel the fear and anxiety. Affirmative action breaks the frustrating cycle of anxiety, since any action leads to reactions that modify the individual's behavior in a realistic rather than in a fantasied manner. Success or failure in that action is of secondary importance to the process of acting—which is the only solution to the double bind of denying naturally occurring anxieties. Writing in the *American Journal of Psychoanalysis,* Akikisa Kondo defines the essential characteristics of neurotic patients: "1) Neurotic individuals are hypochondriacal; 2) attempt to make the impossible possible; 3) do not want to face anxiety directly; 4) do not accept facts and learn from them and do not accept situations that do not suit their demands; 5) tend to think of themselves set apart and different from others; 6) wish to have happiness without effort; and, 7) are troubled by a feeling of inferiority or incapacity" (Kondo 1953). Little or no attempt is made to interpret or analyze these symptoms; rather, the patient is encouraged to engage in a graduated series of activities despite the persistence of his anxiety. Kora summarizes this position of the Morita therapist: "Even if the patient had all these symptoms, and no matter how he felt about these symptoms, he should not let the symptoms get the better of him and so distort his attitude in life, but he should try to do by all means anything he needs to do" (Kora 1965).

Accomplishment of *arugamama* can be more fully explained by a brief overview of the techniques of Morita therapy.

Strong emphasis is placed on the two basic tenets of Zen Buddhism: (1) the importance of life in and with nature and (2) the immersion of the individual in the family, group, and community (Veith 1972). These values are translated into use in Morita therapy, which bases its treatment on three related principles: (1) the curative effects of nature, (2) manual labor, and (3) the importance of developing an attitude of acceptance (Kondo 1953). Acceptance here is analogous to *mushin*, or controlled spontaneity, and is considered to be the goal of all therapeutic interventions. There are four phases of therapy designed to operationalize these principles and to achieve the stage of acceptance. All treatment is conducted on an inpatient basis over a short period of time, rather than prolonged for months or years. This procedure reflects the basic Eastern belief that the specific problems of a neurotic are not alleviated by analyzing them but by cultivating an attitude of acceptance toward those anxieties and fears. Therefore, the intensive four-phase treatment is designed to induce that attitude.

Therapy consists of (1) absolute rest, (2) light physical activity, (3) moderate physical activity, and (4) discipline, by coping with the complex, unpredictable problems of life (Jacobson and Berenberg 1952). Phase one lasts from several days to a week of absolute rest, in which the patient is prohibited from speaking, writing, or any form of distraction. This period is similar to Janov's prescription for sensory isolation prior to Primal therapy. Between the fourth and seventh day, the patient usually exhibits pronounced symptoms, and an accurate diagnosis is then possible. During phase two, the patient is still isolated from socializing, speaking, and reading. However, he now begins to write in a diary every evening and must continue to do so until the end of his treatment. Phase two lasts from seven to fourteen days, and, during that time, the therapist reads the diary every day and writes a commentary in it. This exchange of information through the diary is the patient's only means of communicating with his therapist for nearly two weeks. Moderate physical activity, such as walking, is allowed only to a limited degree because the therapist's intention is to involve the patient in his subjective thoughts and fantasies without distraction. Recently, Japanese psychiatrist Keigo Yokoyama reported that he prescribes thirty minutes of Zen meditation at seven every morning and at eight-thirty every night (Yokoyama 1968). This use of *zazen* during the second phase of Morita has resulted in a decrease in the time required for a patient to become more deeply involved in his subjective fantasies. Usually toward the end of phase two, patients demand to be allowed to perform some manual labor to avoid the sheer boredom of being immersed in the cycle of their futile fantasies.

After two weeks, phase three is initiated: the patient is allowed to perform some moderately heavy work for one week. When the patient reaches this stage, "the sufferings arising from tedium that is caused by being prohibited to do anything become stronger than the sufferings arising from his symptoms. In this fashion, the patient realizes that abulia runs counter to his true nature and that activity is something natural to him" (Kora 1965, p. 18). Work consists of gardening, cleaning rabbit cages, and other activities that involve the patient in nature. In it, he can experience the integrated complexity of nature that functions smoothly, as he must learn to do. In this stage, the patient and therapist do speak directly with each other, but the actual dreams and fantasies are given scant attention and sources of conflict are not sought or examined. Japanese therapists examine the patient's activity in this phase as a condensed expression of his total personality and resources. Therapists engage in explicit directives designed to enhance the patient's ability to function spontaneously without recourse to excessive rumination. Heavy emphasis is placed on flexible solutions to problems that arise in the course of the manual labor. Unfortunately, there are no articles concerning the specific techniques by which the attitude of *arugamama* is elicited in this stage of therapy. Finally, phase four is initiated in which the patient becomes an outpatient and leaves the hospital for one or two days at a time. This stage lasts from one to two weeks, and the therapist's role is to encourage the patient to react less rigidly in meeting his everyday problems (Jacobson and Berenberg 1952). One key principle, which is also common to Zen Buddhism and is graphically illustrated in this last stage of Morita therapy, is that an individual should perform each task of his life with such complete absorption that he is hardly aware of the effort. Involvement in action of this intensity is thought to abolish the duality of the doer of an action and the action itself. Two Zen Buddhist poems are often cited by Morita therapists in order to explain the stage of acceptance or controlled spontaneity:

While alive, Be a dead man, Thoroughly dead; And act as you will, And all is good.

Kill, kill yourself, Kill thoroughly, And when there is nothing, Be a teacher of man (Master Bunan 1603–1676).

Death is not feared, since the Eastern therapies based on Zen advocate nonjudgmental involvement in experience. That is only possible when the incessant analytic stance of the ego is killed. Analytic awareness is accepted as a necessary aspect of human functioning when it is subject to control rather than out of control and obsessive. Obviously, Morita patients do not literally die, but they have been taught to abandon and let die their former behavior patterns and to experience a rebirth into a more effective mode of behavior.

Based on ten years of records from Kyushu University Hospital in Tokyo, research affirms that Morita-therapy patients do assume more constructive behavior. Average time for treatment is 73.2 days, with 76.2 percent of the patients improved on a nonremissive standard, and 7.6 percent improved but remissive (Jacobson and Berenberg 1952). Similar results are reported from the 1929–1937 records of the Kora Koseun Clinic of Tokyo (Kora 1965). Additionally, there is an extensive body of research to support the efficacy of Morita therapy, but it is unnecessary to review that literature except as evidence that Morita therapy is effective with a significant number of Oriental patients. Above all, it is important to note that Morita therapy is a complex, highly evolved system of treating neurosis that has received little attention from Western psychotherapists. In light of the fact that the imagery therapies and Morita are based on many of the same assumptions, it may prove useful to explore Morita therapy as an adjunct and addition to the evolving therapies based on the patient experiencing his subjective fantasies as a precursor to behavioral change. Evaluation of the efficacy of Morita therapy in treating Western patients is complicated by the cultural factors of Japan, which are so prominent in that therapy. Another drawback of Morita therapy is that it is predicated as a treatment for inpatients only, although recent applications to individual long-term outpatient therapy have been reported (Kora 1965). Additionally, the time of treatment is approximately two complete months, although it seems possible that the Western systems of deep relaxation, such as Autogenic Training, may be used to shorten the total time of hospitalization. Also, more active participation by the therapist in interpreting the patient's fantasies in phase two might shorten the time for the course of treatment.

All of these speculations are intended to point out that several Eastern and Western psychotherapies are attempting to formulate a therapy that has the following fundamental characteristics: (1) the use of a method of sensory isolation or deep relaxation intended to heighten the patient's experience of his subjective fantasies, (2) therapists assume an experimental emphasis rather than an analytical stance, (3) the therapist serves as a minimally intrusive guide, (4) spontaneous and/or induced fantasies are the means of diagnosing and treating the patient, (5) patients are encouraged to develop a state of responsibility and acceptance of their anxieties and fears, and (6) acceptance leads the patient to the point of potentially deciding to act with controlled spontaneity. No one system fulfills all of the criteria, but each system does address itself explicitly or implicitly to these issues and, for that reason, it seems that any comprehensive system of psychotherapy needs to recognize and formulate theories and procedures for dealing with those requisites. It would be quite impossible for any one therapist or system of psychotherapy to be all encompassing and comprehensive, nor is that state advocated as ideal. Hopefully, therapists of any given orientation will make themselves aware of alternative systems of therapy for purposes of making insightful referrals. Unnecessary antagonisms between systems of psychotherapy could be mediated by realizing that differences are largely a matter of emphasis rather than of systems being mutually exclusive and competitive. We do not deny that there are differences between systems of psychotherapy and that the subtle differences in theory and technique render certain therapies more effective for certain patients. The enumeration of the common underlying principles of the various imagery therapies is intended to demonstrate the importance of these factors in any therapeutic system and to provide a schema by which any therapist may examine the assumptions and values on which he bases his therapeutic method. Recognition of the similarities among various systems can serve as a means to appreciate the common endeavor of healing and to be aware of various perspectives of behavior that therapists attempt to modify.

Several systems of imagery therapy have illustrated the general principles discussed at the beginning of the chapter. At this point, it would be useful to formulate several conclusions and hypotheses pertaining to evidence that supports the insight of the imagery therapies. Among these considerations are (1) imagery therapies can best be understood by reference to communications theory; (2) the concepts of communications theory are useful in understanding the connections between contemporary neurology and the imagery therapies; (3) it has been demonstrated that imagery can have a profound effect on unconscious psychological processes and physiological autonomic processes; (4) symbolic processes and fantasies are the "language" that links psychological and physiological processes; (5) there is extensive evidence that fantasy techniques are effective in treating a wide variety of psychological and psychosomatic disorders; (6) it may become possible to isolate specific fantasies that would be useful in treating specific disorders; there are a few indications in Psychosynthesis that this may become possible; (7) parallels between observable neurological activity and certain fantasy activity may indicate a promising area of research concerning the nature of mind-body interaction; and (8) it could be that controlled fantasies are the means for exploring the phenomenology of human consciousness. Perhaps the hypothesized psychic energy, or libido, can be understood through exploring how patients are able to transform threatening images into beneficent ones during fantasy experiences and to obtain profound insights as well as a strong sense of personal efficacy and confidence as a result of that experience.

All of the above considerations are highly speculative but are inferred from observed facts from research and clinical records. These hypotheses are not intended to be conclusions but potential directions for future research and therapeutic applications. In actuality, it seems very likely that confirmation and modification of these hypotheses will be emerging within the next decade. One psychotherapeutic system seems to offer the most potential for providing answers to the issues that have been raised here—that system is Biofeedback. It has already demonstrated impressive results using a combination of the older fantasy techniques with the newer innovations in neurological and physiological monitoring instrumentation. Through a combination of these techniques, Biofeedback offers the potential for exploring some of the most fundamental issues concerning the nature of mind-body interaction. We will now discuss the theory and research evidence from Biofeedback in order to demonstrate the far-reaching implications of a psychotherapeutic system based on it.

MEDITATION AND PSYCHOTHERAPY

"I conceptualize meditation as 'meta-therapy': a procedure that accomplishes the major goals of conventional therapy and yet has as its end-state a change far beyond the scope of therapies, therapists, and most personality theorists—an altered state of consciousness" (Goleman 1971). Goleman's article is perhaps the most imaginative and comprehensible synthesis of the ancient Eastern practice of meditation and Western psychotherapy. After a comprehensive review of the literature on meditation, we felt it worthwhile to quote the following excerpts from this selection.

In 1934 Edmund Jacobson . . . propounded the principle—that relaxation is the direct physiological opposite of tension—on which is founded the behavior therapy technique most closely resembling meditation. The technique is "systematic desensitization" as practiced by Joseph Wolpe and Arnold Lazarus (1966).

Systematic desensitization involves three principal operations: (1) Training in deep muscle relaxation. The method is taught as Jacobson designed it, and requires training the patient to relax in sequence the various muscle groups throughout the body. The training takes about six interviews, and the patient practices at home for two fifteen-minute periods a day. (2) The construction of an anxiety hierarchy—a graded list of anxiety-eliciting stimuli. The hierarchy systematically orders the situations, events, thoughts, or feelings in any way distressing to the patient according to the degree of anxiety elicited by each. The patient is taught to visualize as vivid an image as possible for the items in the hierarchy. (3) Graduated pairing, through mental imagery, of anxiety-eliciting stimuli with the state of relaxation. Each item is presented in order, starting with the least anxiety-eliciting, and is repeated until all anxiety is eliminated, and the next item presented. The hierarchy is thus ascended from weakest to strongest stimuli until there is no anxiety elicited by any item. . . .

. . . With the inward turning of attention in meditation, the meditator becomes keenly aware of the random chaos characteristic of thoughts in the waking state. The train of thought is endless, stops nowhere, and has no destination. The meditator witnesses the flow of psychic events, plannings, paranoias, hopes, fantasies, memories, yearnings, decisions, indecisions, observations, fears, scheming, guilt, calculations, exaltations, and on and on and on. The whole contents of the mind compose the meditator's "desensitization hierarchy." The contents of this hierarchy are organic to the life concerns of the meditator; they are drawn from the stored pool of his total experience. This hierarchy is inherently self-regulating; the organizing principle for item presentation is literally "what's on one's mind," and so optimal salience is guaranteed.

As in the desensitization paradigm, the "hierarchy" is presented coupled with the deep relaxation of deep meditation. Unlike the therapy, desensitization is not limited to those items which therapist and patient have identified as problematic, though those are certainly included, but extends to all phases of experience. Apart from the element of physiological relaxation, the mental stance of the meditator toward his thoughts can be one of three sorts: (1) totally immersed in one's thoughts; (2) wholly oblivious to thought, having transcended it through use of mantra or by other means. This state is "pure consciousness" as Lesh (1970, p. 46) described it: "There is no cognition, no dreaming, no hallucinations, no data input (via normal sensory modalities), no information processing, no conscious activity at all, just full waking attention." On the basis of physiological evidence, Wallace (1970b) proposes this transcendental state as "a fourth major state of consciousness." (3) The third is to be in this transcendental "fourth state" and simultaneously witness thought.

There are two ways in which meditation "desensitizes." In the first state the meditator is deeply relaxed while exposed to a hierarchy, much as in conventional behavior therapy. In the third mental stance one is in the position which Maslow (1969, p. 57) discusses as the sense in which one "transcends" in psychotherapy: "This parallels the process in psychotherapy of simultaneously experiencing and of self-observing one's own experience in a kind of critical or editorial or detached and removed way so that one can criticize it, approve or disapprove of it and assume control, and therefore, the possibility of changing it exists." Maupin (1965, p. 144) in a study of Zen meditation, notes "subjectively felt benefits similar to those resulting from relaxation therapies were reported by several subjects." In meditation, relaxation is deep, the hierarchy of thoughts is innately experience-encompassing, self-observation conditions are such that inner feedback for behavior change is optimal. It is natural, global self-desensitization.

Goleman on Meditation and the "Psychophysiological Principle"

Freud believed in the "mysterious leap from mind to body," and based his early theory of anxiety on the transformation of physical into mental. But though he saw the brain and nervous system as "the bodily organ and scene of action" of mental life he saw no means of connecting acts of consciousness with their physiological substrata. He despaired of finding systematic connections between consciousness and the nervous system (1938, p. 44): "Everything that lies between these two terminal points is unknown to us and, so far as we are aware, there is no direct relation between them." From Freud on, mainline psychoanalytic practice if not thinking, has focused on the intra-psychic to the exclusion of the body.

Beginning with Wilhelm Reich (1948), refocusing attention on the patient's "character armor" as revealed in his posture, movements, facial expressions, etc., a growing therapeutic school has begun to chart and use the direct relations between mind and body. With the contributions of Lowen's (1958) bioenergetic analysis, Perls' (1969) gestalt therapy, Pesso's psychomotor therapy, and others, that leap has become increasingly less mysterious. The theoretical underpinning and key to the mind-body leap of these approaches is summarized in the "psychophysiological principle" (Green et al. 1970b): "Every change in the physiological state is accompanied by an appropriate change in the mental-emotional state, and conversely, every change in the mental-emotional state, conscious or unconscious, is accompanied by an appropriate change in the physiological state."

In meditation, the psychophysiological principle can be used to understand the significance of "unstressing," a term used by practitioners of TM. Unstressing takes the form during meditation of completely involuntary, unintended, and spontaneous muscular-skeletal movements and proprioceptive sensations: momentary or repeated twitches, spasms, gasps, tingling, tics, jerking, swaying, pains, shaking, aches, internal pressures, headaches, weeping, laughter, etc. The experience covers the range from extreme pleasure to acute distress. In TM, unstressing is gradual during regular daily meditation, so that it is not always discernible. During special extended meditation sessions where one meditates throughout much of the day, more extreme forms of unstressing can occur. When Maupin taught zazen to a group of college students as part of an experiment, they mentioned to him the emergence of "hallucinoid feelings, muscle tension, sexual excitement, and intense sadness" (1965, p. 145). Because of the unpredictable nature of unstressing, meditators who are unprepared for it, or who are in the midst of others who do not understand the process, can become agitated when it occurs in disturbing forms. For this reason teachers of TM and other systems recommend day-long meditation only in supervised and secluded situations. Psychiatric clinics are beginning to get new patients who have been meditating on their own all day for many days, and are brought in by others who can't understand and are disturbed by behavior changes they see; the dynamics of this influx are parallel to the continuing wave of "bad trips" due to drugs. As with acute drug cases, the psychiatric intervention may worsen and prolong distress rather than alleviate it, while someone familiar with meditation can reassure the person and alleviate the crisis without recourse to the paraphernalia of psychiatry.

The fundamental assumption in understanding the function of unstressing is, as in psychoanalytic thought, that all past experience leaves its mark on present behavior. In accord with the psychophysiological principle, mental-emotional events are paralleled by physiological changes, and so the organism is shaped by the events of a lifetime. The nervous system is the repository of all experiences of emotional strain, pleasure, fatigue, tensions, stresses, etc., whether of "physical" or "mental" origin. It is through reading extensions of the nervous system such as musculature that the gestalt or bioenergetic or psychomotor therapist gets to the major issues in a person's life—literally, to what has shaped him—and begins the work of freeing the person from the grip of the past events that have left that particular mark.

In meditation this same process of liberating the nervous system from past stresses is undergone without effort, volition, or intention. As the meditator reaches a level of profound relaxation and pure awareness with no thoughts, a wide range of kinesthetic sensations, vague feelings, or any of the array of psychic events can be triggered at random. Autokinesthesia may be accompanied by thoughts or may occur alone; or one may notice only thoughts but no move-ment. . . .

. . . If attention is turned to scanning the body when thoughts alone are experienced, underlying proprioceptive kinesthetic sensations invariably will be noticed.

Lerner (1967) has proposed that kinesthetic sensations of this sort are, in fact, the stuff dreams are made of. In one of Dement and Kleitman's (1957) first REM-EEG studies, they noticed very fine digital movements in sleeping subjects. Wolpert (1960), follow-ing up on this lead, compared dream reports with muscle-potential activity and found that the fine movements executed, described as "slight, abortive muscular stirrings," were appropriate to the content of the dreams. Conceptualizing dreams as "kinesthetic fantasy" (i.e., fantasy in the kinesthetic modality, as opposed, say, to the visual or auditory), Lerner points out that in sleep, gross body movements build up to a peak just before the onset of the dream state, terminate abruptly with the onset of dreaming, and reappear when the dream REMs cease. This pattern is just the reverse of the fine muscular stirrings, which occur primarily during dreaming but are negligible other times (or which may fade into the background when gross movements are present). Dement and Wolpert (1958) report that gross body movements indicate an absence of dreams. On this basis, Lerner suggests that gross, overt motor activity is antithetical to kinesthetic fantasy, and that the key factor in the facilitation of kinesthetic fantasy is physical immobility.

Dement (1960) has shown that persons deprived of dreaming time in sleep exhibit symptoms of personality disorganization, includ-ing heightened levels of tension, anxiety, and irritability, difficulty in concentrating, impaired motor coordination, and so on. They also make increasingly frequent efforts to dream; when allowed to do so their total dream time rose significantly and stayed high until the time lost was made up. Thus dreaming is in some way a vital function for the maintenance of personality organization. Lerner suggests that "one may sleep in order to dream," and proposes (p. 98) "that body image forms the basis of ego and that in order to maintain the coherence of body image and thus of personality organization, kinesthetic activity must be supplemented by the sort of kinesthetic fantasy which takes place in and is facilitated by the dreaming state."

Lerner assumes that the crucial restorative effects of dreaming can occur only in sleep because only then is the normal person in a "relatively profound, sustained, and pervasive state of physiological

immobilization." This affords the opportunity to engage in kinesthetic fantasy that is fully elaborated, as opposed to the truncated
kinesthetic fantasy that fleetingly may occur in the waking state.
Wallace (1970*a*) in his study of TM found evidence that the
decrease in metabolic rate during meditation is in some ways *more*
profound a physiological immobilization than that of sleep. In their
EEG study of zazen, Kasamatsu and Hirai (1969) found the
cerebral excitatory level gradually lowered as it is in sleep, but in a
way fundamentally distinct from the sleep pattern. Thus meditation
would also qualify as a time when kinesthetic fantasy, with all its
beneficial effects, could occur: the basic pre-condition of physiological
immobilization prevails. But because the meditator maintains awareness during the process, his experience can encompass the kinesthetic
byplay as well as any accompanying thoughts or fantasies; and so
he reports "unstressing." The dreamer, in part because of a Western
cultural tendency to ignore kinesthetic experience, recalls mainly
visual and auditory elements of the same process. Another factor
distinguishing the experience of dreaming from unstressing is that
rapid eye movements—an indicator of dreaming—while themselves
kinesthetic, provide an unstructured visual stimulus which the
dreamer shapes into meaningful configurations in dream construction; in meditation there are no REMs (Wallace 1970*a*).

I propose that unstressing serves the same psychological function
for the meditator as do dreams for the dreamer. In keeping with
the psychophysiological principle, each movement in unstressing
signals the release of a stored mental-emotional state, event, or
impression, and each such psychic event indicates the release of
stress on the level of nerve-and-muscle. That is, each kinesthetic
event is paralleled by a psychic one, and each psychic event by a
kinesthetic one. Just as Wolpert (1960) found that muscle movements in dreaming are systematically related to the content of
dreams, and as Freud (1956) noted that the content of dreams may
derive from a residue of that day's events or from events in the
dreamer's remote past, so with unstressing: movements and thoughts
are related to each other and to past events.

MEDITATIVE TECHNIQUES IN PSYCHOTHERAPY

Happich (1932, 1939), Desoille (1945), Frederking (1948),
and Mauz (1948) have all made use of meditation within a depth

psychological framework most similar to the conceptualizations of Jung. As all are rather detailed systems, and hence beyond our scope, the reader is referred to the sources above as well as to the works of Carl Jung. In essence, we may say that the orientation of these therapeutic utilizations of meditative techniques has been synthetic rather than analytic. As Kretschmer (1962) has stated, the characteristics these systems have in common are the following: (1) the patient is actively involved in the provocation of the unconscious; that is, the spontaneous production of relevant symbolism as in dream analysis is deemed unnecessary; instead, the patient is asked to meditate on certain symbols chosen by the therapist in an attempt to investigate their full meaning for the individual; (2) much stress is placed on the inclination toward health in the psyche as stated in numerous Eastern philosophies as well as in the works of Jung; (3) there is a frequent attempt to run the gamut from physiology to religion within the scope of these meditative systems. Their all-encompassing perspectives enhance the possibility of a natural unfolding of the religious dimension of the psyche, with increased experience in the meditative state.

Clearly, the therapeutic use of meditation is still on the fringe of the mainstream of conventional psychotherapy. It would appear likely, however, that one result of the increased attention being given to meditation in Western culture will be the systematic attempt to integrate this revered practice of Eastern antiquity into psychotherapeutic use. To say that this might effect a substantially positive change in the essence of psychotherapy is indeed an understatement!

MEDITATION AND DRUG ABUSE

Winquist (1969) studied 484 student practitioners of TM who had been meditating for a period of more than three months. He evaluated three categories of drugs:

1. Marijuana
2. Hallucinogens (LSD, DMT, STP, hashish, peyote, psilocybin, morning glory seeds, and woodrose seeds)

3. Hard drugs (heroin, opium, methedrine, and barbiturates). A regular user was defined as one who (*a*) used marijuana twice a month for three consecutive months immediately prior to commencing TM, (*b*) used hallucinogens or hard drugs once a month for three consecutive months immediately prior to commencing TM.

Based on these criteria, 143 of the 484 subjects (or 30 percent) were classified as regular users. In brief, it was found that of the 143 subjects who used marijuana, 84 percent terminated use, 14.5 percent decreased, and 1.5 percent increased. Of the 111 subjects who used hallucinogens other than marijuana, 86 percent stopped and 14 percent decreased. Of the 42 subjects who used hard drugs regularly, 86 percent stopped and 14 percent decreased. It was found that 49 percent of the regular drug users maintained that their use of drugs was altered following TM because life became more fulfilling. Approximately one-fourth (24 percent) claimed the change was due to the fact that the drug experience became less pleasurable. Eight percent stated that the change was due to disappearance of their desire for drugs. Wallace (1970*b*) notes that some of the subjects in this investigation stated that

Drugs have naturally fallen by. I didn't try to stop—after awhile I just found myself not taking them anymore.

Life after meditation finally became satisfying. I no longer needed drugs.

Because all aspects of my life have become better; in school, at work, my inner personal life—everything.

Benson and Wallace (1970) at Harvard Medical School also examined the drug habits of meditators. Some 1862 individuals responded to a questionnaire concerning their use of hallucinogens (such as LSD and marijuana), narcotics (such as heroin), amphetamines, barbiturates, alcohol, and cigarettes. The results of the survey indicated a marked decrease in drug use within three months after commencing the practice of TM. This decrease was progressively maintained until, after 21 months, almost all the subjects claimed to have terminated their drug use completely. The use of cigarettes and alcohol also declined during this period, but less dramatically. Most subjects indicated that TM was largely responsible for the curtailment of their drug use. In a report before a select Congressional Committee on Crime given during the Ninety-second Congress, Benson (1971) offered the following:

> Individuals who regularly practiced transcendental meditation (a) decreased or stopped abusing drugs, (b) decreased or stopped engaging in drug selling activity, and (c) changed their attitudes in the direction of discouraging others from abusing drugs. The magnitude of these changes increased with the length of time that the individual practiced the technique. Similar decreases were noted in the use of "hard" alcoholic beverages and cigarette smoking. A high percentage of the individuals who did change their habits felt that transcendental meditation was very or extremely important in influencing them to change.

> During transcendental meditation oxygen consumption and heart rate significantly decrease, skin resistance significantly increases and the electroencephalogram shows predominantly slow alpha wave activity with occasional theta wave activity. Thus, the practice of transcendental meditation is physiologically distinguished from sitting quietly with eyes open or closed, from sleeping or dreaming and from suggesting relaxation or rest through hypnosis. During transcendental meditation subjects report that their awareness is spontaneously drawn to "finer" or "more abstract" levels of the thinking process.

> There are no simple explanations of the factors which lead to drug abuse. The types of motives which initiate and prolong drug abuse range from such things as social pressure, curiosity, desire for "kicks," rebellion against authority, escape from social and emotional problems to more philosophical motives such as self-knowledge, creativeness, spiritual enlightenment or expansion of consciousness. Student drug users are, as a group, knowledgeable about the undesirable effects of drug abuse. In general, it is not difficult for most student drug abusers to stop. The issue is to get them to want to stop. For a drug abuse program to be effective it must provide a nonchemical alternative which can at least fulfill some of the basic motivations behind student drug abuse.

CONSCIOUSNESS: EAST AND WEST

Transcendental meditation is acceptable among youthful drug abusers. It is offered as a program for personal development and is not specifically intended to be a treatment for drug abuse: the alleviation of the problems of drug abuse is merely a side effect of the practice. Thus, it may not threaten those beliefs of the committed abuser who condones the use of drugs. Since the introduction of transcendental meditation into the student community 5 years ago, over 40,000 individuals have allegedly begun the practice. Further, the movement continues to grow. It is presently being presented through campus organizations at some 300 colleges and universities and at several universities it is offered in the context of an accredited course.

Involvement in other kinds of self-improvement activities may also lead to decreased drug abuse. The motivation to start meditation may have influenced the subjects to stop drug abuse. The subjects in the present study may have spontaneously stopped, continued, or increased taking drugs independently of transcendental meditation.

However, since there are few effective programs which alleviate drug abuse, transcendental meditation should be investigated as an alternative to drugs by a controlled, prospective study.

PSYCHOTHERAPEUTIC APPLICATIONS OF BIOFEEDBACK

In the last fifteen years, Biofeedback has emerged as a prominent area of theory and research; this area is largely based on the research cited in chapter 8. It is altogether fitting that C. G. Jung, who was the first Western therapist to explore the Eastern disciplines, was the first theorist to suggest the convergence of Eastern and Western systems:

> Western civilization is scarcely a thousand years old and must first of all free itself from its barbarous one sidedness. This means, above all, deeper insight into the nature of man. But no insight is gained by repressing and controlling the unconscious, and least of all by imitating methods which have grown up under totally different psychological conditions. In the course of the centuries the West will produce its own yoga, and it will be on the basis laid down by Christianity (1969*b*, p. 535).

Although Jung was not aware of it, Biofeedback could certainly be described as Western yoga, combining Eastern meditation with Western technology. Biofeedback has not supplanted imagery techniques but has affirmed the potency of such methods in establishing voluntary control of psychological and physiological processes.

Before enumerating the principles of Biofeedback, it is necessary to qualify the concept of *autonomic control*. Control is a Western preoccupation that has intruded into the area of Biofeedback—where it seems most inappropriate. Since all the research literature uses the term in such references as "voluntary control of autonomic functions," it is important to clarify the definition of control as it is used here. A more enlightened phrase for what occurs in Biofeedback might be the *harmonious integration of voluntary and autonomic processes,* since *control* of autonomic functions is only established by surrendering all efforts to control those functions. This paradoxical situation is most analogous to *mushin,* or controlled spontaneity, and control is a most inappropriate description of the phenomenon. Western man is suffering from a split between his conscious and unconscious processes that he assumes can be remedied by the conscious assuming control over the unconscious. Unfortunately, the very cause of the split is a profound distrust of unconscious or autonomic processes, and this distrust cannot be alleviated by means of control. The assumption that Western man must control the unconscious is a mistaken one; in fact, what is needed is the reestablishing of a more harmonious integration of these functions. Harvard psychiatrist Andrew Weil recognized this same difficulty: "The problem is not to learn to control the autonomic nervous system; the problem is simply to open the channels between the conscious and the unconscious minds" (1972, p. 62). This issue is more tangible than theoretical, since all of the Biofeedback research supports the observation that control of autonomic functions is achieved only when control is relinquished. Therefore, the definition of the conventional word *control* in Biofeedback denotes an act of allowing communications between conscious and unconscious processes, in order for a harmonious integration to occur. Anyone who has been in an emergency or dangerous situation has experienced the necessity of relying on his autonomic reflexes. Through the use of Biofeedback and meditation, individuals are capable of expanding that reliance by learning how to interpret consciously their autonomic reactions more accurately. In that way, an individual can learn to make more subtle discriminations in his subcortical reactions, begin to recognize the correlation between subcortical and cortical responses, and act accordingly. Rather than being subjected to gross physiological alterations that must be consciously interpreted, an individual could learn to make subtle differentiations of his physiological state and recognize the correspondence between physiological and psychological states. Physical sensations and symptoms could be more readily understood, and, thus, the threatening or unknown quality of autonomic or unconscious processes would be greatly alleviated.

It is our intention to demonstrate that there are numerous theoretical and clinical links between Biofeedback, meditation, and the imagery therapies. All of the imagery therapies are dependent on the therapist's ability to induce and monitor a patient's state of deep relaxation and subsequent fantasy productions. Biofeedback instrumentation is the means for inducing deep relaxation and probing those states with unprecedented accuracy. Increasingly, clinicians are using a combination of fantasy techniques and Biofeedback with remarkable success in treating psychological and psychosomatic disorders (Budzynski and Stoyva 1971). Exact references will be cited later; at this point we wish to clarify the basic principles of Biofeedback techniques. We will emphasize the research in Biofeedback that has been demonstrated to have clinical or therapeutic application rather than review the equally extensive literature concerning more theoretical issues in neurology and physiology (Miller 1964). Before the advent of psychophysiological instrumentation, imagery therapists were entirely dependent on their intuition and the patient's subjective reports for monitoring internal states. Now it is becoming possible to have a more objective assessment of those states and to make more accurate inferences concerning the relationship between subjective images and fantasies and their physiological concomitants.

PRINCIPLES OF BIOFEEDBACK

Conceptually, Biofeedback is based on two basic principles: (1) "every change in the physiological state is accompanied by an appropriate change in the mental-emotional state, conscious or unconscious, and conversely, every change in the mental-emotional state, conscious or unconscious, is accompanied by an appropriate change in the physiological state" (Green, Green, and Walters 1969); and (2) any physiological process that can be monitored, amplified, and made visible to an individual can be voluntarily controlled by that individual. Physiological instrumentation is a system of electronic equipment that enables a person to perceive a physiological activity that ordinarily occurs below the threshold of awareness. By detecting and amplifying these signals, the instruments allow an individual to be aware immediately of the subtle shifts in his physical state. In a brief time, individuals are capable of noting correlations between these physiological fluctuations and the accompanying psychological states, which are usually in the form of specific images or fantasies. Then, it becomes possible to use the mental image to produce the physiological change at will, and the success or failure of that attempt is immediately registered by the physiological monitoring device. Immediate feedback is the desired result; there is a continuous and instantaneous source of information, and the individual becomes involved in a "closed biofeedback loop" (Gattozzi 1971). Thus, the link between psychological and physiological processes is made quite explicit. Since establishing this link is the key to exploring mind-body interaction, psychosomatic disorders, and a basic assumption of the imagery therapies, Biofeedback becomes an important methodology for resolving some of those issues. Within Biofeedback, emphasis is always on an individual's internal states as the means for establishing voluntary control: "In actuality there is no such thing as training in brain wave control, there is training only in the elicitation of certain subjective states. . . . what are detected and manipulated (in some as yet unknown way) are subjective feelings, focus of attention, and thought processes" (Green, Green, and Walters 1970). By emphasizing subjective imagery, the Biofeedback researchers and clinicians have differentiated voluntary control from conditioning. Psychophysiologist Elmer E. Green of the Menninger Foundation has summarized this distinction: "It is important to differentiate between: a) voluntary control of internal states, as reflected in cranio-spinal, autonomic, and central nervous system indicators, and b) conditioned control of such indicators as in working with animals. . . . Voluntary control moves toward increased inner freedom, conditioned control moves toward loss of freedom" (Green, Green, and Walters 1970). Despite the use of instrumentation, the goal of Biofeedback is the same as that of the imagery therapies—to acquaint the individual with his internal processes so that he might gain insight into his psychological and physiological states.

Neurological indices of the link between psychological and physiological functions have received the most attention in research and in the popular press. An electroencephalogram reveals four major identifiable brain-wave patterns, which are measured in Hz, or cycles per second: (1) delta (0.5–4 Hz), from the central and parietal regions of the brain; (2) theta (4–8 Hz), also from the central and parietal regions of the brain; (3) alpha (8–13 Hz), which originate in the occipital region; and (4) beta (13–22 Hz), which originate in the cerebral cortex. In actuality, the rage of beta waves extends from 13 Hz to infinity, although all research to date has adopted the convention of setting the upper limit between 20 and 40 Hz. During periods of waking activity, beta and alpha waves overshadow theta and delta waves; the latter are more prominent during sleep. Detection of EEG patterns is derived from two electrodes, one on the scalp and one attached to a "neutral" area of the head, such as the ear. The neutral electrode senses electrical noise, which is also picked up by the live electrode. EEG tracings show the electrical difference between the two electrodes after the electrical interference has been canceled out. The origin of the electrical activity has been most commonly attributed to the firing of neurons within the brain, although their real source remains an enigma. Most research has focused on the alpha (8–13 Hz) rhythm because production of that frequency is associated with a subjective sensation of deep relaxation and mental tranquility; it has been described as "active passivity."

Beginning in 1960, Joe Kamiya of the Langley Porter Neuropsychiatric Institute first demonstrated that individuals were capable of controlling their brain rhythms by means of Biofeedback. Volunteers were instructed to guess whether they were in alpha or not, following a brief description of the alpha state. At each guess, the experimenter would tell the subject if he was in alpha according to the EEG tracings. Quite rapidly, the subjects increased the accuracy of their guesses until they were able to predict their state correctly. Next, Kamiya wanted to see if the subjects could learn to control their alpha rhythms once they had learned to recognize the accompanying subjective feelings. To this end, subjects were instructed to induce alpha waves when a single tone sounded and to suppress them when a double tone sounded. This phase of the process was also successful, and Kamiya then established a constant tone indicative of EEG alpha activity. The same subjects were divided into two groups in which one was told to keep the tone off (that is, alpha) and the other was required to keep the tone on, for as long as possible. With the aid of the constant feedback tone, most of the subjects were able to turn the alpha waves on or off after a series of twelve training sessions (Kamiya 1962). When subjects were questioned about their experiences, they described the alpha state as serene, pleasant, devoid of imagery, and accompanied by a relaxed vigilance. Moreover, they noted that in order to turn off the alpha rhythm, it was necessary only to exert some mental effort, such as problem solving or invoking mental images. Since Kamiya, several experimenters have affirmed the ability of subjects to learn to control alpha production after several hours of training (Green 1972; Peper 1971a; Pelletier 1974). Voluntary induction of a state of deep relaxation accompanied by mental alertness is a state advocated by meditation, Autogenic Training, Psychosynthesis, and other imagery techniques in varying degrees. Since such a state is assumed to be pleasant and beneficial, it is of particular significance to note research conducted in Japan several years prior to Kamiya's independent observations at the Langley Porter Neuropsychiatric Institute, University of California Medical School.

In 1957, Akira Kasamatsu recorded the EEGs of one Zen and one Yoga meditator and compared them with two control subjects (Kasamatsu et al. 1966). As the two experts began their meditation, the percentage of their alpha waves increased markedly, even with their eyes open. In contrast, the alpha waves of the controls showed no detectable change, except for statistically insignificant increases in alpha waves when they closed their eyes. Additionally, it was noted that the alpha waves of the Zen and Yoga practitioners were not significantly disrupted by external stimuli, such as hand claps or bells ringing, while they were meditating. Another study (Anand, China, and Singh 1961) monitored four yogis, and all of them demonstrated persistent alpha activity with well-marked increased amplitude during meditation. In this study, Anand also attempted to induce alpha blocking (that is, to change the high-amplitude low-frequency alpha to low-amplitude high-frequency beta waves) by introducing very intrusive external stimuli, such as bright light, loud noises, and hot glass tubing on the skin. None of the yogis produced any blockage of alpha waves due to these intrusions while they were meditating. Furthermore, when these same stimuli were presented to the yogis when they were not meditating, the EEG did not record the habitation response that is usually observed in all individuals. Each stimulus was received with equal intensity each time it was introduced, and the yogis did not indicate any adaptation to the repetition of the same stimulus. This is a most significant result because it indicates that the yogic goal of perceiving each event in the world with equal intensity and appreciation is affirmed by the EEG record. Furthermore, these two pilot studies were the first indications of a convergence of Eastern meditation and Biofeedback, since Biofeedback produced states similar to those states of relaxation and receptivity that were occurring in meditation.

It was the neurological parameters of meditation states that were receiving the most attention from researchers until one study focused belatedly on a number of physiological indices. EEG, electrocardiogram, electromyogram, plesthysmogram, respiration, GSR, and blood-pressure readings were obtained from forty-five yogis in ninety-eight sessions (Bagchi and Wenger 1957). Each physiological variable indicated that the meditators achieved states of control over these functions, which were thought to be autonomic and not subject to voluntary control. Achievement of this control had taken years of concerted effort; the maintaining of the alpha state allowed the meditator to will his physiological functions to operate far below the normal thresholds—for example, there was a twenty-three percent decrease in respiration rate while he remained alert and awake, according to the EEG record. In light of the observation that alpha production was linked to these abilities, researchers began to speculate that Kamiya's Biofeedback system for alpha-wave enhancement might allow individuals to achieve this state of alpha control in an abbreviated period of time. This state of alpha control is considered to be beneficial because it has been demonstrated to alleviate nervous-system stress more effectively than deep sleep (Kanellakos 1970). Whether Biofeedback is a short cut to achieving meditation states is a debatable issue, but it is clear that there are marked similarities between the two systems and that both systems provide the means of exploring psychological and psychophysiological processes with unprecedented accuracy.

Most impressive of all the research conducted on the psychophysiology of meditation states is a fifty-six-page book compiled by Yoshiharu Akishige of Tokyo University. Drawing on research conducted in Japan from 1920 to 1968, Akishige documents research ranging from Rorschach tests of Zen monks to studies showing a decrease in blood acidity during meditation. Each study indicates that meditation practice has allowed people to obtain a remarkable degree of control over various autonomic functions in order to concentrate on the fantasies that emerge when the physical body remains in a state of quiescence. Altogether, there are over two hundred research articles demonstrating that the alpha state of meditation is accompanied by such physiological responses as: (1) a reduction of the metabolic rate (Anand, China, and Singh 1961; Kasamatsu and Hirai 1966; Akishige 1970), (2) reduction of total oxygen consumption by 20 percent (Wallace 1970), (3) a reduction of the breathing rate to four to six breaths per minute from twelve to fourteen per minute (Allison 1965; Pelletier 1974c), (4) an increase in the number of alpha waves (8–12 Hz) in the brain (Akishige 1970; Kamiya 1968; Green 1971; Kasamatsu and Hirai 1966; Pelletier 1974c), (5) the appearance of theta waves in the cerebral cortex (Wallace 1970; Green 1972), (6) a twenty percent reduction of blood pressure in hypertensive patients (Datey et al. 1969; Pelletier 1974e), and other related reports that need not be reviewed here. What these reports consistently demonstrate is that individuals can learn to control autonomic functions and that this state of control allows them to experience and comprehend more fully the relationship between their mental and physical processes.

To date, there have been very few purely psychological studies correlating specific personality dimensions to observed physiological patterns. According to psychologist Edward W. Maupin (1965), positive response to meditation was correlated with the "capacity for regression" and "tolerance for unrealistic experience," as indicated by Rorschach testing. In a series of experiments, psychiatrist Arthur J. Deikman trained four naïve subjects in meditation over a period of twelve weeks and compared their subjective reports with those of four untrained subjects who sat quietly for equal amounts of time. Each subject in both groups "meditated" for forty-five minutes a day and were interviewed immediately after each session. Control subjects were given no specific instructions, while the meditators were instructed in Zen techniques of meditation. Based on clinical interviews, Deikman (1963, 1966a, 1966b) reported that each of the meditation subjects underwent a "mystical" experience that induced a more positive attitude toward themselves and others. These two studies comprise all the research concerning psychological variables accompanying the meditation state, and it is clear that more research is needed before any sound conclusions may be drawn concerning the psychological aspects of meditation states. One promising area of research that has demonstrated a link between physiology, psychology, and meditation has been undertaken by David Galin and Robert Ornstein. Their research proceeds from the neurological observation that "clinical data suggest that speech, reading, language, and mathematical abilities require the activity of the left hemisphere while the right hemisphere predominates in spatial orientation, recognition of shapes and relations, in tonal memory, and Gestalt thinking" (Galin and Ornstein 1973). Furthermore, they observe that EEG alpha waves are found in greater amounts over the right hemisphere than over the left. These observations lead Galin and Ornstein to hypothesize a personality typology based on hemispheric dominance, where right-hemisphere individuals are characterized as synthetic, emotional, spatial, analogic, subjective, and passive and left-hemisphere individuals are characterized as verbal, analytic, abstract, rational, digital, and objective (Bakan 1971). It is possible that individuals who exhibit right-hemisphere dominance by EEG monitoring will also be those who can enter into meditation states more readily. This possible link between physiological processes and psychological parameters remains untested but offers the possibility of defining the links between mind and body. Perhaps a high alpha index in the right hemisphere on a baseline measure indicates that one's habitual cognitive style involves the use of a more passive, nonanalytic stance toward the world and is more readily disposed toward deep-relaxation imagery techniques or meditation exercises. On the other hand, the high alpha index over the left hemisphere may indicate that the individual would be more amenable to a more structured verbal therapy, such as psychoanalysis, or to meditation that involved concentration on an external stimulus, such as a mandala figure. These observations seem plausible, based on the research of Galin and Ornstein, and it is possible that the EEG may prove to be useful as a diagnostic tool for matching patients with a particular type of therapy.

RESEARCH AND PSYCHOTHERAPEUTIC APPLICATIONS OF BIOFEEDBACK

Using Biofeedback as an adjunct to psychotherapy, especially the imagery therapies, is already in practice, and it promises success. Merging Biofeedback and therapy is anticipated by Joe Kamiya:

> In this age of technological sophistication, there seems to be no good reason why a beginning cannot be made toward courses in "physiological awareness," in which students are taught the subjective feel of changes in heart rate, EEG waves, sleep stages, electrodermal changes accompanying social stimuli, gastric contractions, etc. The dictum "Know Thyself" could be made easier to follow with techniques that make the covert internal processes of brain and body directly observable to the person (1968).

While meditators train to achieve this insight for many years, Biofeedback makes these states accessible in a matter of hours or weeks. Most promising is the psychotherapeutic application of Biofeedback to psychosomatic disorders. A few of the more prominent examples are: (1) decreased systolic blood pressure of essential hypertension (Benson et al. 1971), (2) control of pain (Gannon and Sternbach 1971; Pelletier 1974c), (3) heart rate and blood-pressure control (Brener and Kleinman 1970), (4) correcting tachycardia (Weiss and Engel 1971), (5) elimination of migraine headaches and inducing more restful sleep (Sargent, Green, and Walters 1972), and (6) reduction of free-floating anxiety (Jacobson 1971). In every application, the appropriate physiological process, such as heart rate in the tachycardia or muscle tension in the migraines, is monitored and amplified for the patient, who proceeds to find the subjective state that allows him to control that physiological process. It is frequently reported (Gattozzi 1971) that patients often say that they can establish control over the process without knowing how they accomplished the feat. However, it has been demonstrated that those patients who are most adept at focusing on subjective imagery or fantasies learn to control their physiological processes in a shorter amount of time than those patients who are unable to detect accompanying imagery (Green 1971). Imagery associated with the control seems to exhibit wide variation between subjects when it is acknowledged as being present. Therefore, it seems a plausible conclusion that the presence of imagery is not a prerequisite to autonomic control, although imagery does speed up the process. Recent research by Thomas Budzynski and Johann Stoyva (1971) suggests that the contentless state of alpha is necessary in order to achieve autonomic control. However, after that state has been achieved, it is then possible to experience the more subtle psychological states of fantasy. In other words, they are proposing a two-step process: relaxing into the alpha state to quiet physiological processes as a precursor to the inducement of subjective fantasies. Such a process is precisely the same procedure advocated in all systems of meditation as well as in Autogenic Training, Psychosynthesis, and Morita therapy. The one essential difference in Biofeedback is that the feedback to the patient is more accurate and more immediate. However, physiological monitoring devices cannot help the patient to understand consciously and to integrate the fantasy material that accompanies the states he achieves by means of deep relaxation or Biofeedback—that is where the imagery therapies serve as an invaluable adjunct to Biofeedback.

At the present time, the most innovative approach to this proposed synthesis of Biofeedback and imagery has been undertaken by Thomas Budzynski and Johann Stoyva of the University of Colorado Medical Center. Their method combines three systems: (1) Jacobson's progressive relaxation (1938); (2) Autogenic Training (Schultz and Luthe 1959); and (3) Biofeedback, especially the use of the electromyogram (EMG). Their major application of that technique has been to disorders such as bronchial asthma, sleep onset insomnia, migraine headaches, angina pectoris, and peptic ulcers. In practice, Budzynski and Stoyva follow Schultz's six-step process (Schultz and Luthe 1959) as a prelude to therapy. According to their research, patients were able to achieve a deeper and quicker state of deep relaxation when EMG feedback was provided for them throughout each stage of Schultz's exercises. Following this state of deep relaxation, they use techniques of behavior modification and systematic desensitization as their most common therapeutic techniques. Deep relaxation is an essential feature of Wolpe's system. His method involves the establishment, at the outset of therapy, of a hierarchy of scenes of an increasing anxiety-provoking quality based on the patient's detailed account of his phobic experience (Singer 1971). Desensitization occurs by encouraging the patient to remain relaxed while imagining the graduated series of frightening events. Wolpe and his followers have extended the use of the technique from classical phobias to a complex series of social behaviors, such as public speaking and aggressive outbursts (Lazarus 1960). What is critically different in Budzynski's system is: (1) the patient monitors his own anxiety level by means of EMG feedback, and (2) emphasis is on understanding and integrating the fantasy material rather than on viewing it simply as the means to the end of extinguishing unwanted behavior patterns. These last two points are extremely important, since the use of the EMG seems to speed the process of relaxation during the fantasy in two ways: "First, since the EMG indicator can be set at a high sensitivity, most scenes can be terminated even before the patient is aware of rising anxiety. Second, the use of EMG feedback between scenes helps the patient to return quickly to a relaxed condition" (Budzynski and Stoyva 1971). Also, the interpretation of the fantasies is important: "About one in five [patients] becomes frightened of the fantasies and sensations accompanying deep relaxation. Certain bodily sensations such as warmth, heaviness, giddiness, feelings of floating or turning may prove alarming. Imagery of a frightening nature may occur" (Budzynski and Stoyva 1971). Rather than attempting to construct desensitization hierarchies, their procedure involves training the patient in deep relaxation by feedback and then encouraging him to engage in fantasizing about whatever is bothering him that day. Contents of the fantasy may or may not have direct relevance to his present complaint, but, eventually, the patient is capable of confronting even his most deeply rooted anxieties and of remaining relaxed and calm. Subjective reports of the fantasies bear a striking resemblance to those of meditators who have learned to view their fantasies with calm detachment in a mode of active passivity. Additionally, patients indicate increasingly high levels of alpha during the rest periods when visualization is not required. Subjective reports of that alpha state are: "letting go," "a relaxed passive awareness," "a lack of criticalness," "some desirable, indescribable state with timeless dimensions" (Peper 1971a). It seems clear from the clinical applications of Budzynski and Stoyva that Biofeedback and imagery techniques constitute powerful therapeutic tools that combine a means of inducing a meditation state plus a means of interpreting the contents elicited during those states. Many patients report control over various autonomic functions either as a direct or indirect result of learning to monitor their internal states with such accuracy. If the Biofeedback and imagery techniques are able to prove their efficacy in anxiety- and stress-related disorders, then the practical consequences are considerable. Budzynski and Stoyva (1971) have based much of their theory on the neurological evidence presented at the beginning of this book, and they conclude:

> Perhaps they [i.e., biofeedback and imagery techniques] will be useful in modifying man's "defense-alarm" reaction, a response which figures prominently in psychological stress. . . . Though adaptive under conditions of primitive living where strenuous physical exertions are necessary for survival, under conditions of civilized living the sustained evocation of the defense alarm reaction seems likely to lead to stress related disorders, an idea advanced by Simeons (1962), Charvat, Dell, and Eklow (1964), and Wolff (1968).

What these two researchers and clinicians are formulating is the "language" by which an individual's conscious-unconscious, voluntary-autonomic processes might be harmoniously integrated in order to reduce conflicting or misunderstood signals that induce stress. This language consists of two parts: (1) a quiescent state of meditation, and (2) spontaneous or induced imagery that has been demonstrated to have a significant effect on an individual's psychological and physiological functions.

Through the synthesis of the older imagery therapies with the newer Biofeedback therapies, a new form of psychotherapy is emerging that promises to be an effective therapeutic intervention and also a means of resolving some profound theoretical and philosophical issues concerning the nature of mind-body interaction and interdependence. So far, only two theorists have integrated current neurological research with theories of psychological processes; they are Harvard psychiatrist Andrew Weil and McGill neurologist Raymond Prince. In a recent book, *The Natural Mind* (1972), Weil suggests the following connection between neurology and psychological theory: "There exist potential circuits (i.e., the RAS) for conducting unconscious impulses upward, as anyone knows who is aware of his daydreams and intuitions. The sealing of these channels by the conscious mind forces unbalanced unconscious energies down the autonomic nerves to produce negative physical effects" (p. 64). Formulations such as these are crude at this point but are indicative of an emerging area of theory and research. Perhaps the most extensive attempt to integrate neurology and psychology has been the research of Raymond Prince, an orthodox psychoanalyst who has conducted extensive research on the reticular activating system. Prince formulates psychoanalytic theory in terms of recent neurological research by noting:

> The defense mechanism of incorporation . . . it is interesting to note that the engram for swallowing is embedded in the reticular column just below the activating or ego portion. We have of course no idea what the physiological basis of the defense of incorporation might be and it might be coincidence that the engram for swallowing lies in close proximity to the area we have felt to subserve the ego. The same remarks would be applicable to vomiting and the defense mechanism of projection. Analysts have often looked upon projection as a kind of spiritual vomiting. The engram for vomiting is also embedded in the reticular column nearby (1971).

What Budzynski, Weil, and Prince all point to is that fantasies and subjective imagery seem to be the phenomenological correlates of central-nervous-system activity. It is not a one-to-one correlation, but evidence strongly suggests a link between psychological symbolic processes and CNS electrical processes. What the exact nature is of their mutual interdependence remains a vast area for research and clinical insight.

In 1915, Freud wrote the following passage as a condemnation of attempts to synthesize anatomy and psychological processes: "Every attempt to deduce from these facts [i.e., anatomy] a localization of mental processes, every attempt to think of ideas as stored up in the nerve cells and of excitations as passing along nerve fibers has completely miscarried. Here there is a hiatus which at present cannot be filled, nor is it one of the tasks of psychology to fill it. Our mental topography has nothing to do with anatomy" (1962). Perhaps the research in neurology and psychology over the last fifty years has provided the information necessary to begin to fill that hiatus and to develop more effective psychotherapeutic systems in the process. Psychophysiological processes are far more subtle than gross anatomical distinctions and have been demonstrated to bridge the gap between psychological and physiological functions. Of course it is possible that no correlation exists between these two functions, but theory and research indicate that there are some clear connections between the two and that more are yet to be discovered. Through the use of imagery techniques and Biofeedback, twentieth-century patients are able to achieve states that have been advocated in meditation since the twelfth-century inception of Zen Buddhism. Induction of the meditative alpha state of "passive concentration" (Luthe 1962) is relatively easy by means of Biofeedback. Once in that state, one is capable of observing and assessing his fantasies and thoughts with a measure of objectivity and detachment. Such a state is clearly a prerequisite to self-understanding and is the basis for constructive alterations in behavior. When such a discipline is undertaken on a regular basis, an individual can learn to recognize and act in accordance with his most fundamental psychological and physiological responses to personal, social, and environmental stimuli. Trusting the self through a thorough knowledge of the self is the fundamental goal of all psychotherapy, as well as of meditation and Biofeedback. Constructive introspection fostered by specific techniques is a prerequisite to functioning with *mushin,* or controlled spontaneity. To react to other individuals and situations with the knowledge that one's response is absolutely clear, open, and honest seems to be the highest goal of both psychotherapy and meditation. Freedom from neurotic indecision and vacillation allows an individual to focus energy and attention on more creative endeavors. Of course, these are highly idealized statements that are not likely to be achieved by any individual—but that does not lessen their value as goals worth seeking.

CONCLUSION

Drawing on the ancient disciplines of Zen Buddhism, the deep relaxation techniques of several European psychotherapies, and the physiological instrumentation of the twentieth-century Western world, a highly sophisticated form of Western yoga or "metatherapy" (Goleman 1971) is evolving. This psychotherapy constitutes an orientation toward a model of therapy rather than of an actual system. Despite the unorthodox heritage of this evolving metatherapy, it constitutes a major innovation because it has been demonstrated to be an expedient means of alleviating a wide array of psychological and physiological disorders.

Each system of psychotherapy and each area of neurological and psychological research discussed here can be viewed as contributing a specific area of expertise and insight toward the construction of a more comprehensive system of psychotherapy. Although this end might never be achieved, such a unified endeavor between researchers and clinicians would promote more cooperation for mutual benefit. Additionally, the antagonisms between systems of psychotherapy might also be alleviated; it can be demonstrated that the similarities and complementarity of the disparate systems far outweigh their differences. There are evident advantages to such cooperation—some have already been realized, while others are yet to be discovered. Speculations concerning the future development of Western yoga can best be undertaken by citing areas of current research and clinical applications that have far-reaching implications. We are in accord with numerous other clinicians and researchers who have defined the frontiers of the psychotherapeutic applications of Western yoga as:

1. Reduction of blood pressure in hypertensive patients, reducing the reliance on drugs and restoring a sense of efficacy to the individual patient
2. A means of alleviating tension and stress during the periods

of sensory restriction or sensory monotony, such as are experienced by astronauts, truck drivers, assembly-line workers, submarine crews, or during general office work by secretaries and executives

3. Meditation-based psychotherapies are a means to reduce effectively the use of stimulants or depressants ranging from hallucinogenic drugs to cigarettes (Wallace 1970). This indicates that the desire to experience alterations in states of consciousness is distinct from the means to reach that end and that meditation does in fact alter an individual's perceptions with no toxic or negative side effects

4. Prolonged lowering of metabolic rates in patients would be an invaluable aid in dietary considerations for long-term space flights

5. Autonomic control is and will become one of the most useful means for researching the psychophysiology of fantasies, hypnagogic images, and dreams

6. Deep relaxation might prove to be an invaluable adjunct in lessening the shock of individuals who have been injured in accidents or after serious surgical operations

7. Psychosomatic disorders, such as ulcers, epilepsy, and tachycardia, can be more carefully researched and treated by allowing the patient to become a more active participant in the healing process

8. Imagery techniques and Biofeedback increase an individual's ability to use his introspection more effectively and to become more self-aware

9. Creativity and improved work output seem to be by-products of individuals engaging in the imagery therapies and Biofeedback. Perhaps this increased productivity is directly correlated with the marked reduction of physical and mental tensions during meditation and biofeedback

10. Patients are encouraged to experience an aspect of themselves that has a constancy above and beyond their more transient thoughts, opinions, and feelings. Such an experience produces

a profound sense of well-being and assurance, which is a prelude to behaving in a more positive and constructive manner.

Although all of the above speculations and most of the research cited here refer to individual cases, these methods of meditation and Biofeedback have been effectively applied in group and community settings. What is most impressive about this newly emerging system of Western Yoga is that its applications and implications seem unbounded. Research and applications of this new psychotherapy offer an exacting, precise, involving, and exciting means for an unprecedented exploration of human consciousness. By allowing individuals to experience the most subtle levels of their psychological and physiological processes, this psychotherapy enables them to truly know themselves as fully functioning units of mind and body. Since all transcendent, inspiring experiences seem to be characterized by a sensation of unity and wholeness, perhaps Western yoga will make this profound experience more readily accessible. This experience is cited by all systems of meditation as a prerequisite for the marked transformation of the individual personality. What ultimately matters is not the experience of wholeness but the fact that such an event is the basis of self-actualization. To live with controlled spontaneity in accord with the highest ideals of man is, perhaps, less of a vision and more of a reality now than ever before in recorded history.

WHITHER ALTERED STATES?

But way off alone, out by himself beyond boat and shore, Jonathan Livingston Seagull was practicing. A hundred feet in the sky he lowered his webbed feet, lifted his beak, and strained to hold a painful hard twisting curve through his wings. The curve meant that he would fly slowly, and now he slowed until the wind was a whisper in his face, until the ocean stood still beneath him. He narrowed his eyes in fierce concentration, held his breath, forced one . . . single . . . more . . . inch . . . of . . . curve . . . Then his feathers ruffled, he stalled and fell.

Richard Bach, *Jonathan Livingston Seagull*

What directions must altered-state theory and research take as man rapidly approaches the twenty-first century? Can we be on the verge of a psychotechnic neorenaissance, or are we closer to confirming the status of Homo sapiens as an "evolutionary mistake, soon to be discarded on Nature's rubbish heap, like other species that failed to adapt?" (Metzner 1971). It seems that within our transcultural nexus called Planet Earth, both alternatives are moving rapidly toward confirmation. If we are to maximize our chances in what may well be a race against species oblivion, we must recognize that the further reaches of the human mind are at least as important as the further reaches of the physical universe. However, as knowledge continues to increase exponentially in both realms, we may find our explorations of both inner and outer space to be asymptotically approaching the same essential upper limit.

For centuries, philosophers and theologians have espoused the belief that man is barred from truly "grokking" the dictum "Know Thyself" by his perpetual state of encapsulation. "If man wishes to gain a more inclusive world-view or to approach ultimate reality it will be necessary for him to break through the several cocoons within which he is inevitably encapsulated. The first step in this process is to recognize that he is, in fact, encapsulated. Unfortunately, this first step is the most difficult" (Royce 1964).

To really comprehend that this initial step is the most demanding, we must entertain the possibility that in our so-called waking state of consciousness, we are but partially awake. Can the age-old metaphor that man operates from within a culturally induced hypnotic state be more than a metaphor? Indeed, is there some transcultural Laingian injunction against recognizing the existence of such a collective hypnosis? Are we stuck with the realization that "no instruction book came with the human biocomputer," and, hence, the inner ecology must remain a mystery surpassing even that of extragalactic space?

While no absolutely valid instruction book is available for programming the human biocomputer, there do exist partial maps pointing toward the eventual construction of a cartography of consciousness. The discussion of psychosis, Biofeedback, hypnosis, meditation, the imagery therapies, and so on has been an attempt to explicate some of the current techniques for partially mapping one's inner space. Our professed intention has been to foster the development of what may be called transpersonal psychology, experimental or pragmatic mysticism, or a Western form of yoga or Zen so that we might become consciously involved in the process of our own evolution. Both the task and mode of expression are consistent with the present state of our own development. The goal is nothing less than

> self-realization, enlightenment, creativity, self-actualization, spiritual development, being authentic, fully functioning . . . to be aware and to respond: to become aware, from one's own immanent, intimate experience, that we are elements of a greater whole and that one has the choice of responding, of saying "yes" to life with the whole of his being, of being responsible (response-able)—and so to choose, and thereby to taste of freedom, to know the origins of love, to find the essence of wisdom, to become authentically man (Harmon 1967).

We have already taken the advice of Lao-tzu that "the journey of a 1000 miles begins with one step," and, indeed, we have taken several. Our current work, or *sadhana,* has taken us to studies of clinical Biofeedback, psychothanatology, altered states of consciousness, implications of quantum physics, arcane systems of meditation, unorthodox systems of healing, and the applications of parapsychology in medicine. We hope to make these segments of our respective journeys available in the near future. We know, along with Jonathan Seagull, that our feathers will get ruffled, that we may stall and at times even fall; but, on a far deeper level, we are secure in the knowledge that this crucial journey must be made because nothing less than species survival is at stake.

> To everything there is a season, and a time to every purpose under the heaven (Ecclesiastes).

For us, the season and time have arrived.

Bibliography

Aaronson, B. S. "Mystic and Schizophreniform States and the Experience of Depth." *Journal for the Scientific Study of Religion* 6(1967):246–52.

———. "Psychosynthesis as System and Therapy." *American Journal of Clinical Hypnosis* 10(1968):231–35.

———. "Some Hypnotic Analogues to the Psychedelic State." In *Psychedelics*, eds. B. S. Aaronson and H. Osmond. New York: Doubleday, 1970.

———, and Osmond, H. *Psychedelics: The Uses and Implications of Hallucinogenic Drugs.* New York: Doubleday, 1970.

Abe, T. "The Relation between Emotions and Bodily Sensations." *Psychologia* 8(1965):187–90.

Aberle, D. "Arctic Hysteria and Latah in Mongolia." *New York Academy Science Series 11*, 14(1952):291–97.

Ackernecht, E. "Psychopathology, Primitive Medicine, and Primitive Culture." *Bulletin of History of Medicine* 14(1943):30–67.

Adelman, F. "Toward a Psychocultural Interpretation of Latah." *Davidson Journal of Anthropology* 1(1955):69–76.

Adler, A. "Individual Psychology." In *Psychologies of 1930*, ed. C. Murchinson. Worcester, Mass.: Clark University Press, 1930.

Adler, G. "Methods of Treatment in Analytical Psychology." In *Psychoanalytic Techniques*, ed. B. B. Wolman. New York: Basic Books, 1967.

Agnew, H., Webb, W., and Williams, R. "The Effects of Stage Four Sleep Deprivation." *Electroencephalography and Clinical Neurophysiology* 17(1964):68–70.

Akishige, Y., ed. "Psychological Studies in Zen." *Bulletin of Faculty Literature of Kyushu University* 5 and 11, Fukuoka, Japan.

Akishige, Yoshiharu. *Psychological Studies on Zen.* Tokyo: Zen Institute of Komazawa University, 1970.

Alexander, J. "Clinical Experiences with Hypnosis in Psychiatric Therapy." *American Journal of Clinical Hypnosis* 7(1965):190–206.

Allison, J. "Cortical and Subcortical Evoked Responses to Central Stimuli During Wakefulness and Sleep." *Electroencephalography and Clinical Neurophysiology* 18(1965):131–39.

———. "Adaptive Regression and Intense Religious Experiences." *Journal of Nervous and Mental Diseases* 145(1967):452–63.

———. "Respiratory Changes During Transcendental Meditation." *Lancet,* no. 7651(1970):833–34.

Alvarez, W. C. *Minds That Came Back.* New York: Lippincott, 1961.

Anand, B., and China, G. "Investigations on Yogis Claiming to Stop Their Hearts." *Indian Journal of Medical Research* 49(1961):90–94.

———, ———, and Singh, B. "Some Aspects of Electroencephalographic Studies in Yogis." *Electroencephalography and Clinical Neurophysiology* 13(1961a):452–56. Reprinted in *Altered States of Consciousness,* ed. C. Tart. New York: Wiley, 1969.

———, ———, and ———. *Electroencephalography and Clinical Neurophysiology* 13(1961b):452–56.

Ando, S. "Zen and Christianity." *Psychologia* 8(1965):123–34.

Arieti, S. *Interpretation of Schizophrenia.* New York: Brunner, 1955.

Aserinsky, E., and Kleitman, N. "Regularly Occuring Periods of Eye Motility, and Concomitant Phenomena, During Sleep." *Science* 118(1953):273–74.

Assagioli, R. *Psychosynthesis.* New York: Viking, 1965.

Atken, R. "Psychology and Zazen." Paper delivered at the Hawaii State Hospital, 1968.

Baba Ram Dass. *Be Here Now.* New York: Crown, 1971.

Bagchi, B. K. "Mental Hygiene and the Hindu Doctrine of Relaxation." *Mental Hygiene* 20(1936):424–40.

———, and Wenger, M. A. "Electrophysiological Correlates of Some Yogi Exercises." In *Electroencephalography, Clinical Neurophysiology and Epilepsy,* vol. 3 of *The First International Congress of Neurological Sciences,* eds. L. von Bagaert and J. Radermecker. London: Pergamon, 1959.

Bakan, D. *The Duality of Human Existence.* Chicago: Rand McNally, 1966.

———. "The Eyes Have It." *Psychology Today* April 1971:64–67.

Barber, T. X. "Hypnosis as a Causal Variable in Present-day Psychology: A Critical Analysis." *Psychological Reports* 14(1964):839–42.

————. "An Empirically Based Formulation of Hypnotism." *American Journal of Clinical Hypnosis* 12(1969*a*):100–130.

————. *Hypnosis: A Scientific Approach.* Princeton, N.J.: Van Nostrand, 1969*b*.

————. *LSD, Marihuana, Yoga, and Hypnosis.* Chicago: Aldine, 1970.

————, and Calverley, D. "Empirical Evidence for a Theory of 'Hypnotic' Behavior: Effects of Suggestibility of Five Variables Typically Induced in Hypnotic Induction Procedures." *Journal of Consulting Psychology* 29(1965*a*):98–107.

————, and ————. "Empirical Evidence for a Theory of 'Hypnotic' Behavior: The Suggestibility-Enhancing Effects of Motivational Suggestions, Relaxation Sleep Suggestions, and Suggestions That the Subjects Will Be Effectively 'Hypnotized.'" *Journal of Personality* 33(1965*b*):256–70.

————, and ————. "Multidimensional Analysis of Hypnotic Behavior." *Journal of Abnormal Psychology* 74(1969):209–20.

————, et al., eds. *Biofeedback and Self-Control: A Reader.* Chicago: Aldine-Atherton, 1971.

————, et al., eds. *Biofeedback and Self-Control, 1970: An Annual.* Chicago: Aldine-Atherton, 1971.

Bateson, G., ed. *Perceval's Narrative: A Patient's Account of His Psychosis.* Stanford, Calif.: Stanford University Press, 1961.

————. *Steps to an Ecology of Mind.* New York: Ballantine, 1972.

————, et al. "Toward a Theory of Schizophrenia." *Behavioral Science* 4(1956):251–64.

Beahrs, J. "The Hypnotic Psychotherapy of Milton H. Erickson." *American Journal of Clinical Hypnosis* 14(1971):73–90.

Beck, A. T. "Role of Fantasies in Psychotherapy and Psychopathology." *Journal of Nervous and Mental Diseases* 150(1970):3–17.

Behanam, K. *Yoga: A Scientific Evaluation.* New York: Dover, 1937.

Bellak, L. "An Ego-Psychological Theory of Hypnosis." *International Journal of Psychoanalysis* 36(1955):373–79.

————. *Schizophrenia: A Review of the Syndrome.* New York: Logos, 1958.

Benedict, R. "The Concept of the Guardian Spirit in North America." *Memoirs.* American Anthropological Association 29(1923).

Benson, H. In *Hearings before the Select Committee on Crime.* House of Representatives, Ninety-Second Congress, 1971.

————, Shapiro, D., Tursky, B., and Schwartz, G. E. "Decreased Systolic Blood Pressure through Operant Conditioning Techniques in Patients with Essential Hypertension." In *Biofeedback and Self-Control, 1971,* eds. J. Stoyva et al. Chicago: Aldine-Atherton, 1972.

————, and Wallace, K. "Decreased Drug Abuse with Transcendental Meditation: A Study of 1862 Subjects." Paper presented at the Drug Abuse International Symposium for Physicians. Ann Arbor, Mich.: 1970.

Berger, H. *Archiv für Psychiatrie und Nervenkrankheiten* 87(1929):527–70.

Berger, P. L., and Luckmann, T. *The Social Construction of Reality*. New York: Doubleday, 1966.

Bernheim, H. *Suggestive Therapeutics*. New York: Putnam, 1895.

Bettelheim, B. "Individual and Mass Behavior in Extreme Situations." In *Personality*, ed. R. S. Lazarus. Baltimore: Penguin, 1967.

Binswanger, L. *Being-in-the-World*. New York: Basic Books, 1963.

Birdwhistell, R. L. "Kinesthetics and Communication." In *Explorations in Communication*, ed. E. Carpenter. Boston: Beacon, 1960.

————. "Body Behavior and Communication." In *International Encyclopedia of the Social Sciences*. New York: Macmillan, 1964.

Bleuler, E. *Dementia Praecox, or the Group of Schizophrenias*. New York: International Universities Press, 1950.

Bleuler, M. "Conception of Schizophrenia within the Last Fifty Years and Today." *International Journal of Psychiatry* 1(1965):505–15.

Boisen, A. "Onset in Acute Schizophrenia." *Psychiatry* 10(1947):159–66.

————. *The Exploration of the Inner World*. New York: Harper & Row, 1962.

Bowers, M. "The Onset of Psychosis—A Diary Account." *Psychiatry* 28(1965):346–58.

————. "Pathogenesis of Acute Schizophrenic Psychosis." *Archives of General Psychiatry* 19(1968):348–55.

————, and Freedman, D. X. "Psychedelic Experiences in Acute Psychosis." *Archives of General Psychiatry* 15(1966):240–48.

Brattøy, T. "The Neuromuscular Hypertension and the Understanding of Nervous Conditions." *Journal of Nervous and Mental Diseases* 95(1942):550–67.

————. "Psychology versus Anatomy in the Treatment of Arm Neuroses with Psychotherapy." *Journal of Nervous and Mental Diseases* 115 (1952):215–45.

————. *Fundamentals of Psychoanalytic Technique*. New York: Wiley, 1954.

Brazier, M. A. B. "The Analysis of Brain Waves." *Scientific American* June 1962:3–9.

Breger, L. *Clinical-Cognitive Psychology*. Englewood Cliffs, N.J.: Prentice-Hall, 1969.

Brener, J., and Kleinman, R. A. "Learned Control of Decreases in Systolic Blood Pressure." In *Biofeedback and Self-Control, 1970*, eds. T. X. Barber et al. Chicago: Aldine-Atherton, 1971.

Brenman, M. "The Phenomenon of Hypnosis." In *Problems of Consciousness*. New York: Josiah Macy, Jr. Foundation, 1951.

————, and Gill, M. M. *Hypnotherapy: A Survey of the Literature*. New York: International Universities Press, 1947.

Breuer, J., and Freud, S. *Studies in Hysteria*. Trans. by A. A. Brill. New York: Nervous and Mental Disease Publishing Company, 1936.

Brody, W. "On the Dynamics of Narcissism." *Psychoanalytic Study of the Child* 20(1965):165–93.

Brown, B. B. "Recognition of Aspects of Consciousness through Association with EEG Alpha Activity Represented by a Light Signal." *Psychophysiology* 6(1969): 442–52.

Bruner, J. S. *On Knowing: Essays for the Left Hand*. Cambridge, Mass.: Harvard University Press, 1962.

Buchsbaum, M., and Silverman, J. "Stimulus Intensity Control and the Cortical Evoked Response." *Psychosomatic Medicine* 30(1968): 12–22.

Budzynski, T. H. "Some Applications of Biofeedback-Produced Twilight States." Paper presented to the American Psychological Association. Washington, D.C.: 1971.

————, and Stoyva, J. M. "An Instrument for Producing Deep Muscle Relaxation by Means of Analog Information Feedback." *Journal of Applied Behavior Analysis* 2(1969):231–37.

————, and ————. "Biofeedback Techniques in Behavior Therapy and Autogenic Training." Denver, Colorado: University of Colorado Medical Center, 1971.

————, ————, and Adler, C. "Feedback-Induced Muscle Relaxation: Application to Tension Headache." *Journal of Behavior Therapy and Experimental Psychiatry* 1(1970):205–11.

Burlingham, D. T. "Child Analysis and the Mother." *Psychiatric Quarterly* 4(1935):69–92.

Burns, D. *Buddhist Meditation and Depth Psychology*. San Carlos, Calif.: Neo-Dhamma Publications, 1966.

Caldwell, W. V. *LSD Psychotherapy*. New York: Grove Press, 1968.

Cannon, W. B. *The Wisdom of the Body*. New York: Norton, 1963.

Carlson, V. R. "Underestimation in Size-Constancy Judgments." *American Journal of Psychology* 75(1962):462–65.

Carothers, J. C. *The African Mind in Health and Disease: A Study in Ethnopsychiatry*. World Health Organization Monograph Series, no.

17. New York: World Health Organization of the United Nations, 1953.

Cassirer, E. *An Essay on Man.* New Haven: Yale University Press, 1967.

Castaneda, Carlos. *The Teachings of Don Juan: A Yaqui Way of Knowledge.* Berkeley: University of California Press, 1968.

———. *Journey to Ixtlan.* New York: Simon and Schuster, 1972.

Chapman, J. "The Early Symptoms of Schizophrenia." *British Journal of Psychiatry* 112(1966):225–51.

Chapman, L. F., and Walter, R. D. "Actions of Lysergic Acid Diethylamide on Averaged Human Cortical Evoked Responses to Light Flash." In *Recent Advances in Biological Psychiatry*, ed. J. Wortis. New York: Plenum Press, 1964.

Chertok, L., ed. *Psychophysiological Mechanisms of Hypnosis.* Berlin: Springer-Verlag, 1967.

———. "L'hypnose animale." In *Abnormal Behavior in Animals*, ed. and trans. by W. Fox. Philadelphia: Saunders, 1968.

———, and Kramarz, P. "Hypnosis, Sleep, and EEG." *Journal of Nervous and Mental Diseases* 128(1959):227–38.

Chwelos, N., Blewett, D. B., Smith, C. M., and Hoffer, A. "Use of D-Lysergic and Diethylamide in the Treatment of Alcoholism." *Quarterly Journal of Study of Alcohol* 20(1959):577–90.

Cirinei, G. "Psychosynthesis: A Way to Inner Freedom." Paper delivered to the International Psychosynthesis Conference. London: 1964.

Coate, M. *Beyond All Reason.* New York: Lippincott, 1965.

Cohen, S. *The Beyond Within: The LSD Story.* New York: Atheneum, 1964.

———. *The Beyond Within: The LSD Story.* Rev. ed. New York: Atheneum, 1967.

———. *Drugs of Hallucination.* London: Paladin, 1970.

———, Silverman, J., and Shmavonian, B. "Psychophysiological Studies in Altered Sensory Environments." *Journal of Psychosomatic Research* 6(1963):259–81.

Cole, J., and Katz, M. "The Psychotomimetic Drugs: An Overview." In *LSD: The Consciousness-Expanding Drug*, ed. D. Solomon. New York: Putnam, 1964.

Conn, J. "Hypnosynthesis: Hypnotherapy of the Hysterical Depression with a Discussion of Sexual Fantasy and Neurotic Hostility in Terms of Interpersonal Attitudes and Relationships." *Journal of Clinical Experimental Psychopathology* 13(1952):152–63.

———. "Historical Aspects of Scientific Hypnosis." *Journal of Clinical Experimental Hypnosis* 5(1957):17–24.

————. "Hypnosis: Principles and Precautions in General Practice." *Medical Times* 88(1960):56–60.

————. "Hypnosynthesis: Psychobiologic Principles in the Practice of Dynamic Psychotherapy Utilizing Hypnotic Procedures." *International Journal of Clinical Experimental Hypnosis* 16(1968):1–25.

Dabrowski, K. *Positive Disintegration.* Boston: Little, Brown, 1964.

Dalal, A. S., and Barber, T. X. "Yoga, Yoga Feats, and Hypnosis in the Light of Empirical Research." *The American Journal of Clinical Hypnosis* 11(1969):155–66.

Datey K., Deshmukh, S., Dalvi, C., and Vinekar, S. "Shavassan: A Yogic Exercise in the Management of Hypertension." *Angiology* 20(1969): 325–33.

Deikman, A. "Experimental Meditation." *Journal of Nervous and Mental Diseases* 136(1963):329–43.

————. "De-automatization and the Mystic Experience." *Psychiatry* 29(1966a):324–38.

————. "Implication of Experimentally Induced Contemplative Meditation." *Journal of Nervous and Mental Diseases* 142(1966b):101–16.

————. "The Meaning of Everything." Unpublished manuscript, 1970.

————. "Bimodal Consciousness." *Archives of General Psychiatry* 25(1971):481–89.

de Laszlo, V., ed. *The Basic Writings of C. G. Jung.* New York: Modern Library, 1959.

DeLuca, J. N. "Direct Measurement of Differential Cognitive Deficit in Acute Schizophrenia." *Journal of Abnormal Psychology* 72(1967): 143–46.

Dement, W. "The Effects of Dream Deprivation." *Science* 131(1960): 1705–7.

————, and Kleitman, N. "Cyclic Variations in the EEG During Sleep and Their Relation to Eye Movements, Body Motility, and Dreaming." *Electroencephalography and Clinical Neurophysiology* 9(1957): 73–90.

————, and Wolpert, E. "The Relation of Eye Movements, Body Motility, and External Stimuli to Dream Content." *Journal of Experimental Psychology* 55(1958):543–53.

DeRopp, R. S. *The Master Game: Pathways to Higher Consciousness beyond the Drug Experience.* New York: Dell, 1968.

Desoille, R. *Exploration de l'affectivité subconsciente par la méthode du rêve eveil.* Geneva: Mont-Blanc, 1938.

————. *The Waking Dream in Psychotherapy: An Essay on the Regulatory Function of the Collective Unconscious.* Paris: Presses Universitaires de France, 1945.

————. *Theorie et pratique du rêve eveil dirigé.* Geneva: Mont-Blanc, 1961.

Deutsch, H. "Some Forms of Emotional Disturbances and Their Relationship to Schizophrenia." *Psychoanalytical Quarterly* 11(1942): 301–21.

Devereux, G. "A Sociological Theory of Schizophrenia." *Psychoanalytic Review* 25(1939):315–42.

————. *A Study of Abortion in Primitive Societies.* New York: Julian Press, 1955.

————. "Cultural Factors in Hypnosis and Suggestion: An Examination of Some Primitive Data." *International Journal of Clinical Experimental Hypnosis* 14(1966):273–91.

DiCara, L. "Learning in the Autonomic Nervous System." *Scientific American,* January 1970: 30–39.

————, and Miller, N. E. "Changes in Heart Rate Instrumentally Learned by Curarized Rats as Avoidance Responses." *Journal of Comparative and Physiological Psychology* 65(1968a):8–12.

————, and ————. "Instrumental Learning of Vasomotor Responses by Rats: Learning to Respond Differentially in the Two Ears." *Science* 159(1968b):1485–86.

————, and ————. "Transfer of Instrumentally Learned Heart-Rate Changes from Curarized to Non-Curarized State: Implications for a Mediational Hypothesis." *Journal of Comparative and Physiological Psychology* 68(1969):159–62.

Dollard, J., and Miller, N. E. *Personality and Psychotherapy: An Analysis in Terms of Learning, Thinking, and Culture.* New York: McGraw-Hill, 1950.

Donnars, J. *Troubles de la sphere ano-genito-urinaire révélés par l'imagerie mentale.* Cortina, Italy: Société Internationale des Techniques d'Imagerie Mentale, 1970.

Edinger, E. F. *An Outline of Analytical Psychology.* Quadrant Reprint no. 1. San Francisco: C. G. Jung Institute, 1968.

Edmonston, W., and Robertson, T. "A Comparison of the Effects of Task Motivational and Hypnotic Induction Instructions on Responsiveness to Hypnotic Suggestibility Scales." *American Journal of Clinical Hypnosis* 9(1967):184–87.

Eliade, M. *Shamanism.* Princeton, N.J.: Ballinger, 1964a.

————. *Shamanism: Archaic Techniques of Ecstasy.* New York: Pantheon, 1964b.

Ellis, A. "New Approaches to Psychotherapy Techniques." *Journal of Clinical Psychology* 11(1955):207–60.

Engel, B. T., and Chism, R. A. "Operant Conditioning of Heart Rate Speeding." *Psychophysiology* 3(1967):418–26.

———, and Gottlieb, S. H. "Differential Operant Conditioning of Heart Rate in the Restrained Monkey." *Journal of Comparative and Physiological Psychology* 73(1970):217–25.

———, and Hansen, S. P. "Operant Conditioning of Heart Rate Slowing." *Psychophysiology* 3(1966):176–87.

Erickson, M. "Hypnotic Investigation of Psychosomatic Phenomena." *Psychosomatic Medicine* 5(1943):67–70.

———. "The Therapy of a Psychosomatic Headache." *Journal of Clinical Experimental Hypnosis* 1(1953):2–6.

———. "Special Techniques of Brief Hypnotherapy." *Journal of Clinical Experimental Hypnosis* 2(1954):109–29.

———. "An Hypnotic Technique for Resistant Patients: The Patient, the Technique and Its Rational and Field Experiments." *American Journal of Clinical Hypnosis* 7(1964a):8–32.

———. "The 'Surprise' and 'My Friend John' Techniques of Hypnosis: Minimal Cues and Natural Field Experimentation." *American Journal of Clinical Hypnosis* 6(1964b):293–307.

———. "The Use of Symptoms as an Integral Part of Therapy." *American Journal of Clinical Hypnosis* 8(1965):57–65.

Evans, F. "Recent Trends in Experimental Hypnosis." *Behavioral Science* 13(1968):477–87.

Fagan, J., and Shepherd, I. L. *Gestalt Therapy Now.* New York: Harper & Row, 1970.

Fairbairn, W. *Psychoanalytic Studies of the Personality.* London: Tavistock, 1952.

Fenichel, O. *The Psychoanalytic Theory of Neurosis.* New York: Norton, 1945.

Festinger, L. *A Theory of Cognitive Dissonance.* Evanston, Ill.: Harper & Row, 1957.

———, Pepitone, A., and Newcomb, T. "Some Consequences of Deindividuation in a Group." *Journal of Abnormal Social Psychology* 47(1952):382–89.

Fingarette, H. "The Ego and Mystic Selflessness." *Psychoanalysis and the Psychoanalytic Review* 45(1958):4–40.

Fischer, R. W. "A Cartography of the Ecstatic and Meditative States." *Science* 174(1971):897–904.

———. "On Creative, Psychotic, and Ecstatic States." In *The Highest State of Consciousness,* ed. J. White. New York: Doubleday, 1970.

Fisher, C. "Dreams and Perception: The Role of Preconscious and

Primary Modes of Perception in Dream Formation." *Journal of the American Psychoanalytic Association* 2(1954):389–445.

————. "Dreams, Images, and Perception: A Study of Unconscious-Preconscious Relationships." *Journal of the American Psychoanalytic Association* 4(1956):5–48.

————. "A Study of the Preliminary Stages of the Construction of Dreams." *Journal of the American Psychoanalytic Association* 5(1957):5–60.

————. "The Effects of Subliminal Visual Stimulation on Dreams, Images, and Hallucinations: Further Observations on the Poetzl Phenomenon." *Evolution psychiatrique* (1960).

————, and Paul, I. H. "The Effect of Subliminal Visual Stimulation on Images and Dreams: A Validation Study." *Journal of the American Psychoanalytic Association* 7(1959):35–83.

Fiske, D. W., and Maddi, S. R., eds. *Functions of Varied Experience.* Homewood, Ill.: Dorsey, 1961.

Fordham, M. "The Relevance of Analytical Theory to Alchemy, Mysticism, and Theology." *Journal of Analytical Psychology* 5 (1960):113–28.

Frank, J. *Persuasion and Healing: A Comparative Study of Psychotherapy.* Baltimore: Johns Hopkins Press, 1961.

Frank, L. K. "Play in Personality Development." *American Journal of Orthopsychiatry* 25(1955):576–90.

————. "Tactile Communication." *Genetic Psychology Monographs* 57(1957):209–57.

Frederking, W. "Deep Relaxation and Symbolism." *Psyche* 2(1948).

Freedman, D. X., and Bowers, M. B. "Psychedelic Experiences in Acute Psychoses." *Archives of General Psychiatry* 15(1966):240–48.

French, J. D. "The Reticular Formation." *Scientific American* May 1957:2–8.

Freud, A. "Four Contributions to the Psychoanalytic Study of the Child." Papers delivered in New York, 1960.

Freud, S. *An Outline of Psychoanalysis.* 23:141–207. *In Standard Edition* London: Hogarth Press, 1938a.

————. *The Interpretation of Dreams.* Trans. by A. Brill. New York: Modern Library, 1938b.

————. *Beyond the Pleasure Principle.* London: Hogarth Press, 1950.

————. *On Narcissism: An Introduction.* In *Standard Edition* 14:67–102. London: Hogarth Press, 1957.

————. *Civilization and Its Discontents.* New York: Norton, 1962.

Fromm, E. "Psychoanalysis and Zen Buddhism." *Psychologia* 2(1959):79–99.

————. *Psychoanalysis and Religion.* New Haven, Conn.: Yale University Press, 1960.

Furst, P. *Flesh of the Gods.* New York: Praeger, 1972.

Galambos, R. "Suppression of Auditory Nerve Activity by Stimulation of Efferent Fibers to Cochlea." *Journal of Neurophysiology* 19 (1956):424–37.

Galin, D., and Ornstein, R. "Hemispheric Specialization and the Duality of Consciousness." In *Human Behavior and Brain Function*, ed. H. Widroe. Springfield, Ill.: Charles C Thomas, 1973.

Gannon, L., and Sternbach, R. A. "Alpha Enhancement and a Treatment for Pain: A Case Study." *Journal of Behavior Therapy and Experimental Psychiatry* 2(1975):209.

Garfield, C. "A Psychometric and Clinical Investigation of Anomie and Frankl's Concept of Existential Vacuum." *Psychiatry* 36(1973): 396–408.

————. *Psychothanatological Concomitants of Altered State Experience: An Investigation of the Relationship between Consciousness Alteration and Fear of Death.* Washington, D.C.: United States Government Printing Office, 1974a.

————. "The Value of Dying." In *Getting Rid of What You Haven't Got*, ed. Sri Gurudev Baba Muktananda. Albany, Calif.: Wordpress, 1974b.

————. "Death and Human Consciousness." In "Rediscovery of the Body: An Inquiry into Body-Mind Processes," eds. C. Garfield and J. Garfield. Unpublished manuscript, 1975.

Gattozzi, A. A. *Program Reports on Biofeedback.* NIMH Program Reports, 5:291388. Washington, D.C.: 1971.

Gerard, R. *Psychosynthesis: A Psychotherapy of the Whole Man.* Psychosynthesis Research Foundation Issue No. 14, 1964.

Goffman, E. *The Presentation of Self in Everyday Life.* New York: Doubleday, 1959.

Goleman, D. "Meditation as Meta-Therapy: Hypotheses Toward a Proposed Fifth State of Consciousness." *Journal of Transpersonal Psychology* 3(1971):1–25.

Gordon, J. "Hypnosis in Research on Psychotherapy." In *Handbook of Clinical and Experimental Hypnosis*, ed. J. Gordon. New York: Macmillan, 1967.

Gorton, B. Autogenic Training." *American Journal of Clinical Hypnosis* 2(1959):31–41.

————. "Autogenic Training." In *Autogenic Training*, ed. W. Luthe. New York: Grune and Stratton, 1965.

Govinda, A. *The Psychological Attitudes of Early Buddhist Philosophy.* New York: Weiser, 1970.

Granit, R. "Centrifugal and Antidromic Effects on the Ganglion Cells of the Retina." *Journal of Neurophysiology* 1(1955):388–411.

Green, E. E. "Preliminary Report on the Voluntary Controls Project: Swami Rama." Unpublished manuscript, 1972.

———, Green, A. M., and Walters, E. D. "Self-regulation of Internal States." In *Proceedings of the International Congress of Cybernetics.* London: 1969.

———, ———, and ———. "Voluntary Control of Internal States: Psychological and Physiological." *Journal of Transpersonal Psychology* 2(1970):1–26.

———, ———, and ———, and Murphy, G. "Feedback Technique for Deep Relaxation." *Psychophysiology* 6(1969):371–77.

———, et al. "On the Meaning of Transpersonal: Some Metaphysical Perspectives." *Journal of Transpersonal Psychology* 3(1971):27–46.

Griffin, F., Archer, R. C., Zinsmeister, S. C., and Jastram, P. S. "Weber Ratio in Gustatory Chemoreception: An Indicator of Systemic (Drug) Reactivity." *Nature* 207(1965):1049–53.

Grof, S. "The Use of LSD in Psychotherapy." *Journal of Psychedelic Drugs* 3 (1970*a*):52–62.

———. "LSD Psychotherapy and Human Culture (I)." *Journal for the Study of Consciousness* 3(1970*b*):100–19. "LSD Psychotherapy and Human Culture (II)." *Journal for the Study of Consciousness* 4 (1971):167–88.

———. "Beyond the Bounds of Psychoanalysis." *Intellectual Digest* September 1972:86–88.

Gubel, I. "Hallucinogenic Drugs and Hypnosis in Psychotherapy." *American Journal of Clinical Hypnosis* 4(1962):169–73.

Gunderson, E. J. "Relaxation in Therapy." *Journal of General Psychology* 38(1948):181–90.

Guntrip, H. "A Study of Fairbairn's Theory of Schizoid Reactions." *British Journal of Medical Psychology* 25(1952):86–103.

Hadfield, J. *Functional Nerve Disease.* London: Frowde, 1920.

Hadley, J. M. "Various Roles of Relaxation in Psychotherapeutics." *Journal of General Psychology* 19(1938):191–203.

Haley, J. "Control in Psychoanalytical Psychotherapy." In *Progress in Psychotherapy* vol. 4, eds. J. Masserman and J. L. Moreno. New York: Grune and Stratton, 1959.

Hall, E. T. *The Hidden Dimension.* New York: Doubleday, 1966.

Happich, C. "Das Bildbewusstsein als Ansatzstelle psychischer Behandlung." *Zbl. psychoter.* 5(1932):663–77.

————. "Bildbewusstsein und schopferische Situation." *Deutsche Medizinische Wochenschrift* 65(1939):68–71.

Harman, W. "Old Wine in New Wineskins: The Reasons for the Limited World View." In *The Proper Study of Man,* ed. J. Fadiman. New York: Macmillan, 1971.

Harris, D. H., Firestone, R. W., and Wagner, C. M. "Brief Psychotherapy and Enuresis." *Journal of Consultant Psychology* 19(1955):246.

Hart, J. T. "Autocontrol of EEG Alpha." Paper presented at the Seventh Annual Meeting of the Society for Psychophysiological Research. San Diego, Calif.: October 20–22, 1967.

————. "Beyond Psychotherapy." In *New Directions in Client-Centered Therapy,* ed. J. T. Hart and T. M. Tomlinson. Boston: Houghton Mifflin, 1970*a.*

————, and Tomlinson, T. M., eds. *New Directions in Client-Centered Therapy.* Boston: Houghton Mifflin, 1970*b.*

Hartman, E. *The Biology of Dreaming.* Springfield, Ill.: Charles C Thomas, 1967.

Hartmann, H. *Ego Psychology and the Problem of Adaptation.* New York: International Universities Press, 1939.

————. "Ego Psychology and the Problem of Adaptation." In *Organization and Pathology of Thought,* ed. D. Rapaport. New York: Columbia University Press, 1951.

Haverland, L. E. H. "The Effects of Relaxation Training on Certain Aspects of Motor Skill." Ph.D. dissertation, University of Illinois, 1953.

Hebbard, F. W., and Fischer, R. R. "Effect of Psilocybin, LSD, and Mescaline on Small, Involuntary Eye Movements." *Psychopharmacologia* (Berlin) 9(1966):146–56.

Heidegger, M. *Existence and Being.* Chicago: Henry Regnery Co., 1950.

Henderson, J. L., and Oakes, M. *The Wisdom of the Serpent.* New York: Collier, 1963.

Hernandez-Peon, R. "Neurophysiological Mechanisms of Wakefulness and Sleep." Paper presented at International Congress of Psychology. Washington, D.C.: 1963.

Herrigel, E. *Zen in the Art of Archery.* New York: Pantheon, 1956.

Hilgard, E. "Lawfulness within Hypnotic Phenomena." In *Hypnosis: Current Problems, ed.* G. Estabrooks. New York: Harper & Row, 1962.

————. "The Motivational Relevance of Hypnosis." In *Nebraska Symposium on Motivation,* ed. M. Jones. Lincoln, Neb.: University of Nebraska Press, 1964.

————. "Hypnosis." *Annual Review of Psychology* 16(1965*a*):157–80.

————. *Hypnotic Susceptibility.* New York: Harcourt Brace Jovanovich, 1965*b*.

————. "A Quantitative Study of Pain and Its Reduction through Hypnotic Suggestion." *Proceedings of the National Academy of Science* 57(1967):1581–86.

————. "Pain as a Puzzle for Psychology and Physiology." *American Psychologist* 24(1969):103–13.

————, et al. "The Use of Pain-State Reports in the Study of Hypnotic Analgesia to the Pain of Ice Water." *Journal of Nervous and Mental Diseases* 144 (1967):506–13.

————, and Tart, C. "Responsiveness to Suggestions Following Waking and Imagination Instructions and Following Induction of Hypnosis." *Journal of Abnormal Psychology* 71(1966):196–208.

Hirai, T. "Electroencephalographic Study on Zen Meditation (Zazen): EEG Changes During the Concentrated Relaxation." *Psychiatrica et Neurologia Japonica* 62(1960):76–105.

Hoch, P. "Aims and Limitations of Psychotherapy." *American Journal of Psychiatry* 112(1955):321–27.

Hoenig, J. "Medical Research on Yoga." *Confinia Psychiatrica* 11(1968): 69–89.

Hoffer, A. "LSD: A Review of Its Present Status." *Clinical Pharmacology and Therapeutics* 6(1965):183–255.

————. "A Comment on the Laing Paper." *Psychedelic Review* 7(1966): 127–28.

————, and Osmond, H. *The Chemical Basis of Clinical Psychiatry.* Springfield, Ill.: Charles C Thomas, 1960.

————, and ————. "Some Psychological Consequences of Perceptual Disorder and Schizophrenia." *International Journal of Neuropsychiatry* 2(1966):1–19.

Hoskovec, J. "A Critical Evaluation of the Pavlovian Theory of Hypnosis." In *Psychophysiological Mechanisms of Hypnosis,* ed. L. Chertok. Berlin: Springer-Verlag, 1967.

Hsu, F. "Americans and Chinese: The Beginnings of Contrast." In *Americans and Chinese,* ed. F. Hsu. New York: Abelard-Schuman, 1953.

Hull, C. *Hypnosis and Suggestibility: An Experimental Approach.* New York: Appleton-Century-Crofts, 1933.

Humphreys, C. *Zen Buddhism.* London: Heinemann, 1949.

————. *Zen Comes West: The Present and Future of Zen Buddhism in Britain.* New York: Macmillan, 1960.

Huxley, J. "Psychometabolism." *Psychedelic Review* 1(1963):183–204.

Ilovsky, J. "Experience with Group Hypnosis on Schizophrenics." *Journal of Mental Science* 108(1962):685–93.

Jacobson, A., and Berenberg, A. N. "Japanese Psychiatry and Psychotherapy." *American Journal of Psychiatry* 109(1952):321–32.

Jacobson, E. "Reduction of Nervous Irritability and Excitement by Progressive Relaxation." *Journal of Nervous and Mental Diseases* 53 (1920):282.

———. "Electrophysiology of Mental Activities." *American Journal of Psychology* 44(1932):677–94.

———. *Progressive Relaxation.* Second Edition, Chicago: University of Chicago Press, 1938.

———. "Cultivated Relaxation in Essential Hypertension." *Archives of Physical Therapy* 21(1940):645–54.

———. "The Physiological Conception and Treatment of Certain Common 'Psychoneuroses.'" *American Journal of Psychiatry* 98(1941): 219.

———. "Cultivated Relaxation for the Elimination of 'Nervous Breakdowns.'" *Archives of Physical Therapy* 24(1943):133–43.

———. "Neuromuscular Controls in Man: Methods of Self-direction in Health and Disease." *American Journal of Psychology* 68:549–61.

———. "The Two Methods of Tension Control and Certain Basic Techniques in Anxiety Tension Control." In *Biofeedback and Self-Control, 1971,* eds. J. Stoyva et al. Chicago: Aldine-Atherton, 1972.

James, W. *The Varieties of Religious Experience.* New York: New American Library of World Literature, 1958.

Jasper, H., and Shagass, C. "Conditioning Occipital Alpha Rhythm in Man." *Journal of Experimental Psychology* 28(1941):373–88.

Johnson, L. C. "A Psychophysiology for All States." *Psychophysiology* 6(1970):501–16.

Jung, C. G. *The Integration of the Personality.* London: Routledge and Kegan Paul, 1950.

———. "Introduction." In *An Introduction to Zen Buddhism,* ed. D. T. Suzuki. London: Rider, 1957.

———. *Psychological Reflections.* New York: Harper & Row, 1961.

———. *Psychology and Religion: West and East.* New York: Bollingen, 1969a.

———. *The Structure and Dynamics of the Psyche.* New York: Bollingen, 1969b.

———, and Hisamatsu, S. "On the Unconscious, the Self, and the Therapy." *Psychologia* 11(1968):25–32.

290 CONSCIOUSNESS: EAST AND WEST

Kalinowsky, L. B., Hoch, P. H., and Grant, B. *Somatic Treatments in Psychiatry*. New York: Grune and Stratton, 1961.

Kamïya, J. "Conditioned Discrimination of the EEG Alpha Rhythm in Humans." Paper presented at the meeting of the Western Psychological Association, San Francisco, April, 1962.

———. "EEG Operant Conditioning and the Study of States of Consciousness." Paper presented at a symposium on Laboratory Studies of Altered Psychological States, American Psychological Association. Washington, D.C.: September 1967.

———. "Conscious Control of Brain Waves." *Psychology Today* April 1968:57–60.

———. "A Fourth Dimension of Consciousness." *Experimental Medicine and Surgery* 27(1969a):13–18.

———. "Operant Control of the EEG Alpha Rhythm and Some of Its Reported Effects on Consciousness." In *Altered States of Consciousness*, ed. C. Tart. New York: Wiley, 1969b.

———, and Salasnek, S. "Meditation and Trained Self-control of Psychophysiological States." Research proposal, 1969.

Kanellakos, D. "The Physiology of the Evolving Man." Speech delivered at Stanford Research Institute, January 26, 1970a.

———. *Voluntary Improvement of Individual Performance*. Stanford Research Institute: IR&D Project No. 933531–01–403, 1970b.

———. "The Psychobiology of Consciousness and Transcendental Meditation." *Proceedings of the First International Symposium in the Science of Creative Intelligence*. Amherst, Mass.: University of Massachusetts, 1971.

Kaplan, B., ed. *The Inner World of Mental Illness*. New York: Harper & Row, 1964.

Karambelkar, P., Vinekar, S., and Bhole, M. "Studies on Human Subjects Staying in an Air-Tight Pit." *Indian Journal of Medical Research* 56(1968):1282–87.

Kasamatsu, A., and Hirai, T. "An Electroencephalographic Study of the Zen Meditation (Zazen)." In *Altered States of Consciousness*, ed. C. Tart. New York: Wiley, 1969. Reprinted from *Folio Psychiatrica Neurologica Japonica* 20(1966):315–36.

Kast, E. C., and Collins, V. J. "Lysergic Acid Diethylamide as an Analgesic Agent." *Anesthesia and Analgesia* 43(1964):285–91.

Keeler, M. "The Effects of Psilocybin on a Test of After-image Perception." *Psychopharmacology* 8(1965):131–39.

Kelman, H. "Zen and Psychotherapy." *Psychologia* 1(1958):219–28.

Kennard, M. "The EEG in Schizophrenia." In *Applications of Electro-*

encephalography in Psychiatry, ed. W. Wilson. Durham, N.C.: Duke University Press, 1965.

Kennedy, D. "Key Issues in the Cross-cultural Study of Mental Disorders." In *Studying Personality Cross-culturally*, ed. B. Kaplan. New York: Harper & Row, 1961.

Kiev, A. *Magic, Faith, and Healing*. New York: Free Press, 1964.

Klein, G. S. "Consciousness in Psychoanalytic Theory." *Journal of the American Psychoanalytic Association* 7(1959):5–34.

Klein, M. *Developments in Psychoanalysis*. London: Hogarth Press, 1952.

———. *New Directions in Psychoanalysis*. London: Tavistock, 1971.

Kleitman, N. *Sleep and Wakefulness*. Chicago: University of Chicago Press, 1963.

Kluver, H. "Neurobiology of Normal and Abnormal Perception." In *Psychopathology of Perception*, ed. J. Zubin. New York: Grune and Stratton, 1965.

Koestler, Arthur. *The Ghost in the Machine*. New York: Macmillan, 1967.

———. *The Roots of Coincidence*. New York: Random House, 1972.

Kondo, A. "Intuition in Zen Buddhism." *American Journal of Psychoanalysis* 12(1952):10–14.

———. "Morita Therapy: A Japanese Therapy for Neurosis." *American Journal of Psychoanalysis* 13(1953):31–37.

———. "Zen in Psychotherapy: The Virtue of Sitting." *Chicago Review* 12(1958):57–64.

Kopp, S. B. *Guru*. Palo Alto, Calif.: Science and Behavior Books, 1971.

———. *If You Meet the Buddha on the Road, Kill Him!* Palo Alto, Calif.: Science and Behavior Books, 1973.

Kora, T. *Morita Therapy*. Tokyo, Japan: Monograph of the Kora Koseiin Clinic, 1808 Simo-ochinai, Shinkikuku, 1965.

———, and Sato, K. "Morita Therapy: A Psychotherapy in the Way of Zen." *Psychologia* 1(1958):219–25.

Kretschmer, W. "Meditative Techniques in Psychotherapy." *Psychologia* 5(1962):76–83.

Krippner, S. "Hypnosis and Creativity." *American Journal of Clinical Hypnosis* 8(1965):94–99.

———. "Hypnosis and Psychedelic Experience." *Journal for the Study of Consciousness* 2(1969a):125–37.

———. "The Psychedelic State, the Hypnotic Trance, and the Creative Act." In *Altered States of Consciousness*, ed. C. Tart. New York: Wiley, 1969b.

————. "Altered States of Consciousness." In *The Highest State of Consciousness*, ed. J. White. New York: Doubleday, 1972.

————, and Hughes, W. "Genius at Work." *Psychology Today* June 1970: 40–43.

Kris, E. *Psychoanalytic Explorations in Art.* New York: International Universities Press, 1952.

Kubie, L. S. *Neurotic Distortion of the Creative Process.* Lawrence, Kansas: University of Kansas Press, 1961.

————, and Margolin, S. "The Process of Hypnotism and the Nature of Hypnotic State." *American Journal of Psychiatry* 100(1944):611–22.

Kuhn, T. S. *The Structure of Scientific Revolutions.* Chicago: University of Chicago Press, 1962.

Laidlaw, R. W. "The Psychiatrist as Marriage Counselor." *American Journal of Psychiatry* 106(1950):732–36.

Laing, R. D. *The Divided Self.* Baltimore, Md.: Penguin, 1965a.

————. "Transcendental Experience in Relation to Religion and Psychosis." *The Psychedelic Review* 6(1965b):7–15.

————. Lectures before William Alanson White Institute, 1966.

————. *The Politics of Experience.* New York: Pantheon, 1967.

Langer, J. "Werner's Comparative Organismic Theory." In *Carmichael's Manual of Child Psychology*, ed. P. Mussen. New York: Wiley, 1970.

Lapkin, B. "The Relation of Primary Process Thinking to the Recovery of Subliminal Material." Ph.D. dissertation, New York University, 1960.

Leary, T. "The Experiential Typewriter." *Psychedelic Review* 7(1966): 70–85.

————, Metzner, R., and Alpert, R. *The Psychedelic Experience.* New York: University Books, 1964.

Leighton et al. *Psychiatric Disorders among the Yoruba.* Ithaca, N.Y.: Cornell University Press, 1963.

Lerner, B. "Dream Function Reconsidered." *Journal of Abnormal Psychology* 72(1967):85–100.

Lesh, T. "Zen Meditation and the Development of Empathy in Counselors." *Journal of Humanistic Psychology* 10(1970):39–74.

Le Shan, L. "Physicists and Mystics: Similarities in World View." *Journal of Transpersonal Psychology* 1(1969):1–19.

Leuner, H. "L'imagerie catathyme: Une psychotherapie utilisant l'imagerie mentale." In *Informations de la Société International des Techniques d'Imagerie Mentale.* Paris: SITIM, 1968.

Levine, A., Abramson, H. A., Kaufman, M. R. and Markham, S. "Lysergic Acid Diethylamide (LSD-25): VI. The Effect on Intellectual Functioning as Measured by the Wechsler-Bellevue Intelligence Scale." *Journal of Psychology* 40(1955):385–95.

Levine, J., and Ludwig, A. "Alterations in Consciousness Produced by Combinations of LSD, Hypnosis, and Psychotherapy." *Psychopharmacologia* 7(1965):123–37.

————, and ————. "The Hypnodelic Treatment Technique." *International Journal of Clinical Experimental Hypnosis* 14(1966):207–15.

————, ————, and Lyle, W. "The Controlled Psychedelic State." *American Journal of Clinical Hypnosis* 6(1963):163–64.

Levine, S. "Sex Differences in the Brain." *Scientific American* April 1966: 84–90.

Levitsky, A., and Perls, F. "The Rules and Games of Gestalt Therapy." In *Gestalt Therapy Now*, eds. J. Fagan and I. L. Shepherd. New York: Harper & Row, 1970.

Lidz, T. "Adolph Meyer and the Development of American Psychiatry." *American Journal of Psychiatry* 123(1966):320–32.

Lilly, John. *Programming and Metaprogramming in the Human Biocomputer.* Menlo Park, Calif.: Whole Earth Catalog, 1968.

Lin, T. Y. "A Study of the Incidence of Mental Disorders in Chinese and Other Cultures." *Psychiatry* 16(1953):313–36.

Lindsley, D. "Electroencephalography." In *Personality and the Behavior Disorders*, ed. J. Hunt. New York: Ronald Press, 1944.

Lippman, H. "The Relation between Early Childhood Development and Psychopathology." In *The Concept of Development*, ed. D. Harris. Minneapolis: University of Minnesota Press, 1957.

Loomis, A., Harvey, E., and Hobart, G. "Potential Rhythms of the Cerebral Cortex During Sleep." *Science* 81(1935):597–98.

Luborsky, L., and Shevrin, H. "Dreams and Day Residues: A Study of the Poetzl Observation." *Bulletin of the Menninger Clinic* 20(1956): 135–48.

Luce, G. G., ed. *Current Research on Sleep and Dreams.* United States Department of Health, Education, and Welfare, No. 1389. Washington, D.C.: Government Printing Office, 1965.

————. *Biological Rhythms in Psychiatry and Medicine.* NIMH-PHS Publication No. 2088. Washington, D.C.: 1970.

————. *Body Time.* New York: Bantam, 1973.

Ludwig, A. M. "Altered States of Consciousness." *Archives of General Psychiatry* 15(1966):225–34.

————, and Levine, J. "A Controlled Comparison of Five Brief Treat-

ment Techniques Employing LSD, Hypnosis, and Psychotherapy."
American Journal of Psychotherapy 19(1965):417–35.

Luthe, W. "Method, Research, and Application of Autogenic Training."
The American Journal of Clinical Hypnosis 5(1962):17–23.

———. *Autogenic Training.* New York: Grune and Stratton, 1965.

MacKinnon, D. W. "The Nature and Nurture of Creative Talent." *American Psychologist* 17(1962):484–95.

———. "Personality and the Realization of Creative Potential." *American Psychologist* 20(1965):273–81.

Maddi, S. R. *Personality Theories: A Comparative Analysis.* Homewood, Ill.: Dorsey, 1968.

———, and Propst, B. "Activation and Personality." Unpublished manuscript read at the American Psychological Association convention, Philadelphia, 1963.

Maneceine, M. *Archives Italiennes de Biologie* 21(1894):322–25.

Mann, H. "Hypnosis in Short-term Therapy." *American Journal of Clinical Hypnosis* 8(1966):169–72.

Marin, P., and Cohen, A. Y. *Understanding Drug Use.* New York: Harper & Row, 1971.

Maslow, A. H. *Motivation and Personality.* New York: Harper & Row, 1954.

———. "Various Meanings of Transcendence." *Journal of Transpersonal Psychology* 1(1969):57–66.

Masters, R. E. L., and Houston, J. *Varieties of Psychedelic Experience.* New York: Holt, Rinehart and Winston, 1966.

———, and ———. "Toward an Individual Psychedelic Psychotherapy." In *Psychedelics,* eds., B. Aaronson and H. Osmond. New York: Doubleday, 1970.

Maupin, E. W. "Zen Buddhism: A Psychological Review." *Journal of Consulting Psychology* 26(1962):362–78.

———. "Individual Differences in Response to a Zen Meditation Exercise." *Journal of Consulting Psychology* 29(1965):139–43.

———. "Meditation." In *Ways of Growth,* eds. H. Otto and J. Mann. New York: Grossman, 1968.

———. "On Meditation." In *Altered States of Consciousness,* ed. C. Tart. New York: Wiley, 1969.

Mauz, F. "Der psychotische Mensch in der Psychotherapie." *Archiv für Psychiatrie und Nevrenkrankheiten* 181(1949): 337–41.

McCain, G., and Segal, E. M. *The Game of Science.* Belmont, Calif.: Brooks Cole, 1969.

McGhie, A., and Chapman, J. "Disorders of Attention and Perception in Early Schizophrenia." *British Journal of Medical Psychology* 34(1961):103–16.

McKellar, P., and Simpson, L. "Between Wakefulness and Sleep." *British Journal of Psychology* 45(1954):266–76.

McPeake, J. "Hypnosis, Suggestions, and Psychosomatics." *Diseases of the Nervous System* 29(1968):536–44.

Mednick, S., and Schulsinger, F. "Factors Related to Breakdown in Children at High Risk for Schizophrenia." In *Life History Research in Psychopathology*, eds. M. Roff and D. Ricks. Minneapolis: University of Minnesota Press, 1970.

Melei, J., and Hilgard, E. "Atitudes toward Hypnosis, Self-predictions, and Hypnotic Susceptibility." *International Journal of Clinical and Experimental Hypnosis* 12(1964):99–108.

Menninger, K. *Man against Himself*. New York: Harcourt Brace Jovanovich, 1938.

Metzner, R. "Mushrooms and the Mind." In *Psychedelics*, eds. B. Aaronson and H. Osmond. New York: Doubleday, 1970.

——. *Maps of Consciousness*. New York: Collier Books, 1971.

Miles, W. *Journal of Applied Physiology* 19(1964):75–82.

Miller, N. E. "Integration of Neurophysiological and Behavioral Research." *Annals of the New York Academy of Sciences* 92(1961): 830–39.

——. "Some Reflections on the Law of Effect Produce a New Alternative to Drive Reduction." In *Nebraska Symposium on Motivation: 1963*, ed M. E. Jones. Lincoln, Neb.: University of Nebraska Press, 1963.

——. "Some Implications of Modern Behavior Theory for Personality Change and Psychotherapy." In *Personality Change*, eds. D. Byrne and P. Worchel. New York: Wiley, 1964.

——. "Learning of Visceral and Glandular Responses." *Science* 159 (1969a):434–45.

——. "Psychosomatic Effects of Specific Types of Training." *Annals of the New York Academy of Sciences* 159(1969b):1025–40.

——, and Banuazizi, A. "Instrumental Learning by Curarized Rats of a Specific Visceral Response, Intestinal or Cardiac." *Journal of Comparative and Physiological Psychology* 65(1965):1–7.

——, and Carmona, A. "Modification of a Visceral Response, Salivation in Thirsty Dogs, by Instrumental Training with Water Reward." *Journal of Comparative and Physiological Psychology* 63(1967): 1–6.

——, and DiCara, L. "Instrumental Learning of Heart Rate Changes in Curarized Rats: Shaping and Specificity to Discriminative

Stimulus." *Journal of Comparative and Physiological Psychology* 63(1967):12–19.

——, and ——. "Instrumental Learning of Urine Formation by Rats: Changes in Ural Blood Flow." *American Journal of Physiology* 215(1968):677–83.

——, and Dollard, J. *Social Learning and Imitation.* New Haven, Conn.: Yale University Press, 1941.

Mogar, R. "Search and Research with the Psychedelics." *Etc.* 22(1965): 393–407.

——. "Psychedelic (LSD) Research: Critical Review of Methods and Results." In *Challenges of Humanistic Psychology,* ed. J. Bugental. New York: McGraw-Hill, 1967.

——. "Psychedelic States and Schizophrenia." *Journal of Existential Psychiatry* 6(1968):401–20.

——. "Psychedelic States and Schizophrenia." In *Psychedelics,* eds. B. Aaronson and H. Osmond. New York: Doubleday, 1970.

Moreno, J., and Enneis, J. *Hypnodrama and Psychodrama.* New York: Beacon House, 1950.

Moss, C. *Hypnosis in Perspective.* New York: Macmillan, 1965.

Mulholland, T. "Occurrence of the Electroencephalographic Alpha Rhythm with Eyes Open." *Nature* 206(1965):746.

——. "Feedback Method: A New Look at Functional EEG." *Electroencephalography and Clinical Neurophysiology* 27(1969):688.

——. "Can You Really Turn On with Alpha?" Paper presented at a meeting of the Massachusetts Psychological Association. Boston: Boston College, May 7, 1971.

——, and Runnals, S. "A Stimulus-Brain Feedback System for Evaluation of Alertness." *Journal of Psychology* 54(1962):69–83.

——, and ——. "The Effect of Voluntarily Directed Attention on Successive Cortical Activation Responses." *Journal of Psychology* 55(1963):427–36.

Muncie, W. "Adolph Meyer's Contribution to Clinical Psychiatry." *Bulletin of the Johns Hopkins Hospital* 89(1951):60–63.

Murphy, G. *Human Potentialities,* New York: Basic Books, 1958.

Murphy, H. B., Wittkower, E., Fried, J., and Ellenbruger, H. "A Cross-cultural Survey of Schizophrenic Symptomatology." *International Journal of Social Psychiatry* 9(1963):237–39

Muses, C., and Young, A. M. *Consciousness and Reality.* New York: Outerbridge and Lazard, 1972.

Myers, F. W. H. "Human Personality in the Light of Hypnotic Suggestion." *Proceedings of the Society for Psychical Research* 4(1887):1–24.

Naranjo, C. "The Healing Potential of Drugs in Psychotherapy." *Journal for the Study of Consciousness* 2(1969a):94–111.

———. "The Unfolding of Man." Stanford Research Institute, research report no. EPRC–6747–3. Stanford, Calif.: 1969b.

———. "Present-Centeredness: Technique, Prescription, and Ideal." In *Gestalt Therapy Now*, eds. J. Fagan and I. L. Shepherd. New York: Harper & Row, 1970.

———. *The Techniques of Gestalt Therapy*. Berkeley, Calif.: SAT Press, 1973.

———, and Ornstein, R. E. *On the Psychology of Meditation*. New York: Viking, 1971.

Natanson, M. *Philosophy of the Social Sciences*. New York: Random House, 1963.

Neki, J. S. "Yoga and Psychoanalysis." *Comprehensive Psychiatry* 8 (1967):160–67.

Neufeld, W. "Relaxation Methods in U.S. Navy Air Schools." *American Journal of Psychiatry* 108(1951):132–37.

Nidich, S., et al. "A Study of the Influence of TM on a Measure of Self-actualization." Unpublished paper, 1971.

Nowlis, D. P., and Kamiya, J. "The Control of Electroencephalographic Alpha Rhythms through Auditory Feedback and the Associated Mental Activity." *Psychophysiology* 2(1970):1–26.

Orme-Johnson, D. "Transcendental Meditation and Autonomic Lability." Paper presented at the First International Symposium on the Science of Creative Intelligence. Arcata, Calif.: Humboldt State College, August, 1971.

Orne, M. "The Nature of Hypnosis: Artifact and Essence." *Journal of Abnormal Social Psychology* 58(1959):277–99.

———. "On the Social Psychology of the Psychological Experiment: With Particular Reference to Demand Characteristics and Their Implication." *American Psychologist* 17(1962):776–83.

———. "Hypnosis, Motivation, and Compliance." *American Journal of Psychiatry* 122(1966):721–26.

———. "What Must a Satisfactory Theory of Hypnosis Explain?" *International Journal of Psychiatry* 3(1967):208–11.

Ornstein, R., and Timmons, B. "Auto-regulation of States of Consciousness for Astronauts." Unpublished manuscript, 1969.

Osmond, H. "A Review of the Clinical Effects of Psychotomimetic Agents." *Annals of New York Academy of Science* 66(1957):418–34.

————. "Mescaline: On Being Mad." In *Psychedelics*, eds. B. Aaronson and H. Osmond. New York: Doubleday, 1970.

————, and Hoffer, A. "A Comprehensive Theory of Schizophrenia." *International Journal of Neuropsychiatry* 2(1966):302–309.

Otto, H. A. *Ways of Growth*. New York: Pocket Books, 1971.

Pahnke, W. N. "The Psychedelic Mystical Experience in the Human Encounter with Death." *Psychedelic Review* 11(1971):3–21.

————. "Drugs and Mysticism." In *The Highest State of Consciousness*, ed. J. White. New York: Doubleday, 1972.

————, and Richards, W. A. "Implications of LSD and Experimental Mysticism." *Journal of Religion and Health* 5(1966):175–208

Pande, S. K. "The Mystique of Western Psychotherapy and Eastern Interpretation." *Journal of Nervous and Mental Diseases* 146(1968): 425–32.

Papez, J. W. "Central Reticular Path to Intralaminar and Reticular Nuclei of Thalamus for Activating EEG Related to Consciousness." *Electrocencephalography and Clinical Neurophysiology* 8(1956): 117–28.

Paul, G. L. "Physiological Effects of Relaxation Training and Hypnotic Suggestion." *Journal of Abnormal Psychology* 74(1969):425–37.

Pe, W. "Mindfulness of Sensation." *Psychologia* 9(1966): 195–98.

Pearce, J. C. *The Crack in the Cosmic Egg*. New York: Julian Press, 1971.

Peberdy, G. "Hypnotic Methods in Group Psychotherapy." *Journal of Mental Science* 106(1960):1016–20.

Pelletier, K. R. "Altered Attention Deployment in Meditation." In *The Psychobiology of Transcendental Meditation*, eds. D. Kanellakos and J. Lukas. Reading, Mass.: Benjamin Press, 1974*a*.

————. "Increased Perceptual Acuity Following Transcendental Meditation." In *Scientific Research on Transcendental Meditation: Collected Papers*, eds. L. Domash, J. Farrow, and D. Orme-Johnson. Los Angeles: MIU Press, 1974*b*.

————. "Influence of Transcendental Meditation upon Autokinetic Perception." *Journal of Perceptual and Motor Skills* 39(1974*c*):1031–34.

————. "Neurological, Psychophysiological, and Clinical Differentiation of the Alpha and Theta Altered States of Consciousness." *Dissertation Abstracts International* 35(1974*d*):520–28.

————. "Neurological, Psychophysiological, and Clinical Parameters of Alpha, Theta, and the Voluntary Control of Bleeding and Pain."

Proceedings of the Biofeedback Research Society. Denver: Biofeedback Research Society, February, 1974*e*.

————. "Neurological Substrates of Consciousness." *Journal of Altered States of Consciousness* 2(1974*f*).

————. "Psychophysiological Parameters of the Voluntary Control of Blood Flow and Pain." In *The Psychobiology of Transcendental Meditation*, eds. D. Kanellakos and J. Lukas. Reading, Mass.: Benjamin Press, 1974*g*.

————. "Diagnosis, Procedure, and Phenomenology of Clinical Biofeedback." *Proceedings of the Biofeedback Research Society.* Denver: Biofeedback Research Society, in press (1975*a*).

————. "Neurophysiological Parameters of the Voluntary Control of Blood Flow and Pain." *Journal of Altered States of Consciousness* 3(1975*b*).

————. "Preface." In *The Reflexive Universe*, ed. A. M. Young. Boston: Seymour Lawrence/Delacorte, forthcoming (1975*c*).

————. "Mind as Healer, Mind as Slayer." In *Lifelong Learning*. Berkeley: University of California, University Extension, 1975.

————. "Theory and Applications of Clinical Biofeedback." *Journal of Contemporary Psychotherapy* 7(1975):29–34.

————, and Peper, E. "The Chutzpah Factor in Psychophysiological Parameters of Altered States of Consciousness." *Proceedings of the Biofeedback Research Society.* Denver: Biofeedback Research Society, February 1974.

————, and ————. "The Chutzpah Factor in Altered States of Consciousness." *Journal of Humanistic Psychology.* In press (1975).

Peper, E. "Feedback Regulation of the Alpha Electroencephalograph Activity through Control of the Internal and External Parameters." *Kybernetik* 7(1970):107–12.

————. "Voluntary Control of Heart Rate: Problem in Feedback." Preprint, 1971.

————, and Mulholland, T. "Methodological and Theoretical Problems in the Voluntary Control of Electroencephalographic Occipital Alpha by the Subject." *Kybernetik* 7(1970):10–13.

————, and Pelletier, K. R. "Frontiers and Concepts of Clinical Biofeedback." *Journal of Transpersonal Psychology.* In press (1975).

Perline, I. "Group Hypnotherapy: A Brief Survey." *American Journal of Clinical Hypnosis* 10(1968):267–70.

Perls, F. *Ego, Hunger and Aggression.* New York: Random House, 1969*a*.

————. *Gestalt Therapy Verbatim.* Lafayette, Ind.: Real People Press, 1969*b*.

Perry, J. W. "Reconstitutive Process in the Psychopathology of the Self."
    Annals of the New York Academy of Sciences 96(1962):853–76.
Peterson, S. *A Catalog of the Ways People Grow.* New York: Ballantine,
    1971.
Piaget, J. *Play, Dreams, and Imitation in Childhood.* New York: Norton,
    1962.
Poetzl, O. "The Relation between Experimentally Induced Dream Images
    and Indirect Vision." *Psychological Issues* 2, no. 3 (1960).
Pribram, K. H. "The Brain." *Psychology Today* September 1971:44–89.
Prince, R. "Interest Disorders." *Journal for the Study of Consciousness*
    4(1971):62–82.
———, and Savage, C. "Mystical States and the Concept of Regres-
    sion." *Psychedelic Review* 8(1966):59–75.
———, and ———. "Mystical States and the Concept of Regression."
    In *The Highest State of Consciousness,* ed., J. White. New York:
    Doubleday, 1972.
Progoff, I. *The Death and Rebirth of Psychology.* New York: Julian
    Press, 1956.

Rao, S. "Metabolic Cost of Head-stand Posture." *Journal of Applied
    Physiology* 17(1962):117–18.
———. "Oxygen Consumption During Yoga-Type Breathing at Alti-
    tudes of 520 m. and 3,800 m." *Indian Journal of Medical Research*
    56(1968):701–05.
Rapaport, D. *Organization and Pathology of Thought.* New York: Co-
    lumbia University Press, 1951.
Reich, W. *Character Analysis.* London: Vision Press, 1948.
Reyher, J. "Brain Mechanisms, Intrapsychic Processes and Behavior: A
    Theory of Hypnosis and Psychopathology." *American Journal of
    Clinical Hypnosis* 7(1964):107–19.
Rhijn, C. H. "Symbolysis: Psychotherapy by Symbolic Presentation." In
    The Use of LSD in Psychotherapy, ed. H. A. Abramson. New York:
    Josiah Macy, Jr. Foundation, 1960.
Rogers, C. R. *On Becoming a Person.* Boston: Houghton Mifflin, 1961.
Rosenbaum, C. P. "Events of Early Therapy and Brief Therapy." *Archives
    of General Psychiatry* 10(1964):506–12.
Rothballer, A. B. "Studies on the Adrenaline-Sensitive Component of the
    Reticular Activating System." *Electroencephalography and Clinical
    Neurophysiology* 8(1956):603–21.
Royce, J. *The Encapsulated Man.* New York: Van Nostrand, 1964.
Ruesch, J., and Kas, W. *Nonverbal Communication.* New York: Basic
    Books, 1956.

Salter, A. *What Is Hypnosis: Studies in Auto and Hetero Conditioning.* New York: Richard R. Smith, 1944.

Sarbin, T. "Contributions to Role-Taking Theory: 1. Hypnotic Behavior." *Psychological Review* 57(1950):255–70.

————. "The Concept of Hallucination." *Journal of Personality* 35(1967): 359–80.

————. "Schizophrenia Is a Myth, Born of Metaphor, Meaningless." *Psychology Today* June 1972:18–27.

————, and Adler, N. "Commonalities in Systems of Conduct Reorganization." Paper presented at the California State Psychological Association. San Diego: January 1967.

Sargant, W., and Slater E. *An Introduction to Physical Methods of Treatment in Psychiatry.* Edinburgh: E. and S. Livingstone, 1944.

Sargent, J. D., Green, E. E., and Walters, E. D. "Preliminary Report on the Use of Autogenic Feedback Techniques in the Treatment of Migraine and Tension Headaches." Unpublished research report. Topeka, Kan.: Menninger Foundation, 1971.

Sartre, J. *Being and Nothingness.* Trans. H. Barnes. London: Methuen, 1956.

Sato, K. "Psychotherapeutic Implications of Zen." *Psychologia* 1(1958): 213–18.

————. "The Teaching of Human Body." *Psychologia* 9(1966):192–94.

————. "Zen from a Personological Viewpoint." *Psychologia* 11(1968): 3–24.

Saul, L. J. "On the Value of One or Two Interviews." *Psychoanalytic Quarterly* 20(1951):613–15.

Schacter, S. "The Interaction of Cognitive and Physiological Determinants of Emotional States." In *Advances in Experimental Social Psychology*, vol. 1, ed. L. Berkowitz. New York: Academic Press, 1964.

————, and Singer, J. E. "Cognitive, Social, and Physiological Determinants of Emotional States." *Psychological Review* 69(1962):379–99.

Schade, M., Hruza, T., Washburne, A., and Carns, R. "Relaxation as an Adjunct to Psychotherapy." *Journal of Clinical Psychology* 8(1952): 338–46.

Schilder, P., and Kauders, O. "A Textbook of Hypnosis." In P. Schilder, *The Nature of Hypnosis*, pt. 2, trans. G. Corvin. New York: International Universities Press, 1956.

Schmiege, G. R., Jr. "LSD as a Therapeutic Tool." *Journal of the Medical Society of New Jersey* 60 (1963):203–07.

Schultz, J. *Das autogene training.* Stuttgart: Georg Thieme Verlag, 1953.

————, and Luthe, W. *Autogenic Training: A Psychophysiologic Approach in Psychotherapy.* New York: Grune and Stratton, 1959.

Sen, I. "The Psychological System of Sri Aurobindo." *Indian Journal of Psychology* 27(1952):79–89.

Shafii, M. "The Pir (Sufi Guide) and the Western Psychotherapist." *R. M. Bucke Memorial Society Newsletter Review,* Fall 1968.

Shakow, D. "Segmental Set." *Archives of General Psychiatry* 6(1962): 1–17.

Shapiro, A. "A Contribution to a History of the Placebo Effect." *Behavioral Science* 5(1960):109–35.

Sharpless, S., and Jasper, H. H. "Habituation of the Arousal Reaction." *Brain* 79(1956):655–80.

Shaw, R., and Kilb, D. Personal communication, 1972.

Shelly, M. Paper presented at the First International Symposium on the Science of Creative Intelligence. Arcata, Calif.: Humboldt State College, August 1971.

Sherwood, J. N., Stolaroff, M. J., and Hamran, W. W. "The Psychedelic Experience: A New Concept in Psychotherapy." *Journal of Neuropsychiatry* 4(1962):69–80.

Siegler, M., Osmond, H., and Mann, H. "Laing's Model of Madness." *Salmagundi,* no. 16(1971):84–105.

Silverman, J. "Perceptual Control of Stimulus Intensity in Paranoid and Nonparanoid Schizophrenia." *Journal of Nervous and Mental Diseases* 139(1964a):5545–49.

————. "The Problem of Attention in Research and Theory in Schizophrenia." *Psychological Review* 71(1964b):352–79.

————. "The Scanning Control Mechanism and 'Cognitive Filtering' in Paranoid and Non-paranoid Schizophrenia." *Journal of Consulting Psychology* 28(1964c):385–93.

————. Personality Trait and 'Perceptual Style': Studies of the Psychotherapists of Schizophrenic Patients." *Journal of Nervous and Mental Diseases* 145(1967a):5–17.

————. "Shamans and Acute Schizophrenia." *American Anthropologist* 69(1967b):21–31.

————. "Variations in Cognitive Control and Psychophysiological Defense in the Schizophrenias." *Psychosomatic Medicine* 29(1967c): 225–51.

————. "A Paradigm for the Study of Altered States of Consciousness." *British Journal of Psychiatry* 114(1968a):1201–18.

————. "Attentional Styles and the Study of Sex Differences." In *Attention: Contemporary Theory and Analysis,* ed. D. Mostofsky. New York: Appleton-Century-Crofts, 1968b.

———. "Toward a More Complex Formulation of Rod-and-Frame Performance in the Schizophrenias." *Perceptual and Motor Skills* 27 (1968c):1111–14.

———. "Facts and Issues in Research with Psychedelic Drugs." *California Mental Health Research Digest* 7(1969a):107–16.

———. "Perceptual and Neurophysiological Analogues of 'Experience' in Schizophrenic and LSD Reactions." In *Schizophrenia: Current Concepts and Research*, ed. D. V. Siva Sankar. Hicksville, N.Y.: PJD Publications, 1969b.

———. "When Schizophrenia Helps." *Psychology Today* September 1970: 63–65.

———, Buchsbaum, and Henkin, R. "Stimulus Sensitivity and Stimulus Intensity Control." *Perceptual and Motor Skills* 28(1969):71–78.

———, and Gaarder, K. "Rates of Saccadic Eye Movement and Size Judgments of Normals and Schizophrenics." *Perceptual and Motor Skills* 25(1967):661–67.

Simeons, A. T. W. *Man's Presumptuous Brain.* New York: Dutton, 1960.

Singer, J. E. "Sympathetic Activation." *Journal of Comparative Physiological Psychology* 56(1963):612–78.

———. "Imagery and Daydream Techniques Employed in Psychotherapy." In *Current Topics in Clinical and Community Psychology*, ed. C. Spielberger. New York: Academic Press, 1971.

———, Brush, C. A., and Lublin, S. C. "Some Aspects of Deindividuation: Identification and Conformity." *Journal of Experimental Social Psychology* 1(1965):356–78.

Singer, M. "Thought Disorder and Family Relations of Schizophrenics." *Archives of General Psychiatry* 12(1965):201.

———. "Communication Styles in Parents of Normals, Neurotics, and Schizophrenics." *Phychiatric Research Reports of the American Psychiatric Association* 20(1966): 25–38.

Sinha, D. "Integration of Modern Psychology with Indian Thought." *Journal of Humanistic Psychology* 5(1965):6–16.

Solamon, I., and Post, J. "Alpha Blocking and Schizophrenia." *Archives of General Psychiatry* 13(1965):367–74.

Solovey, G., and Milechnin, A. "Concerning the Criterion of Recovery." *Journal of Clinical Experimental Hypnosis* 6(1958):1–9.

Spanos, N., and Chaves, J. "Hypnosis Research: A Methodological Critique of Experiments Generated by Two Alternative Paradigms." *American Journal of Clinical Hypnosis* 13(1970):108–27.

Spilker, B., Kamiya, J., Callaway, E., and Yeager, C. L. "Visual Evoked Responses in Subjects Trained to Control Alpha Rhythms." *Psychophysiology* 5(1969):683–95.

Stace, W. *The Teachings of the Mystics.* New York: New American Library, 1960.

Starzl, T. E., and Magoun, H. W. "Organization of the Diffuse Thalamic Projection System." *Journal of Neurophysiology* 14(1950):133–46.

Stoyva, J. M. "The Public (Scientific) Study of Private Events." *International Psychiatry Clinic* 7(1970):355–68.

————, and Kamiya, J. "Electrophysiological Studies of Dreaming as the Prototype of a New Strategy in the Study of Consciousness." *Psychological Review* 75(1968):192–205.

Sullivan, H. *Conceptions of Modern Psychiatry.* New York: Norton, 1953*a*.

————. *The Interpersonal Theory of Psychiatry.* New York: Norton, 1953*b*.

Supple, L. "Hypnodrama—A Synthesis of Hypnosis and Psychodrama: A Progress Report." *Group Psychotherapy* 15(1962):58–62.

Sutliffe, J. "Credulous and Skeptical Views of Hypnotic Phenomena: Experiments on Esthesia, Hallucination, and Delusion." *Journal of Abnormal Psychology* 62(1961):189–200.

Suzuki, D. T. *Living by Zen.* Tokyo: Sanseido Press, 1949*a*.

————. *The Zen Doctrine of No-Mind.* London: Rider, 1949*b*.

————. *Zen Buddhism.* New York: Doubleday, 1956.

Takesiso, K. Personal communication to Joe Kamiya, 1965.

Takeuchi, K. "On 'Naikan' Method." *Psychologia* 8(1965):2–8.

Tart, C. T., ed. *Altered States of Consciousness: A Book of Readings.* New York: Wiley, 1969.

————. "Scientific Foundations for the Study of Altered States of Consciousness." *Journal of Transpersonal Psychology* 3(1972):93–124.

Townes, C. H. "The Convergence of Science and Religion." *California Monthly* February 1970:10–19.

Turner, W. J. et al. "Chemotherapeutic Trials in Psychosis." *American Journal of Psychiatry* 11(1959):261–262.

Underhill, E. *Mysticism.* New York: Dutton, 1961.

Van Dusen, W. "Wu-wei, No-mind, and the Fertile Void in Psychotherapy." *Psychologia* 1(1958*a*):253–56.

————. "Zen and Western Psychotherapy." *Psychologia* 1(1958*b*):229–30.

————. "LSD and the Enlightenment of Zen." *Psychologia* 4(1961):11–16.

————. "Hallucinations of Psychotics." *Journal for the Study of Consciousness* 4(1971*a*).

———. "Hallucinations as the World of Spirits." *Psychedelic Review* 11(1971*b*):59–71.

———. *The Natural Depth in Man.* New York: Harper & Row, 1972.

Van Nuys, D. "Proposal for a Program in Advanced Studies in ASC." Unpublished paper, 1968.

———. "A Novel Technique for Monitoring Attention During Meditation." Ph.D. dissertation, University of Michigan, 1970.

Veith, I. "On the 'Principles of the Heart' and the Psychiatric Insights of Zen." *New England Journal of Medicine* 285(1971):1458–60.

———. "Zen Psychotherapy." *Behavior Today* January 24, 1972: 3.

Venables, P. "Input Dysfunction in Schizophrenia." In *Progress in Experimental Personality Research,* ed. B. Maher. New York: Academic Press, 1964.

Vinacke, W. *The Psychology of Thinking.* New York: McGraw-Hill, 1952.

Virel, A. *Histoire de notre image.* Geneva: Mont-Blanc, 1968.

Von Uexkull, J. "A Stroll through the Worlds of Animals and Men." In *Instinctive Behavior,* ed. C. Schiller. New York: International Universities Press, 1957.

Walkup, L. E. "Creativity in Science through Visualization." *Perceptual and Motor Skills* 21(1965):35–41.

Wallace, A. F. C. "Revitalization Movement." *American Anthropologist* 58(1956):264–81.

Wallace, R. K. "Physiological Effects of Transcendental Meditation." *Science* 167(1970):1751–54.

———, and Benson, H. "The Physiology of Meditation." *Scientific American* February 1972:85–90.

Wapnick, K. "Mysticism and Schizophrenia." *Journal of Transpersonal Psychology* 1(1969):42–68.

Watson, L. D., and Guthrie, D. M. "A New Approach to Psychopathology: The Influence of Cultural Meanings on Altered States of Consciousness." *Journal for the Study of Consciousness* 5(1972):26–34.

Watts, A. W. *Zen Buddhism: A New Outline and Introduction.* London: Buddhist Society, 1947.

———. *Psychotherapy East and West.* New York: Ballantine, 1961.

———. "Asian Psychology and Modern Psychiatry." *American Journal of Psychoanalysis* 13(1966):25–30.

———. *The Book on the Taboo against Knowing Who You Are.* New York: Macmillan, 1966.

Weil, A. "The Natural Mind." *Psychology Today* October 1972:51–97.

Weiss, T., and Engle, B. T. "Operant Conditioning of Heart Rate in

Patients with Premature Ventricular Contractions." In *Biofeedback and Self Control, 1971,* eds. J. Stoyva et al. Chicago: Aldine-Atherton, 1972.

Weitzenhoffer, A. "Some Speculations Regarding the Nature and Character of Hypnotic Behavior." *American Journal of Clinical Hypnosis* 4(1961):69–89.

————, and Hilgard, E. *Stanford Hypnotic Susceptibility Scale, Forms A and B.* Palo Alto, Calif.: Consulting Psychologists Press, 1959.

————, and ————. *Stanford Hypnotic Susceptibility Scale, Form C.* Palo Alto, Calif.: Consulting Psychologists Press, 1962.

————, and ————. *Stanford Profile Scales of Hypnotic Susceptibility, Forms 1 and 11.* Palo Alto, Calif.: Consulting Psychologists Press, 1963.

Wenger, M. A., and Bagchi, B. K. "Studies of Autonomic Functions in Practitioners of Yoga in India." *Behavioral Science* 6(1961):312–23.

————, ————, and Anand, B. K. "Experiments in India on 'Voluntary' Control of the Heart and Pulse." *Circulation* 24(1961a):1319–25.

————, ————, and ————. "Voluntary Heart and Pulse Control by Yoga Methods." *International Journal of Parapsychology* 5(1963): 25–41.

Werner, H. *Comparative Psychology of Mental Development.* New York: International Universities Press, 1948.

Whatmore, G. "Tension Factors in Schizophrenia and Depression." In *Tension in Medicine,* ed. E. Jacobsen. Springfield, Ill.: Charles C Thomas, 1967.

White, J. *The Highest State of Consciousness.* New York: Doubleday, 1972.

White, R. W. "Two Types of Hypnotic Trance and Their Personality Correlates." *Journal of Psychology* 8(1937):265–77.

————. "A Preface to the Theory of Hypnotism." *Journal of Abnormal Social Psychology* 36(1941a):477–505.

————. "An Analysis of Motivation in Hypnosis." *Journal of General Psychology* 24(1941b):145–62.

Whitehorn, J. "The Concepts of 'Meaning' and 'Cause' in Psychodynamics." *American Journal of Psychiatry* 104(1947):289–92.

Whyte, L. *The Unconscious before Freud.* New York: Doubleday, 1962.

Wienpahl, P. "Identity as Atonement." *Psychologia* 8(1965):135–44.

Wikler, A., et al. "Reaction Time ('Mental Set') in Control and Chronic Schizophrenic Subjects and in Post-Addicts under Placebo, LSD-25, Morphine, Pentobarbitol, and Amphetamine." *Psychopharmacologia* 7(1965):423–43.

Winnicott, D. *Collected Papers*. London: Tavistock, 1958.

Winquist, T. "The Effect of the Regular Practice of Transcendental Meditation on Students Involved in the Regular Use of Hallucinogenic and 'Hard Drugs.' " Unpublished report, Department of Psychology, UCLA, 1969.

Witkin, H. A. "Psychological Differentiation and Forms of Pathology." *Journal of Abnormal Psychology* 70(1965):317–36.

Wolberg, L. *Hypnoanalysis*. New York: Grune and Stratton, 1945.

———. *Medical Hypnosis*. New York: Grune and Stratton, 1948.

———. *Short-term Psychotherapy*. New York: Grune and Stratton, 1965.

Wolff, C. *The Hand in Psychological Diagnosis*. New York: Philosophical Library, 1952.

Wolpe, J., and Lazarus, A. *Behavior Therapy Techniques*. New York: Pergamon, 1966.

Wolpert, E. "Studies in the Psychophysiology of Dreams: II." *Archives of General Psychiatry* 2(1960):231–41.

Wynne, L., and Singer, M. "Thought Disorder and Family Relations of Schizophrenics." *Archives of General Psychiatry* 9(1963):191.

———, and ———. "Schizophrenic Impairments in Sharing Foci of Attention." The Bertram H. Roberts Memorial Lecture, Yale University. New Haven, Conn.: 1966.

Yap, P. "The Latah Reaction: Its Pathodynamics and Nosological Position." *Journal of Experimental Science* 98(1952):515–64.

Yates, D. H. "Relaxation in Psychotherapy." *Journal of General Psychology* 34(1946):213–38.

Yokoyama, K. "Morita Therapy and Seiza." *Psychologia* 11(1968):179–84.

Young, A. M. "Some Reactions to Arthur Koestler's *The Ghost in the Machine*." *Journal for the Study of Consciousness* 2(1969):58–71.

———. *A Theory of Process*. Boston: Seymour Lawrence/Delacorte, forthcoming.

Zilboorg, G. "The Emotional Problem and the Therapeutic Role of Insight." *Psychoanalytic Quarterly* 21(1952):1–24.

Ziller, R. C. "Individuation and Socialization." *Human Relations* 17 (1964):341–60.

Zimbardo, P. G. *The Cognitive Control of Motivation*. Glenview, Ill.: Scott Foresman, 1969*a*.

———. "The Human Choice: Reason and Order versus Impulse and Chaos." Nebraska Symposium on Motivation, 1969*b*.

Zimmer, H. *Myths and Symbols in Indian Art and Civilization*. Series 6. New York: Bollingen, 1946.

KENNETH R. PELLETIER

Kenneth R. Pelletier, Ph.D., is a Clinical Psychologist, and is a Research Psychologist at the Langley Porter Neuropsychiatric Institute and Department of Psychiatry, University of California School of Medicine, San Francisco. He is Director of the Psychosomatic Medicine Center of Gladman Memorial Hospital, Oakland, and is in private practice in Berkeley. During graduate school at the University of California, Berkeley, he was a Woodrow Wilson Fellow; studied at the C. G. Jung Institute in Zurich; and became Director of the Institute for the Study of Consciousness, Berkeley. He has published numerous articles in clinical biofeedback, psychosomatic medicine, and altered states research.

CHARLES GARFIELD

Charles Garfield received his Ph.D. in clinical psychology from the University of California, Berkeley, after receiving previous graduate degrees in mathematics and education from Adelphi University. He formerly taught mathematics at the New York Institute of Technology and worked as a mathematician and computer analyst on the Lunar Earth Module (LEM) project of the Apollo Space Program. He has published articles in psychology, psychiatry, and mathematics as well as developed humanistic approaches to inner-city education. For his doctoral dissertation research, entitled "Psychothanatological Concomitants of Altered State Experience," he investigated the effects of long-term meditation and psychedelic drug use on one's fear of death. He recently spent two years investigating and participating in the Eastern schools of Tibetan Vajrayana and Zen Buddhism in an effort to integrate the insights of these traditions with modern psychotherapeutic practice.

Presently, Dr. Garfield is teaching courses on altered states of consciousness, psychology of death, and futurologic and ecologic approaches to personal growth at the University of California campuses at Berkeley, Davis, and Santa Cruz and is organizing a multidisciplinary Center for Death and Dying. He is also engaged in post-doctoral research and study at the University of California, Berkeley, in the areas of meditative and somato-psychic approaches to healing and behavior change and the relationship between consciousness alteration and subjective orientation to physical death.